D0757977

Library of Congress Cataloging-in-Publication Data

Haney, Marsha Snulligan
    Islam and Protestant African American churches : responses and challenges to religious pluralism / Marsha Snulligan Haney.
      p. cm.
    Includes bibliographical references and index. (hc.alk.paper) and Index.
    ISBN 1-57309-300-9
    1. Islam—United States. 2. Afro-Americans—Religion. 3. Black Muslims—United States. 4. Afro-American churches—United States. 5. African Union Methodist Protestant Church (U.S.) 6. Islam—Relations—Christianity. 7. Christianity and other religions—Islam. 8. Religious pluralism—United States. I. Title.

BP67.U6H36 1998
261.2'7'08996073—dc21

98-36396
CIP

Editorial Inquiries:
International Scholars Publications
7831 Woodmont Avenue, #345
Bethesda, MD 20814
website: www.interscholars.com
To order: (800) 55-PUBLISH

Dedicated to

My husband ~ ~
Willie C. Haney

My parents ~ ~
Jesse B. Snulligan and Phyllis W. Snulligan

My sisters ~ ~
Phyllis L. Wilson
Danita J. Snulligan

and in memory of
my mother ~ ~
Princess M. Snulligan

My family has given me life, love and the desire to serve God.
I hereby seek to honor them by passing on to others some portion
of what they have passed on to me, combined with some portion
of what I have done with their investment in me.

M.S.H.

CONTENTS

Chapter

Chapter

A Holistic Concern for the Total Person
A Biblical Approach to Religious Pluralism
A Theoretical Framework for Addressing Religious Pluralism
Basic Approaches and Assumptions Concerning Reality
A Criteria for Assessing Religions
A Criteria for Assessing Contextualization
A Theological Model and Method
Mission and Theology
A Faithful Witness
Worship As Viewed Through Ritual Prayer
Justification by Grace vs. Justification by Law
Additional Themes of Concern
Urban Models of Authentic Approaches

Appendix

LIST OF ILLUSTRATIONS

FOREWORD

I think that this book, *Islam and Protestant African-American Churches: Responses and Challenges to Religious Pluralism*, is a timely, comprehensive, required text for those concerned about religion in the 21st century. In clear, accessible language, Marsha Snulligan Haney helps us understand the most acute challenges of the new millennium within an African-American religious framework which is both Islam and Christian, and analyzes essential aspects of both traditions which will allow us to meet the demands of the new century. The fundamental question, *"Can we be different but not alienated?"*, lies at the center of the Black community today, and is the thesis of this first-class book.

Katie G. Cannon, PhD
Associate Professor of Religion
Temple University

PREFACE

The conceptual framework for this study emerged while serving as a mission worker with the Sudan Council of Churches (Juba) from 1979 to 1981. While living in this country torn by a long history of Muslim and Christian conflict and destruction, I became aware of the growth of Islam worldwide, and the various responses to religious pluralism. I have also had the opportunity to work with the Presbyterian Church in Cameroon, a country where Muslims and Christians peacefully co-exist. As Islam becomes the second largest faith community in the United States, the African-American Protestant community has an unprecedented opportunity to provide leadership and guidance to North American churches as they seek to respond faithfully to this new religious pluralism in our context. On the threshold of a new century, the African-American Christian Church is called upon to utilize its unique history, gifts, experiences, spirituality and faith to assist the Church in responding to the challenge of Islam with a sense of integrity, biblical faithfulness and social relevancy. The faith tradition and strength of the African-American Christian Church (visible and invisible) has demonstrated its power throughout history, and if it chooses to, can continue to demonstrate its commitment to the mission and ministry of the church in light of this new phenomena of religious pluralism.

Presently, the contemporary state of Protestant African-American churches indicate a low awareness of where they are presently situated in a religiously plural society. This has resulted in the churches' seemingly inability to meet the new challenges of Islamic growth within the African-American community. However, as Muslims actively engage in mission and ministry within the North American context, they present opportunities as well as obstacles that must be faced by the Church. This historical investigation reveals determining factors both internal and external to the churches that have shaped the growth of Islam in the African-American community, and the multifaceted existential inquiry identifies factors which are responsible for the Islamic appeal among African Americans who see that religious faith is a viable option. The results of the evaluations indicate the areas of change needed for the churches to develop a relevant mission and ministry to Muslims.

This manuscript presents a systematic means by which the criteria for the development of an authentic and appropriate model of Christian contextualization might be identified and formulated as a resource for the mission of evangelization and re-evangelization in the African-American community in the midst of the contemporary challenge of the Islamic faith. Two analytical models will be used: the worldview theory model and the contextualization model. The theological, religious and leadership challenges presented by Islam provides the context for missiological analysis. Finally, a missional model is recommended that might possibly provide a means by which the Protestant African-American churches could bear witness of the Incarnational Christ within a religiously diverse society.

ACKNOWLEDGMENTS

The preparation and writing of a manuscript such as this entails many years of work. In a very real sense, the prayers, assistance and contributions of family, friends and colleagues are an integral part of this study.

I would like to express my gratitude to my mentors at the Fuller Theological Seminary, School of World Mission, for the guidance and encouragement that led to the completion of this work in its initial form as a dissertation. I want to thank my colleagues on the faculty of the Interdenominational Theological Center for their support and encouragement as I sought to complete this manuscript in its present form. A special measure of gratitude goes to Reta Lacy Bigham for her invaluable typing and editorial assistance. I also want to acknowledge the contributions of Muslims in the Los Angeles area for their probing questions and discussions which nurtured many of the ideas in the pages that follow.

Finally, I must give an inexpressible appreciation to my spouse, Willie C. Haney, Jr., to my biological family, and to my extended church family in the Sudan and Cameroon. As I complete this manuscript, I also realize I am more indebted to a great circle of God's peoples around the world whose names, unfortunately, space does not allow me to list.

CHAPTER 1

INTRODUCTION

The primary purpose of this manuscript is to identify the need for the Protestant African-American churches to develop a contextualized theology of mission and ministry within an increasingly multi-religious society. The contemporary state of these churches indicates a low awareness of where they presently are situated in a pluralistic world. An examination of the religious and social challenges presented by the expansion of Islam within the North American context will provide a case study for missiological analysis. With a new knowledge of Islamic motivation and goals, what would an authentic and relevant model of Christianity contextualized for the mission of evangelization and re-evangelization of African Americans look like? The goal of this study is toward the development of a missional approach and model that would enable the Protestant African-American churches to bear witness of the Incarnational Christ within the religiously diverse African-American community.

Background

Today there are over 1,313 different religious groups in the United States (Melton 1985). Christianity, until very recently, was considered the only significant religion with which African Americans generally identified. However, whether the African-American churches are aware of it or not, there is a multitude of missional activities taking place, appealing to both the religious and social aspects of life. This religious pluralism is extremely active within the African-American community. Activities generated by religious and missional concerns are taking place in communities which traditionally have had a strong historic Christian presence and influence. This is not only occurring in the North American context, but also in other parts of the world where people are impacted by globalization and modernity.

It is within the urban setting, where there are changing religious affiliations and persons seeking new faiths that the challenges presented by religious pluralism are greatest. For instance, within a five block radius of a particular neighborhood in central Los Angeles the following churches can be found: First Church of Rasta (symbolic of several "New" world religions), Trinity Baptist (representing a historic black denomination), Westminister Presbyterian (an African-American congregation located in a predominantly Anglo denomination), Masjid Ibaadillah (an Islamic mosque), and the Deliverance Church of Christ (Pentecostal). For some churches, the presence of the orthodox Islam, and the tremendous growth among African Americans who have embraced orthodox Islam, are seen as threats. The activities of orthodox Muslims in recent years in Los Angeles County have included the developments of neighborhood mosques, community centers, elementary schools, stores and bookstores. Some pastors and church leaders in various geographic locations throughout Los Angeles County are having to struggle with the meaning of faithful Christian congregational mission and witness as they watch religious pluralism unfold before their eyes within the African-American community.

However, in its current state and understanding of biblical mission amid religious diversity, the church is unaware of how Islam has been contextualized within the African-American community. The following account, excerpted from Bebe Campbell (*Essence*, December, 1992) illustrates some of the typical issues which are being raised in the African-American community. It is focused on the more concrete observational aspects of missiological research and is fundamental to the understanding of the more abstract realm of theory building related to Christian mission among Muslims.

"Is Jesus the only way?" is a thought that perplexes more and more African-American Christians as a result of living in an increasing religiously plural society. As the women sipped their coffee, Patrice pondered this question. She listened quietly as each of the others spoke of their personal religious journeys, and she became reflective. Patrice is a Christian who was brought up in the Baptist church. She had stopped going to church for several years, and now has returned to the church. As she shared her faith with the others, she acknowledged:

> I realized that the music and the celebratory spirit of the Baptist church gives me strength. I can actively participate in what's happening by responding any way I choose. I feel very connected to all African people when I'm in church. The ritual of a black Baptist minister preaching the gospel is sustaining to me. I like the cadence of the preacher's voice; it excited me. I can get a message that will help me get through my problems. When I was younger, I used to think that God hated me because I was bad. My church has taught me that God is love (Campbell 1992:56).

With commitment, and strong in her Christian faith, Patrice, listened to the others as they now shared, with surprise and confusing. How could they not see the truth of Christianity? Jesus is the only way, isn't He?

The Reality of Religious Pluralism

Tina who had departed from the Methodist church and was now a Science of Mind practitioner, was speaking. "My religion takes God out of the heavens and places him in the center of our being. Science of Mind says that Jesus Christ wasn't the great exception, but the great example. . . . It teaches us that the world is in divine order, that all our needs will be met when we respond to the very tangible presence of God within us" (Campbell 1992:56).

Then there was Barbara. She grew up attending the Episcopal Church, and discovered Buddhism in her twenties while living in Los Angeles. "When I was younger, I never really understood the concept of Jesus being divine; I just went along with it," she said. According to Barbara, her faith has brought her a new sense of enlightenment that has an impact on her daily life. "It's empowering to know that there is cause and effect, because it makes me more conscious of my thoughts and words. I've begun to realize that I am the reason for my problems" (Campbell

1992:56). And regarding chanting which she says uplifts her, "Somehow when I'm chanting, everything comes out, my truest, deepest feelings."

Raised in the African Methodist Episcopal Church, another friend, Dianne, turned to the religion which she describes as one which helped her to embrace her own culture. Dianne says that "rather than replacing Christianity, Yoruba enhances her understanding of it. It's very empowering for me to be able to call upon the strength of my ancestors. In my house I have an ancestral table with pictures of all my relatives. I say their names and ask them for guidance. When I walk by that table I feel that I can overcome every struggle because they did" (Campbell 1992:122).

Concerning the Yoruba religion, it is described in the following manner. Cause and effect is the centerpiece of this faith: followers of Yoruba believe that you reap what you have sown. Yorubas pay homage to Olodumare, the highest power. They also acknowledge and give offerings to other deities, known as Orishas. There are Obatala, Shango, Oshun, Yemoja and many others.

Sheba, another young lady seated around the table, proudly points out that she is a third generation Ethiopian Hebrew. She attends Friday evening services at the synagogue, believes in one God, and does not believe in Christ.

> We follow the Old Testament of the Bible. We consider our bodies holy and eat only kosher food, food that is clean according to Hebraic law. And we dress modestly. . . . Yom Kippur is a day that strengthens our faith. . . . Growing up as a Black Hebrew in America is hard. It is easy to stray away from the religion, but I never wanted to, because my beliefs have made me feel better about myself. I feel that everything I'm doing is for the Almighty (Campbell 1992:122).

The Particular Challenge of Islam

However, perhaps no other testimony moved (and yet disturbed) Patrice as much as the one given by Halima, who is a Sunni Muslim. She professes Islam, a faith based on the teachings of the prophet Muhammad, as described in the Qur'an.

> When I discovered Islam, I was very moved. . . . I loved the focus on family and the interconnectedness of all things. My religious perspective permeates all facets of my life. The Five Pillars of Islam give me strength. The foundation of Islamic belief, the first pillar, states that there is no God but God. Knowing that helps me to put all my problems into perspective. . . . There is no power worthy of worship other than God (Campbell 1992:122).

The challenge that Islam presents to the African-American community is one that has just recently been discovered by discerning persons committed to the mission of the African-American churches. The growth of Islam among African Americans is a phenomena that calls for more research and understanding from the Christian community. C. Eric Lincoln and Lawrence Mamiya were correct in their significant observation made in 1990. "The Black Church . . . must not underestimate the Islamic challenge on the horizon. Islam is a proven universal religion that is undergoing a worldwide fundamental resurgence and the Muslims in the black communities have proven themselves to be highly motivated evangelists" (1990:397). In addition, it is not only within the United States that African Americans are embracing Islam. African Americans serving in predominantly Somalia have also converted to Islam; however, because the Department of Defense does not keep track of such conversions, the number of converts is not known (Alexander 1993:4).

As we have seen in the introductory dialogue, the religiously pluralistic society in which we live is one that has impacted African-American churches as never before. The Jehovah Witnesses, the Baha'is, the Black Hebrews, the Falashas (Black Jews of Ethiopia), the Yoruba religious followers, the Muslims and other religious groups are among the various peoples of faith actively engaging in several ministries and missions (some strategically) aimed at converting both Christian and non-Christian African Americans. More often than not, the new recruits in these various non-Christian religious bodies are from second, third, and even fourth generation Christian families.

6

Problem Statement

The most successful of the mission minded religious faiths is Islam. In theory, Muslims proclaim that "all" people are created Muslims by nature. Most Christians are surprised when they discover that Islam, according to some experts, is the fastest growing religion in the world. The current rapid growth rate of Islam through conversion in North American is staggering. Dudley Woodberry observes, however, that the numerical growth of Islam is far more biological than the result of conversions. According to Woodberry, "While in fact more people are becoming Christians each year, they are not enough to maintain the same percentage difference by the turn of the century" (March 1994). However, as Muslims actively engage in mission and ministry within the African American community, Islam and Muslims present challenges and obstacles that must be faced by the Church. The national motto of the American Muslim Society is "Bringing Humanity Together in Moral Excellence with Truth and Understanding." The motto captures the themes of life emphasized in the presentation of the Islamic faith: unity of humanity (under One God, known as Allah); the need for a program of moral excellency; and the quest for truth and reason. Muslims are attempting to make a difference based on growing religious convictions, emphasizing solutions for relevant living.

This manuscript will address the problem of the lack of awareness by Protestant African-American churches of Islamic missionary activities within the African-American community. Decreased awareness seems to have resulted in the church's inability to meet the new challenge of Islam within an increasingly religiously pluralistic society. "While it is acknowledged that Islam has offered many positive benefits to its converts, the fact cannot be denied that it has drawn people away from a personal commitment to the biblical God as revealed in Jesus Christ" (Birchett 1992:34). Therefore, the critical challenge before the contemporary African-American Protestant churches is to gain knowledge of Islam as a missionary religion. It is through a missiological understanding of Islamic faith and practices that the church will become conscious and empowered to respond with an authentic and appropriate model of contextualization. The goal of this manuscript is to discern how the church should respond within a religiously plural environment in order to address this question: What contextualized missional response should the African-American Protestant churches take that will lead to an authentic and biblical response to religious pluralism?

Additional Religious Concern: Nominalism

The presence of an active environment of religious pluralism tends to emphasize particular religious and spiritual themes that emerge from a secular context. The result is Christian nominalism. This issue, along with those previously identified need to be incorporated into an appropriate framework for identifying and analyzing a theological response to religious pluralism. Issues related to Christian nominality ("I never really understood the concept of Jesus. I just went along with it") are evidenced in the following terms: **the divinity of Jesus Christ** ("Jesus is a great example, not the great exception"); **personal identity and humanity** ("I feel connected with all Africans". . . "and with my ancestors"); **the relationship between religious belief and rituals** ("chanting . . . five pillars . . . dietary laws"); **reason and religion** ("My religion takes God out of the heavens and places him in the center of our being") ; and, the need for **a holistic perspective of life** ("the connectedness of life").

As Joseph V. Crockett reminds us, though, the aim of Scripture is for learners to claim the life of Jesus as their own and to embrace an identity in the fullness of their lives: "the formative and transformative processes must not ignore the cultural context through which identity emerges or faith is expressed" (1991:1). Specific religious and theological concerns such as those identified in the opening dialogue are being raised anew by a critical generation of African Americans. In light of the growing multi-cultural and multi-religious environment in which the Church is called to mission, awareness of orthodox Islam must be addressed to provide the means for formulating an authentic and appropriate Christian model of contextualization.

The Research Goal

Samuel P. Schlorff has stated in regard to Christian mission to Muslims, that "What is needed to meet this challenge is a contextualized apologetic that presents the case for Christian faith in relation to Muslim ideology. This has been called 'cultural-specific apologetics' " (Schlorff, quoting Netland, 1988:297). A contextualized apologetics should enable and empower these churches to respond with biblical faithfulness in both belief (an appropriate apologetic) and in practice (appropriate contextualized models). With intentionality, this study will focus on historic and contemporary Muslim leadership in an effort to address the concerns, motives, and means of mission as they relate to the indigenous Muslims of North America, including their worldview and approaches to contextualization.

The overall goal is to develop criteria leading to an authentic and appropriate model of biblical contextualization for African Americans among the present Islamic movements utilizing historical and contemporary ethnographical factors that might assist the Protestant African-American churches in meeting the challenge of Islam within their communities. In the process of examining the mission of evangelization and re-evangelization of African Americans in the midst of religious diversity and missional activities, the characteristics of authenticity and appropriateness of a contextuzalized model will emerge.

Furthermore, the additional goals of this study are: (1) to study the major theoretical mission models of contextualization, with special attention given to the differences of usage among Muslims of both the Nation of Islam and the American Muslim Society (i.e., the House of Islam); (2) to indicate the applied nature of contextual approaches currently influencing African-American churches; and (3) to identify missiological criteria that will assist in the formulation of a biblically faithful and appropriate model of Christian contextualization for the communication of the Christian gospel.

Objectives

The introductory scenario has been offered to describe not only the various voices of religious pluralism that exist within the contemporary African-American community, but is also descriptive of the dilemma that pluralism presents to the wider Christian community. As stated previously, the purpose of this manuscript is to identify the need for the Protestant African-American churches to develop a contextualized theology of mission and ministry within the face of the Islamic challenge. Significant objectives guiding this study are: (1) to re-appraise African American religious history; (2) to determine the nature of the contemporary challenge of Islam; (3) to understand Muslim contextualization and mission approaches; and, (4) to determine the present state of Protestant African-American churches. These four objectives will direct this inquiry.

To Re-Appraise African-American Religious History

It appears that the missional challenge that Islam poses for the African-American churches cannot be comprehended through the traditional academic presentation and interpretation of American Religious History. Therefore, one objective of this study is to re-think and re-order this history as it relates to Islamic missiological experiences and influences. The African-American religious tradition has not been homogeneous. The presence of Muslims and the witness to Islamic practices existed within African-American communities as early as the 1700s, in a variety of forms.

Islam has had a long and complex history in the United States and it is this history that needs to be revisted and re-ordered in order to understand how it has functioned in the African-American community. There have been at least five major Islamic movements spanning less than a century, each one aimed directly at the African-American community. It is significant that these Islamic and proto-Islamic groups have set the stage for the influx of orthodox Islam. A careful study of each of the major movements should indicate whether or not each has portrayed Islam as a viable religious faith, and the means by which Islam, either as formal or popular, has been seen as a relevant and viable religious option available to African Americans.

To Determine the Nature of the Contemporary Challenge of Islam

A second objective is to understand the nature of the Islamic appeal to African Americans, especially among Christians. It is important to discern historically whether Islamic elements have produced conflict or cooperation within the African-American community, and to evaluate the consequences of the differences in the original message and context. Such discernment might contribute to a comprehensive understanding of the contemporary Islamic challenge, offering information that might be used to assist in the education and empowerment of the Christian community.

A few scholars such as C. Eric Lincoln and Lawrence Mamiya (1990) and Birchett (1992) have acknowledged the reality of the religious challenge presented to Christianity by the Muslims. While these are able to give credence to the religious dynamics occurring in the African-American community, and to take the Muslims seriously, this is not always the case. Carl Ellis (1983) has attempted to tackle this very issue from an evangelical perspective; however, he stands among those who all too lightly dismiss the missional and universal appeal of Islam, claiming that apart from the Arabic cultural wrappings, Islam can have no appeal.

> . . . the very essence of Islam is rooted in a language and culture which is neither Afro-American nor African, but Arab. Thus Islam cannot take on itself the identity of any non-Arab culture. Islam and Black culture would have functioned in an "oil and water" relationship, the oil layer of supra-culture being Islam and the water layer of culture being Black humanism. They never blend (Ellis 1983:112).

As long as African-American Protestant Christians continue to deny both the universal appeal and missional nature of Islam and naively believe that this world religion is incompatible with the African-American experience, we will fail to grasp the significance of the evolution of Islam in North America toward Sunni Islam. The

Christian churches must take Islam seriously in the African-American community if we are to be faithful to our missionary calling.

Religious leaders are the main avenues through which religious beliefs and knowledge are taught, along with the defining of religious practices. It is important therefore, to give attention to the examination of the current Islamic leadership influencing African-American Muslims and potential converts to Sunni Islam. One of the critical challenges before the contemporary African-American Protestant churches is to gain a greater knowledge and understanding of the Islamic leadership within the North American context. This process requires an increased awareness of Muslim leaders and their behaviors and styles that reveal a complicated and intelligent world view.

Muslim Contextualization

The third objective is concerned with understanding Muslim contextualization. The term contextualization has been used freely by Christians. Within the context of Christianity, the following definition is offered:

> Contextual theology is the dynamic reflection carried out by the particular church upon its own life in light of the Word of God and historic Christian truth. Guided by the Holy Spirit, the church continually challenges, incorporates, and transforms elements of the cultural milieu, brining these under the lordship of Christ. As members of the body of Christ interpret the Word using their own thoughts and employing their own cultural gifts, they are better able to understand the gospel as incarnation (Gilliland 1989:12).

However, even without Christian theology and doctrine, these concepts can be generically conceived and utilized by any missional religious community. Therefore, in order to understand the dynamics and potential of Islamic missionary activities, and in an effort to formulate an appropriate Christian response, generic concepts of mission models and approaches must be considered. Selected models will be identified as they relate to the experiences of contextualization by both the Nation of Islam, and the Sunni Muslims.

Specific models and approaches will be identified based on their implications for Christian utilization for the mission of evangelizing and re-evangelizing African Americans in the midst of the contemporary challenge of the Islamic faiths. The insights of this study will be presented in the two final chapters of summaries and a recommendation. They will be based on the determination as to whether the Protestant African-American churches are unable or unwilling to respond to the current missional challenge of Islam. The summary and conclusions provided will be designed to affect an increased awareness of need to respond to the missional efforts of the Muslim in a holistic nature that is both biblical and effective. Elements of a faithful response (holistic and appropriate) to the missiological activities of the Muslims in the African-American communities of Los Angeles will be identified and applied to the development of a biblical response to the missional efforts of Muslims.

Understanding the Present State of Protestant African-American Churches

A fourth objective identifies the need to assess the church's willingness and ability to address the challenge presented by Islam. This can only be obtained by a determination of the present state of Protestant African-American churches. Knowledge is needed concerning these churches, not only in relation to the concerns and challenges facing the African-American community, but in relation to other religious faiths, especially that of Islam. *The State of Black America*, produced by the National Urban League, comments that:

> Because a religious orientation or perspective is not readily amenable quantitative measurement, it is not possible for us to be precise about its influence on black families over the past decade. Nevertheless, it appears that the black church continues to play a major role in black communities across the nation. Each Sunday it continues to attract the largest number of African Americans at one time. In some communities, cutbacks in funds for social services and community action agencies have led many black churches to assume the historical role as a key provider of social, psychological and economic support to black families. . . . Moreover the black ministry continues to be the vanguard of the struggle on behalf of African Americans (1980:54).

From the perspective of most of the social service agencies and organizations which have historically served the African-American communities, there is a continued affirmation of the positive and central role of the African-American churches. "The Black Church in America" in *Progressions*, a report of the Lilly Foundation, also supports this positive view of the church, observing that "Problems aside, African-American churches are still the strongest institutions left in many inner-city neighborhoods" (1992:1). However, what is the actual state of the African-American churches from a missiological perspective? The primary question pertaining to this area of the study is this: Do the African-American churches understand their present historical context as well as the environment of religious pluralism?

These questions are certainly crucial ones considering the pluralistic society in which the African-American churches must seek to be faithful to their Christian calling. As churches begin to reflect on ministry and mission in the year A.D. 2000 and beyond, it is possible to have a vision of what the church can become. However, it is impossible to shape and influence churches for faithful ministry and mission unless these churches are aware of their present state. Once churches acknowledge their present condition it becomes possible to bring about recognition, remedy to actualize visions, and to address challenges effectively.

The Purpose

The purpose of this study is to determine how the Protestant African-American churches can missiologically respond to the Islamic challenge currently taking place within the African-American community. This will be accomplished by providing a means by which the criteria for the development of an authentic and appropriate model of Christian contextualization could be identified and formulated as a resource for the mission of evangelizing and re-evangelizing African Americans in the midst of the contemporary challenge of the Islamic faith. As indicated in the opening dialogue, Islam has found a permanent foothold in the North American context among the African-American population. According to recent statistics, 42% of the current 6 million Sunni Muslims in the United States are African

Americans (see Appendix A). This study seeks to identify several key factors, historical, sociological, and cultural, as well as religious, which are responsible for the continued growth of Islam among African Americans who see that religious faith as a viable religious option.

Significance

The challenge of pluralism today has caused key issues to surface that African-American congregations must struggle to address if they are to witness faithfully within religiously diverse communities. Among them are the prevalent issues of social justice, urbanization, cultural diversity and economic disparity. It is, however, the issue of religious pluralism within the African-American communities that is challenging the church most from the perspective of theological relevancy. A biblical response to Christian mission within religious diversity might enable the contemporary African-American church to discover a foundation upon which to respond to the current challenge of religious pluralism, specifically that of Islam.

In a social environment where other religious believers are also striving to give witness to the "uniqueness" of their beliefs, what are appropriate biblical models of living within religious pluralism? Does the Bible provide a theoretical framework for guiding Christians as they live within a religiously plural society? These questions raise timely issues to which African-American churches must seek to respond. Posed within the context of a pluralistic society--one that is religiously plural, and in the case of African-American Muslims, racially and culturally diverse as well-- questions about God, God's nature, and goals abound. Addressing the issue of pluralism in general, Lesslie Newbigin has written:

> Pluralism is conceived to be a proper characteristic of a secular society, a society in which there is no officially approved pattern of belief or conduct. It is therefore also conceived to be a free society, a society not controlled by accepted dogma but characterized by the critical spirit which is ready to subject all dogmas to critical (and even skeptical) examination (1989:1).

Though pluralism is one of the dominant features of our culture, as Newbigin observes, the principle of pluralism is not universally accepted in our culture. The growth of Islam in the United States can be attributed to certain aspects of Western culturalism, both the rejection of it by African-American Muslims and the embracing of opportunities for Islam to develop by immigrant Muslims. Significant is the observation made by ethnographer James P. Spradley.

> Our culture has imposed on us a myth about our complex society--the myth of the melting pot. Social scientists have talked about "American Culture" as if it included a set of values shared by everyone. It has become increasingly clear that we do not have a homogeneous culture: that people who live in modern, complex societies actually live by many cultural codes (1979:12).

One additional observation needs to be made in order to understand the reaction of North Americans in general to the Islamic presence. What historian Thomas Sowell has observed about cultural diversity holds true also about religious diversity in this culture. "American pluralism was not an ideal with which people started, but an accommodation to which they were eventually driven by the destructive toll of mutual intolerance in a country too large and diverse for effective dominance by any one segment of the population" (1981:10). The tolerance of North Americans in the area of technology and the willingness to experiment, for example, is not reflected in attitudes regarding religious pluralism. Given these realities, the Great Commission sends forth the church within the given plurality to obediently and faithfully engage in the mission of Jesus Christ in word and deed.

In addition, although there is such information available about the expansion of Islam in other cultural contexts (such as Bosnia, the Sudan, Indonesia, and in east and west Africa), and in historical circumstances such as the Crusades to mention one, only recently have scholars given any attention to the development of Islam in North America, and specifically among African Americans. This study seeks to remedy this concern.

Research Questions

The research questions guiding this study are:

1. What historical influences have shaped the growth of Islam in the African-American community?

2. Why may African Americans be more vulnerable to orthodox Islamic missionary outreach (*daw'ah*) today?

3. What is the nature of the Islamic appeal to African Americans?

4. What challenges does Islam pose for Christianity in the African-American community?

5. What segment of the Los Angeles churches will respond to the Muslims as a religion whose followers need to be converted?

Definition of Terms

Whenever possible, the particular context or speaker will be identified within the discourse to help ensure clarity of understanding. There are three principle terms that must be clarified to avoid confusion and prevent relevant dialogue.

African American

According to the *Harvard Encyclopedia of American Ethnic Groups,* the following observation is made:

> There were an estimated 24 million Afro-Americans in the United States is the mid-1970's, a figure making them not only the largest ethnic group in America, but second only to Afro-Brazilians in the Western Hemisphere and larger than any single ethnic sub-group in Africa. However, not their tremendous number, but their minority status has governed the position of blacks in America (Thernstorm 1980:5).

This definition is significant, not only quantitatively, but sociologically. Its implications for worldview themes are key. It is appropriate to speak of the "African-American community," not on the basis of race or ethnicity, but rather on the communal foundation of a people bound together by a shared history, collective self needs, and a common experience of the same kinds of struggles. Warith D. Muhammad summed it up in these words:

> The difference between our spirits and the spirit of an achieving society like the Jews, the Asians and many of the European races, is that we have been cutoff from natural social progression. We were taken out of the social mold

of life by slavery. Slavery broke up the social pattern of the lives of those who were enslaved and made them conscious of themselves as properties dependents of their masters. . . . . We were cut off too abruptly, too thoroughly to have the kind of sensitivity we find in other ethnic groups.... We have taken all of our signals from the new environment that offered us little or nothing from the past except negative things (1988:56-57).

Thernstorm's definition is significant because the "minority status" continues to be supported by the current Human Development Index (of the United Nations Development Program) which ranks African Americans on the basis of standards of living which include poverty levels, nutrition, health, education, gender disparities and income distribution, with those of some second and third world countries. In response to the forced transportation of Africans from Africa, the African holocaust (including the Middle Passage which resulted in the deaths of 1/3 of the estimated 15-50 millions of Africans removed from the continent from 1482- 1888), there has risen several philosophical schools of thought represented in the African-American churches. Schools of thought have also been influenced and developed out of the ambiguities related to the life experiences of segregation, injustices and discrimination within the U.S.A. and the Church.

Worldview and Worldview Change

The concept of worldview is based on the difference between reality on the one hand and the way humans perceive this reality on the other hand. Charles Kraft has defined world view as follows:

Cultures pattern perceptions of reality into conceptualizations of what reality can or should be, what is to be regarded as actual, probable, possible, and impossible. These conceptualizations form what is termed the "worldview" of the culture. The worldview is the central systematization of conceptions of reality to which members of the culture assent (largely unconsciously) and from which stems their values system. The worldview lies at the very heart of culture, touching, interacting with, and strongly influencing every other aspect of the culture (1979:53).

This anthropological perspective undergirds the fact that all people have a world view from which they see the totality of life. Often when it comes to the discussion of the Africans kidnapped and forcibly brought to North American, world view has often been over looked or discredited because the Africans were seen as merely blank pages in a book.

Muslims

Within the United States, there are two Islamic groups that are considered orthodox, and numerous Islamic sects. The largest majority are Sunni Muslims who follow the *Sunna*, meaning, "the way of the Prophet." The second largest group are the Shiites (also called the Shi'a Muslims). The division between the Sunnis and the Shiites was originally political and developed from a struggle over succession to the secular rule of the the prophet Mohammad. A third group, though not orthodox, consists of the Sufi order, which developed in the thirteen century, and are represented in the United States in the forms of the Maktab Tarighat Oveyssi Shahmaghsoudi and the Naqshbandi fellowships.

Among the non-orthodox Islamic groups are listed the following: the Ahmadiyya Movement in Islam; the Ahmadiyya Anjuman Ishaat Islam, Lahore, Inc.; the Ansaaru Allah Community; the Hanafi Madh-Hab Center; the Moorish Science Temple of America; the Moorish Science Temple Reincarnated, Founder; the Nation of Islam (The Caliph); the Nation of Islam (Farrakhan); the Nation of Islam (John Muhammad); and, the Nation of Islam (Silas Muhammad). Each has its own history of development within the United States, a headquarters in addition to local places of worship, and publications.

The African-American Muslim is often referred to as the indigenous North American Muslim primarily because the first persons to practice Islam in North America were Africans and early African Americans. Even today the largest number of African converts to Islam are from the African-American population. There are three primary groups of Muslims active within the African-American community.

These are (1) members of the Nation of Islam, a "proto-Islamic" movement, to borrow a term coined by C. Eric Lincoln in 1973; (2) immigrant (and naturalized) Muslims and international students; and (3), the African-American Muslims who identify their movement as "American Muslim Society", a Sunni Muslim branch of Islam. The latter two groups, representing official Islam, are separated only by cultural, worldview and linguistic differences. They are united by Islamic orthopraxy and Qur'anic beliefs as generally interpreted. The Nation of Islam Muslims and orthodox African-American Muslims of the American Muslim Society have a common origin and history, but are mutually divided over the issues of Islamic orthodoxy.

Official (or Formal) Islam

Theologically, there is only one Muslim community, one Islamic confession, one Islamic orthopraxis. However, as it has previously been discussed, there are within the North American context several forms of Islam. Emphasis of this point is made for the benefit of Muslim readers who have insisted that Islam is one religious faith and that it does not divide itself along racial lines or into sects. As one imam has shared with me: "Consequently, the term 'orthodox' Islam has no meaning for us. The term orthodox is a term that is frequently used in conjunction with Judaism. A Muslim is either a believer or a non-believer. We follow the sunna of Muhammad (S.A.W.)" (Abdul-Qadir Morris, April 14, 1992:2). Denny affirms this when he states that orthodoxy is not the best term to use when characterizing Islam's sense of right religion. He sees that the better term might be "orthopraxy," because it comes closer to the reality of Muslim devotion and obedience to God (1985:989). Within the context of this study, orthodoxy and orthopraxy are interchangable and both are identified with official Islam. Denny observes that:

> Generally, for the majority, "true" Islam has been considered to be Sunnism, based on the Qur'an and adith, the interpretations and teachings of the early jurists, and the four great law schools. Together these compromise the Shari'a and its instrutionalized expressions. . . . At the ritual level, the Shi'i minority have also been included as full and equal participants, as it makes much more

sense to view the two dimensions as an essentially unified tradition but offering a variety of emphasis and style (1985:336).

The distinctions presented between immigrant Muslims and African-American Muslims are for clarity and analytical purposes only. One of the largest community of orthodox/orthopraxy Muslims in North America is found among African-American Sunnis who are the subject of this study. The second largest group of Muslims are the Sunni immigrants, many of whom will eventually become naturalized citizens, and international students, representing Islamic communities from more than 65 nations.

The thinking and writing of Warith D. Muhammad, a national Muslim leader in the U.S.A., will be researched in an effort to determine the direction that orthodox Islam has taken within recent history. As an imam with much vested power and authority, he has a primary responsibility of representing Muslims in the United States and both immigrant and indigenous American Muslims worldwide. Having sought orthodoxy wholeheartedlly since the 1960s, he has received some of his life-long Islamic education in Egypt. He is a well trained student of the Qur'anic and Islamic studies, and serves on the Supreme Council of Masjids of the prestigious and scholarly Muslim World Leage of Mecca and New York (Mohammed 1988:1). In addition to having been awarded the "Gold Medal of Recognition" by the Ministry of Waqfs by Muhammad Hosni Muburack, president of Egypt, and the Walter Reuther Humanitarian Award, religious endowments, W. D. Muhammad was invited to pray at Congress and during President Clinton's Inaugural Celebration.

Proto-Islamic Movements

Popular Islam refers to Islamic teachings that appear to conform within the boundaries of Islam, but whose belief and/or practices in part indicate roots based on societal or cultural influences. The veneer of Islamic references are presented to appear in harmony with cultural ideas and practices that emerge and are presented as a type of orthodox Islamic standard. 'Proto-Islam' is a term used by C. Eric Lincoln to refer to Islamic groups, such as the Nation of Islam, which contribute to a "pronounced awareness of Islam, its power and its potential" (1989:347). Throughout African-American religious history, there have been key persons who have prepared the soil in which Sunni Islam has taken root, and have contributed to the formation of a more general knowledge of Islam-- historical, theological, social and geographical. Concerning the Nation of Islam, Lincoln has stated:

> Under Elijah Muhammad, the Nation of Islam became the prevailing Islamic presence in America. It was not *orthodox Islam*, but it was by all reasonable judgments, *proto-Islam* ; and therein lies a religious significance that may well change the course of history in the West (1989:348).

Significant proto-Islamic movements are analyzed in this study in regards to those elements that have contributed to a sustantial awareness of Islamic beliefs and practices. While this study is not necessarily concerned with the members of the Nation of Islam, it becomes obvious that one of the main distinctions being made, particularly by the imams is between the African-American Muslims of the orthodox American Muslim Society and the Nation of Islam. Both Christians and non-Christians are often confused about formal and popular Islam, and the distinction between the two is sometimes lost.

It was sociologist C. Eric Lincoln who coined the term "Black Muslims" in 1956, and even today, his unprecedented work entitled *The Black Muslims in America* (1961, 1973, 1991) continues to prove extremely valuable in understand the origins and rationale of the Nation of Islam movement. It has, however, led to some sharp misconceptions and generalization regarding all African Americans who happen to be Muslim, without differentiating between other streams of Islam (such as the Hanafis and Ahmaddiyas) and members of the Nation of Islam.

> While the name Black Muslims has been in vogue since its coining by sociologist Eric Lincoln in the 1960s, it is not a term that has been consciously adopted by the African-American community, and suggests a homogeneity that can be deceptive. In fact, there are today African Americans who are members of the Hanafi confession, as well as other groups of practicing Muslims (Haddad 1984:258).

This points to the need for careful examination and analysis of information and knowledge presented if we are to understand today's African-American orthodox Muslim with accuracy and integrity.

The Nation of Islam, in its various forms (the largest group is headed by Louis Farrakhan), has chosen to remain outside of orthodox considertions, and its members are called Black Muslims. According to Farrakhan:

> My brothers in the East were never subjected to the conditions of slavery and systematic brainwashing by the Slavemasters for as long a period as my people here were subjected. I cannot, therefore, blame them if they differ with me in certain interpretations of the message of Islam (Lincoln 1973:243).

Farrakhan simply could not reconcile the social conditions of African Americans with a religious doctrine such as orthdox Islam that lacked a direct and vigorous political message (Lee 1988:86).

African-American Churches

The African-American Christian community is by no means homogenious. It is diverse, complex and contains several theological beliefs and doctrine that can be classified into two primary religious communities.

Indigenous African-American Denominations

Represented among the indigenous African-American denominations, according to C. Eric Lincoln and Lawrence H. Mamiya, are the African Methodist Episcopal Church (AME), African Methodist Episcopal Zion (AME Zion), Christian Methodist Episcopal (CME), National Baptist Convention, USA, Incorporated (NBC), the Progressive National Baptist Convention (PNBC), and the Church of God in Christ (COGIC) (1990:1). More than 80% of all African Americans worship in these denominational churches. Included in this category are African-American Christians who worship in lesser known denominational assemblies, such as the Cumberland Presbyterian Church in America (fomerly the Second Cumberland Church). These churches, according to theologian James Cone, rejected the teachings of Euro-American Christianity in favor of a gospel in which "preaching the gospel, doing Christian theology, and speaking the truth" were interrelated (1986:vii). In recent years, there has been a growth in the number of independent Afrocentric/Africentric Christian communities such as The Church of the Black Madonna (founded by Rev. Albert Cleage), and the Imani Temple (founded by Rev. George Augustus Stallings).

There is a clear distinction made in this study between Pentecostal and Protestant African-American churches. As Lincoln and Mamiya observe:

> Among the seven historic black denominations, the black Pentecostals have a unique historical origin. Unlike black Methodists and Baptists, they trace their origins not o white denominatins, but to a movement initiated and led by a black minister. Also unlike black Methodists and Baptists, these black Pentecostals began not as a seperatist movement, but as part of a distinctly interracial movement from which whites subsequently withdrew.
> The modern Pentecostal movement in the United States, inclusive of black and white people, dates from the Azusa Street Revival held in Los Angeles from 1906 to 1909 under the leadership of William J. Seymour, a black Holiness preacher. Pentecostalism, in turn, as suggested by Seymour's background, had roots in the Holiness movement of the latter part of the nineteenth century (1990:76-77).

What this distinction intends to suggest is a theoretical and critical discussion serving to indicate how African-American Pentecostals (mainly represented in the Church of God in Christ, and the Apostolic fellowships), and Protestant African Americans think, understand and participate in God's mission from the perspective of religious pluralism.

African-American Churches in Predominately White Religious Bodies

African-American churches located in primarily Anglo religious denominations continue to engage in a threefold ministry. This includes: (1) ministering with the Anglo members of the church in areas of common calling, mutual concern and committed ministry, (2) ministering to the Anglo majority within the church whose Euro-centric view of theology and culture are frequently insensitive to the concerns and perspectives of racial and ethnic Christians within their church body, and (3) ministering within these denominations to the African-American population within and surrounding the local congregation.

From the Reformed tradition, Randal M. Jelks speaks with clarity to the particular issues facing African Americans in predominately Anglo churches.

> Important cultural and spiritual issues lurk behind our conversations. The first is whether the predominately Anglo-Christian heritage can speak meaningfully to the spiritual-political quest for freedom of the great-grandchildren of African- American freedmen and ex-slaves. Second, are the values we find in the Anglo-Christian heritage better spoken outside the rubric of a nearly all white denomination? Being African American in a predominantly white denomination points out the dilemma that W. E. B. Du Bois posed at the turn of the century: How could Americans of African descent be both American and African without damaging either our Americanness or our Africanness? To be part of a predominately white church raised all kinds of questions about which side we fall on and who we are in the definitional struggle in the African-American community between social class and cultural heritage (*A Journal of Reformed Thought Perspective* May 1992:7, adapted).

Any talk about pluralism therefore demands a critical understanding of the role of ethnic, racial, and the historical process of socialization in the North American context. Without this deliberate intentionality, the ability to contextualize the Christian faith, by persons who seek to impact others with the core message of Christianity, particularly as we enter the twenty-first century, will find their efforts ineffective.

In addition, the following definitions are offered for further clarity.

1. <u>Protestant African-American Churches</u>: Church denominations or individual congregations in the United States whose constituent memberships/parishioners are predominately composed of persons of African descent.

2. <u>Pentecostal African Americans</u>: In addition to that above, Pentecostal Christian theology has historically involved a belief in God, miracles and the power of the Holy Spirit present in the life of every believer. L. Grant Mc Clung, Jr. has identified five major characteristics of pentecostal missions. They are: a literal

biblicism, an experiential Christianity, belief in the personality and power of the Holy Spirit, a strong Christology, and an urgent missiology (1988:2).

3. Black theology: Black theology is a distinct theological position within Christianity which uses the experience of Black people as the starting point for all discussion about God and Divine relationship to and involvment in the universe. It is based upon a sociopolitical and economic context apart from that which is generally identified as (so- called) traditional Western theology, but which is, in fact, White western theology. White western theology, by contrast, has been structured primarily in keeping with the sociopolitical and economic events in Europe or theological tenets growing out of that context.

4. Africentricity/Afrocentricity: A worldview, or perspective of the universe that places Africa at the center for persons of African descent (as for Asians, an Asian oriented center or Europeans, an European-oriented worldview). This perspective makes Africa the subject rather than object of all inquiry and investigation. Instead of using other cultural perspectives by which to evaluate and compare, Africa becomes the standard by which other cultures, histories and sociopolitical systems are compared.

5. Afrocentric Church: An African-American congregation whose proclamation of the Gospel of Jesus Christ is informed and shaped by an Afrocentric consciousness. It points out Africa's role in giving birth to Judeo-Christian theological tenets in ways generally overlooked by traditional Eurocentric scholarship. Evangelism, mission, Christian education, nurture, and stewardship in the Afrocentric congregations all emphasize the distinctive contributions of Africa in the formation of the Gospel.

6. Religion: Religion provides a set of instructions about how to live life, as well as a particular perspective on the nature of things created, as well as the Creator. Through religion, faith involves not only a way of looking at the world, but also a personal trust in God.

Assumptions

There are four key assumptions undergirding this manuscript on the encounter of Islam and the response of the Protestant African-American churches. The distinctions help determine the shape of God-talk that is concerned with how humans seek to understand God, the universe, their relationship with one another, and their responsibilities within the world. This affirms that theology must therefore be culturally bound and relative, as Richard Busse notes "if that is not admitted, then theology becomes idolatry" (1993:2).

Today's pluralistic social environment is one where Muslims and other religious believers or advocates are also striving to give witness to the "uniqueness" of their religious beliefs and practices. They, like Christians, discover that secularization (the impact of science, nationalism, humanism, urbanization and the decline of western influence) is having an impact on the religiosity of North Americans in general, to such a degree that we are now living in what has been defined as a "controlled secularity."

> The dominant religion in the United States is a folk religion which deifies traditional American values. This civil religion retains and uses the symbols of traditional Christianity, but with the meanings changed. So in the nineteenth century, Christian symbols were used to support American imperialism as 'Manifest Destiny.' In the twentieth century, Christianity is widely equated with the religiosity of Readers Digest, and some churches with large attendance reinforce this heretical equation, rather than liberate people from their cultural idolatry into biblical faith (Hunter 1992:32).

Islam: Perceived As a Viable Faith Alternative

A first assumption is the belief that only by understanding the religious worldview of the Muslim can Christian witness among Muslims and potential Muslims be effective. The Christian witness must be cognitive of the fact that for the Muslim, law and tradition are as central to their belief system as are grace and faith to Christianity. In spite of this major religious worldview difference, Christian and Muslim dialogue can find common ground in defining the nature of God as Creator, Sustainer and Judge. The underlying premise of this study begins with an acknowledgment of the important and universality of the spiritual dimension of humans beings (Muck 1991:9). However, as Umar A. Hassan astutely noted, "Islam has been given a racial definition, one which in coined in the terms of cultural rejection, social resistance, rebellion, Black nationalism, and a simmering anger which, in turn, frightens those who have invested their identities in a white America" (1980:293). The attention focused on the race factor often fails to reveal that the typical Muslim is usually a devout religious person seeking to live right before God. Just as Christianity denies that it is a religion and defines itself as a relationship with God through Jesus Christ, so also does Islam deny that it is a religion.

Advocates of Islam claim instead, that Islam is a way of life, "which takes practical steps to organize a movement for freeing man" (Sayyid Qutb 1991:137). Warith D. Muhammad describes the purpose in life for Muslims in the following manner.

God has given us a purpose. And the highest purpose is to fulfill community, not personal life. The highest purpose for man is to fulfill community life under God as He intended. You might ask, "How can I know how God intended my life to be?" You have to trust Revelation, trust what God has revealed (1985:56).

This becomes a crucial concern, particularly when one realizes that Islam has an estimated two to three million worshippers within the United States. Forty-two percent (42%) of all Muslims in American are African Americans (_USA Today,_ March 10, 1993), (see Appendix A). A focus will be on discerning the religious worldview and theological presentation of similarities and dissimilarities existing between Islamic and Christian beliefs and practice as discovered through ethnographical research.

The Nation of Islam and its model of mission will be considered briefly because of what it represents--a powerful and influential "popular" Islam, that has frequently become the step ladder leading to formal Islam. The various models and approaches evident in these two Muslim movements will be analyzed in the process of developing a framework for identifying criteria for the development of an authentic and relevant model of Christianity contextualized for the mission of evangelization and re-evangelization of African Americans in the midst of the contemporary challenge of the Islamic faith.

The Act of Muslim Prayer

Because prayer, the act of addressing God with adoration, confession, supplication, or thanksgiving, is a central religious belief common to both Christianity and Islam, a focus on prayer will provide a specific means of understanding some theological aspects of Islam that are important to Muslims. Special emphasis will be brought to bear on this Islamic practice of ritual prayer, performed five times a day by the faithful Muslim. This understanding of religious thought and behavior might assist Christians in their understanding of Muslims.

Because the majority of my ethnographic research took place at the Masjid Bilal mosque (Los Angeles), the information gained there will be utilized, in conjunction with *The Prayer Made Simple* (1983), written by Tajuddin Shu'aib. Sheikh T. Shu'aib is a graduate of the Islamic University (Medina, Saudi Arabia) who was sent in 1977 to work with the American Muslim Mission. Since then, he has been working as the head of the Islamic Studies Department at the Masjid Bilal in Los Angeles. It is intended that this particular method of studying the Islamic ritual prayer practice will assist the church is understanding and meeting the challenge of providing a contextualized approach that presents the case for Christian faith in relation to the Muslim theology that is described within this study.

African-American World View

Another assumption is that there is a unique African-American worldview. As a result of affirming the transitional factors that characterizes the current historical position of African Americans, Muslims appear to be articulating the Islamic faith and addressing African-American worldview felt needs more satisfactory than most religious communities. It is in understanding both the positive and negative attitudes and actions of Muslims regarding the presentation of that faith that clarity will be gained. Persons who use "worldview" seek to define it in terms that capture the significance of "the insider in interpreting his/her own reality." The contributions of the emic/epic theories of interpretation (Pike and Harris) have helped to shape this assumption.

The assumptions of this research call attention to the fact that while the worldview perspectives, personal experiences, and concerns of African Americans as a whole have had a common historic, cultural, and social experience within the North American context, African-American Muslims and African-American Christians differ with regards to the theological framework from which they view life. As a result, Islam will be approached as a perceived viable religious option. The African- American Muslims, as found in the American Muslim Society (Sunni orthodox), represent an authentic relationship with God through religious expression. If the spiritual journey of Malcolm X could by used to represent the "typical Muslim," we would have to acknowledge that there is the possibility of at least a third generation of Muslims believers who advocate Islam.

A Review of Historical Considerations

A third assumption is that the current religious attitudes, beliefs and practices of Christians today toward Muslims is an ambiguious response to the historical nature of relationship that has existed between African-American Muslims and Christianity within the context of the United States. The growing presence of Islam is in part, a response to a violent historic past of racism and discrimination which has been undergirded by the use of Christian theological beliefs and practices (C. Eric Lincoln, 1973; J. Cone, 1993). While the Christian response is historical fact, the non-Christian response, especially in the form of Islam, has not been well presented in any systematic historical analysis. The Christian theology of African Americans that gave birth to the indigenous African-American denominations and churches in the late 18th and early 19th century, continued to reflect the theological and cultural problems that the African-American experience encountered with "orthodox American Christianity." As a result, key persons and movements, exemplified in James Cone's *Black Theology* and William Jones's *Is God a White Racist?*, and Albert Cleage's founding of the Shrine of the Black Madonna churches reflect the affirmation of the biblical God, within the Christian tradition, contextualized, as does the traditional eight indigenous African-American denominations.

But what of the key persons behind the proto-Islamic movement which also expressed religious belief in God? It is necessary to investigate the historic Islamic movement within the African-American community. Lessons from the past will be examined to determine theological, social, political and economic issues that shaped the various Muslim movements in the United States, with an emphasis on their missional response.

The Failure of the African-American Churches

Fourthly, the African-American churches must also claim their responsibility in failing to communicate and to pass on to present generations, in relevant and authentic ways, foundational Christian beliefs and values. A critical look at the state of African-American churches will indicate that there are some key internal factors related to the degree of contextualualization that will significantly determine the outcome of these churches as they encounter religious pluralism. Factors internal to the church, specifically those related to indigenous theology and worship, inadequate evangelism, the failure to develop an authentic African-American church, the church's lack of identification of the Christian faith with persons who are oppressed and powerless, and specific leadership issues cannot afford to be under-estimated. While the appeal of Islam (formal) to the African-American religious person as an external factor cannot be denied, the external factors also must be considered, for the future of the African-American churches are at stake.

Delimitations

This study on Muslims and Islam is written from the etic perspective of a Christian. I am well aware that the very factors that might have distorted the vision of other missiologists, past and current, are also the same factors--religious, gender, age, contextual--that may influence my own understanding of Muslim beliefs and practices. As an ethnographic researcher concerned with both credibility and usefulness, my academic work and experiential living in two Islamic countries and visits to others provides some stability and objectivity in understanding and presenting the religious system of Islam in the United States.

The primary focus is on comprehending the nature of the development and expansion of Islam within the African-American community. The social and religious relationships between Christians and Muslims in different historical and social contexts, and their missiological activities will inform this study as necessary for illuminating how the church is to be faithful in carrying out its commandment among and to Muslims. Global factors, especially with a focus on Africa, related to this topic may also be employed, but only as they have direct bearing on issues related to the topic. In addition, the political aspects of Muslim and Christian activities are beyond the focus on this study and will not be addressed.

Unless otherwise noted, the terms Muslim or Muslims will be used to identify African-American Muslims, who are the majority of Muslims within orthodox Islam. Although it is noted that there is a "growing number of Anglo converts to the indigenous Muslim community, estimated up to seventy-five thousand" (Haddad and Lummis 1987:3), neither they nor their conversion to Islam is of interest to this study.

Since it is not possible to study all African-American Muslims and Protestant churches, the study will be limited to the county of Los Angeles. Christians from both historic Protestant denominations and Pentecostal churches will be selected for various responses to religious pluralism. Los Angeles is an ideal geographical location for studying the impact of Muslim missional efforts and to make recommendations for the church. This is because Los Angeles represents a typical and natural setting where such multi-religious activities are being carried out nationwide. The impact of urbanization, secularization, and nominality among Christians, in addition to the religious pluralism, assist in creating an ideal environment where Christians and Muslims in community can be analyzed, and a recommendation for general application can be obtained.

Orthodox Islam, in the form and practice known as Sunni Islam, is present in the African-American community across the nation, and it is alive and growing. While there are other forms of Islam practiced by African-American Muslims within the African-American community, this study will limit its primary focus to the study of Sunni Islam as representative of orthodoxy/orthopraxy in Islam. The Nation of Islam (NOI) will be included as the embodiment of popular Islam, that is, a form of the Islamic faith more concerned with local cultural issues rather than religious.

There is a third concern which cannot be addressed due to the limitations of this research. It refers to the desire to understand the Muslims from a biblical as well as theological perspective. Clinton Bennett points to God's promise to Ishmael and the covenant that carried both spiritual and material blessings. According to him, the thoughts of Charles Foster and John Frederick Dennison Maurice's theological premises thus prepare the way for the reception of Christianity (Clinton 1991:116-117).

In addition, it must be recognized as Kenneth Cragg reminds us, that neither the Christianity nor the Islam present in the United States today should be conceived or will be treated as ideals (1993:163). The Christian Islamicist Yvonne Haddad speaks of this based on her comparative study of Islamic values in the United States which demonstrates the changes that some Islamic practices undergo in this country (1987). Also, Luzbetak (1991) speaks to this issue from the Christian perspective, recalling the historical dimension of the syncretization of Christianity in America. As Woodberry reminds us, God begins where the Muslim (and Christian) start, and this is the mission of the church--to journey with our Muslim "companions in travel, and be used by our Divine Companion to open our minds to understand the scriptures" (1989:xv).

Methodology

The methodology presented in this chapter represents a pluri-form approach to providing explanations and predictions (the criteria for the development of an authentic and appropriate model of biblical contextualization). It is created on the premise that successful descriptions and hypothesis testing is dependent on the judicious mixing of quantitative and qualitative research materials (Pelto and Pelto 1989:xiv). The overall methodology is a multi-instrumental research which constitutes the blueprint for the collection, measurement and analysis of data within a framework of contemporary attitudes and practices related to religious beliefs and religious inquiries.

The major missiological implications of each unit of study (two identified with Islam, two identified with Christianity, and one neutral) will be cross-referenced, compared and contrasted in an effort to determine criteria for an effective Christian mission to Muslims. A single framework such as this, encompassing such diverse units of study enabled me to compare one with another, to determine the reliability of each, and to analyze the complex responses and predictions concerning religious pluralism in the African-American community. However, the study of the present situation alone would not provide the depth of understanding needed to address the research problem from a holistic perspective. Therefore the historiographic methodology must also be employed.

The Historical Method

The historical method will be used primarily to seek answers to questions framed by history as an academic discipline. The historic determinants that have influenced current Protestant African-American attitudes and practices toward Muslims will be researched, with an emphasis on identifying elements conducive to cooperation as well as to conflict. The goal in utilizing this method is to pursue data of the past which will provide partial answers identifying historical determinants related to the current low awareness of African Americans toward Muslim contextualization. The data will then be ordered in a sequence that is both meaningful and true. As suggested by missiologist Paul Pierson, attention to key persons as well as mission structures reveal much about the composition and character of mission movements (Pierson 1988). Following the presentation of historical determinants which have shaped the African-American religious experience and worldview, a presentation on history as the present (focused on Los Angeles) will serve as a means for the expression of global Muslim contextualization.

The primary objectives of the historiological method are three-fold. The first is to discover truths revealed by the experiences of persons who have identified themselves as Muslims in the past which may not be recognized in the current experience. The second is to reveal elements of past key leaders and their dynamic missional influences as represented within the Nation of Islam (and its predecessors) as well as Sunni Islam as practiced among contemporary African-American Muslims. And the third objective is to identify elements or variables which produce conflict and cooperation, and to evaluate the consequences of the differences in their original context. This historical analysis will assist greatly to understand the Muslims' presence in the United States in the past, and thereby contributing to a more comprehensive understanding of the contemporary scene.

Data Collection And Validity

I have chosen a sample of materials, and subjected them to critical analysis. The sample comprised two kinds of documents--those which contained specific information about key persons, places or events written by Muslims themselves, and those written by non-Muslims. Available information was evaluated on basis of a preferred mixture of emic and etic sources and categories. Whenever possible, the bias of the sample toward Muslim materials was compared with other sources. The documents in this study are weighed heavily toward individual perceptions of people and events. Both primary and secondary sources were utilized. Primary sources of information beginning with the historical period of the enslavement of Africans for North America, until recent times, are much more readily available than for their preceding periods of history. Yet the attempt was made to collect relevant data pertaining to the earlier periods of history, namely early Muslim and Christian encounters. Materials contemporary to the various historical periods under study were examined, including among other things, diaries, letters, newspapers, unpublished materials, magazine articles, tape recordings and maps. The bias toward primary sources was expected.

Secondary sources, including the accounts of reporters and textbooks were used also. Works of secondary scholarship were sought to find relevant materials as well as clues that lead to original source materials. They were helpful as guides because records for the majority of early Muslim thoughts and actions in history have not been kept. The lack of much recorded information regarding the early African religious experiences within the context of the United States is but yet another reminder that all histories are distorted, imperfect reflections of the past, reflecting the historian's perspective and interpretation of events.

The study is concerned with the broader national Islamic movements among African Americans and the influences that shaped them. Pertinent are those persons and movements from the 1920s to 1994 in American religious history which helped to create and sustain an Islamic identity. These movements included the leadership of Noble Ali Drew, Wadi Fard Muhammad, Elijah Muhammad, and Warith D. Muhammad, in addition to key persons such as Malcolm and Betty Shabazz, and Louis Farrakhan. This study is not simply concerned with the roots of Islamic religious beliefs and missional practices, but more importantly it is concerned with the background of the wider union of contemporary African-American Muslims whose identity is substantially grounded in, but now distinct from the Muslim experience of earlier eras. As the research questions have indicated, the experience of Muslims in history is a major factor shaping not only the contemporary Protestant African- American attitudes and practices of response, but also the current growth and expansion among Sunni Muslims.

Current Research for This Study

Los Angeles, California represents an ideal geographical location for studying the impact of Muslim missionary efforts on African Americans because its pluralism makes it more attractive to Muslim penetration. The impact of urbanization, secularization, nominality among Christians, and the religious pluralism in Los

Angeles help to create an environment where Muslims and mosque can be studied and carefully analyzed.

<u>Research Operation</u>

The contemporary data has been provided through three sources--the direct observation of human behavior; listening to and noting the contexts of human speech, and the examination of the products of human behavior. Each source will be identified, along with the use of several research tools and techniques. This enthnographic observation provides a general conceptual framework for sorting and organizing behavioral elements.

The research tools utilized for observation in this study are what Pelto and Pelto refer to as "multi-instrument research." While several different research tools were required in this investigation, the first employed was that of participant observation of both Christian (Pentecostal and Protestant), and Muslim (Nation of Islam and American Muslim Society) communions. For three years (1990-1993), formal and informal field experiences provided opportunities, scheduled and unscheduled, to gain insights and clues into topics related to the experiences of faith and life of Muslims and Christians. This information was recorded, filed and later utilized in the development of ideas, definitions, explanations and predictions.

For observation of the Muslim population, I immersed myself in a local mosque community on weekends during the third year of research. As the primary field worker, I attended classes at the mosque. My husband also attended and assisted in the observation of both verbal and non-verbal behaviors of Muslims. Because of the attitudes held by Muslims toward women in general, it was to my advantage to have my husband accompany me in those aspects of the research that took place at the mosques and public events.

I was able to observe details of Muslim worship and the educational aspects that took place at the mosque. By attending classes, visiting and interviewing with Muslims, many of the habits and concerns were discovered. Through direct participation in classes, lectures, and other learning opportunities, information was processed from subjects such as the Muslims greetings, preparation for prayer (*wudu*), performance of *salat*, and additional insights pertinent to the understanding of the Islamic law and tradition. This was extremely helpful in that it allowed me to check and monitor information received against information concerning Muslims found in both popular and academic literature.

I recognized that the data from a single grouping (such as orthodox Muslims) can only be used for suggesting relationships. In order to establish more abstract theoretical propositions, it is necessary to consider primary descriptive data from other religious groupings as well. The same process described above was also applied to the other religious communities (Pentecostal, Protestant, Nation of Islam) and as well, to the non-Muslim/non-Christian group. Each community was subjected to the same procedure of participate observation with an emphasis on the nature of group prayer, domain analysis determined by key-informant interviewing and a questionnaire, and projection techniques. The projective technique (see Appendix A) was chosen based on the the assumption that humans have a basic psychological tendency to project their personal needs, inclinations, and themes into their verbal responses and behavioral styles (Pelto and Pelto 1993:89). The testing of my research hypotheses could be carried out only if the descriptive data from all four religious communities contain the same kind of observation and descriptive materials as those available for the orthodox Muslims. The problem of making systematic comparisons was greatly reduced by operating in the one cultural worldview.

Research Population

The Muslims and Christians sampled consisted of African-American adults, women and men. They ranged in ages from 18 through the 70s. Their educational levels were diverse, as were their economic social classes. My direct and formal contacts were with five primary Sunni Muslim environments: The Altadena Taraweeh Mosque, the Los Angeles Masjid Bilal, the Islamic Adult Community Center in Inglewood, the Daw'ah Bookstore and the Multi-Cultural Islamic Center in Los Angeles. The Muslims of the NOI were studied based on three primary sources: Louis Farrakhan event (Los Angeles), Save The Children Headquarters (Los Angeles), and the Shabazz Cafe (Altadena).

Concerning the Christian community, the Interdenominational Ministerial Alliances of both the Los Angeles and Greater Pasadena chapters were studied, in addition to several ecumenically sponsored events. In particular, the following congregations informed this study through careful and intentional observations, identified by the geographical area from which most of their membership is drawn: Second Baptist (Los Angeles, CA), Grace Community (Pasadena), First African Methodist Episcopal (Los Angeles); and Redeemer Presbyterian (Compton). The Pentecostal African-American churches include the Church of God (Inglewood), the Church of God in Christ (Los Angeles), and the Apostolic Miracle Church (Altadena).

CHAPTER 2

THE HISTORICAL DETERMINANTS OF THE AFRICAN-AMERICAN
ISLAMIC RELIGIOUS WORLDVIEW

Most surveys of American religious history, with few exceptions, have practically omitted the development of Islam. This fact alone makes the subject of this research difficult, yet challenging. However, it is this fact of omission in much of the systematic teaching of world civilization and Eurocentric history in the United States that allows the contemporary Muslim to build a case based on how the "knowledge of the true religion of the people of African descent" was denied them intentionally by the bearers of Christianity. Several African-American scholars throughout the twentieth century beginning with W. E. B. Du Bois, and including John Hope Franklin, Lerone Bennett, and a cadre of recent academics, have sought to remedy this problem by appropriately interjecting the limited but available knowledge of early Islamic beliefs and practices into current presentations of American religious history.

In this chapter a holistic historical account of the development of Islamic influences and their relationship to African Americans and their African heritage will be presented. The findings of the historic determinants which have shaped the African-American worldview and religious self-understanding will be identified and analyzed. The broader historic perspective allows for the examination of how the various parts come together to form the current Islamic expansion and impact.

Precolonialized Africa

Africa is known as the cradle of civilization. It is historian Lerone Bennett, Jr. who most succinctly identifies the ethnic and cultural significance that this acknowledged fact offers the African-American community.

For Olduvis Gorge in East African from caves in the Sahara and excavations in the Nile Valley, have come bits on bone and husks of grain which speak more eloquently than words of the trials ands triumphs of the African ancestors of the American Negro. . . . The discoveries by Dr. L. S. B. Leakey and other scholars indicate that man was born in Africa, that he began to use tools there and that this seminal invention spread to Europe and Asia . . .(1964:4).

Acknowledging the sites of various contributions made to the human race in the Nile Valley . . . the Congo . . . the Sahara . . . and later discoveries in Africa, Bennett and other scholars concluded that Black people were influential contributors to Egyptian dynasties, Ethiopian kingdoms, and that they were known and honored throughout the ancient world.

Biblical historian Charles B. Copher in "Three Thousand Years of Biblical Interpretation with Reference to Black Peoples" makes the case for reviweing the history of the Bible and its interpretation with refence to Black people (1989:106-128). Kenneth Cragg also states how the Sudan deeply affected the life of a vast region of Africa during the sixth to the fourteenth century in more ways than we know (1985:230-231). The European ideologies of natural theology, racism, colonization and imperialism have coincided and merged with philosophies of economic exploitation and religious and social theories that have debased Africa and the people of that continent. For example, today there are only two European countries, Poland and Spain, that still honor the Black Madonna. It was during the Napoleonic empire that "hundreds of thousands" of black paintings of Mary and Christ were destroyed (Johnson 1991:203).

Christian and Muslim Relations

Historically there has existed an ambivalent, but accommodating, relationship between Muslims and Christians that dates to their earliest relationship in Arabia. Early on in the development of Islam, Christians (and Jews) were given the special status of "the people of the Book" as viewed in the Qur'an. This indicated that the prophet Muhammad had a knowledge of Christianity which, according to Kenneth Cragg, was "wholly oral in origin" (1985:236). According to Islamicist Donald S.

Tingle, the Prophet Mohammad's call to religious and theological renewal and revival, and to the worship of God as Allah was so strict that it left no room for the Christian belief in the Trinity. And yet, when Muhammad had to flee from Mecca to Medina the Christians in Ethiopia offered him hospitality. Particular references to Jesus and Mary, and some of the recorded miracles of Jesus, support the view that Muhammad did have contact with some Christian theology. However, the nature of the Christianity which Muhammad rejected in favor of the new faith he founded is also questionable:

> Christianity on the borders of Arabia was torn by ecclesiastical disputes that poisoned theological controversies. It was embittered by partisanship and compromise. The Ghassanids and the Hira Christians on the Syrian and Iraqui frontiers of Arabia were responsible for some Christian penetration, but they occupied buffer areas in uncertain relations with Byzantine and Persia. The southern Arabian Christianity of Najran and Yemen is known to have suffered much persecution and did not succeed in making any lasting foothold in the Hijas itself. The pre-Islamic Arab poets refer to Christian hermits, Christian wine, and Christian bells (Cragg 1985:237).

By the end of the first century of Islam, the Muslims possessed a great empire in newly conquered areas of Persia, Mesopotamia, Syria, Egypt and Northern Africa. An analysis of why Islam was able to spread so rapidly has been the focus of recent research. While it is not my intention to dwell on this issue in depth, the following quote offers much insight:

> The history of Islam, by contract, contains no Constantine. Muhammad was from the outset its Constantine as well as its Prophet. From the time when Islam established itself as a city-state in Medina, it was a form of rule as well as of worship. It came upon the Eastern world not simple as a creed, but as an allegiance, a state, and a sovereignty. Its tokens were not baptism and the bread and the wine; its tones were prayer and the caliph. It would, therefore, be un-historical and un-Islamic to suppose that when multitudes of Christians, in ancient Christian bishoprics turned to Islam, they did so merely out of intellectual persuasion and never out of prudential realism, or that what they accepted was a creed only and not also a conquest (Cragg 1985:230).

The North African Experience

Calvin E. Shenk in an article entitled "The Demise of the Church in North Africa and Nubia and Its Survival in Egypt and Ethiopia: A Question of Contextualization" (1993) presents a relevant observation. This article suggests that internal factors, as well as the degree of contextualization offered by the external challenge of Islam, significantly determined the future outcome of the churches: two which survived and two which eventually died as they encountered Islam. The factors included inadequate evangelism; the failure to develop an authentic national church; the fact that Christian literature was mainly in Latin; the identification of the Christian faith with imperial powers; the suppression of the Donatist Christians' attempt to contextualize; and, the appeal of Islam to the indigenous popular. Concerning the Nubian Church, factors such as the precarious state of relations between the church and the state; the dependence upon the Church of Alexandria which stifled leadership development; and the fact that the church lacked sufficient depth in the indigenous culture all contributed to the demise of the church.

However, the study of the two churches which did survive in the face of Islam, Egypt and Ethiopia, indicate successful contextualization, which could be attributed, at least in part, to the vision of the leadership. The leader's concern for the evangelization of the peasant population; the use of vernacular language and literature; the development of monasticism; the development of indigenous leadership; and, the development of an indigenous Christian theology did not happen by accident, but rather reflect thoughtful consideration. When the church in Ethiopia was considered, the contextualization of the Christian faith was evidenced in at least six ways: widespread evangelization; an indigenous monasticism; literature, art, music and architecture were localized; relationships developed with the Coptic Church of Egypt; an appropriate relationship between the church and state; and, theological inculturation. In conclusion, Shenk observes, "North African and Nubia abandoned Christian faith for Islam which appears to be more affirming of their culture. Egypt and Ethiopia developed a faith congruent with their culture. That embodiment enabled the Church to survive" (1993:152). Missiological implications for the African-American churches are clear. It is imperative that the African-American churches engage in a bold, self-evaluation based on the aspects of contextualization presented by Shenk's comparisons of the historical Christian churches of Africa.

Islam South of the Sahara

Carley and Kilson have noted that "Islamic civilization and European colonization are both historical experiences of the traditional African society" (1970:205). Even prior to the conquest of the Old Kingdom of Ghana (1076) Muslims were found along the regions of western Africa and the Sahara Desert. During the great Islamic era of ancient Africa, three powerful states rose which have significance for this study. They were the states of Ghana, Mali and Songhay in the western Sudan of Africa. Islamic influence was greater upon the upper classes and the leaders first , and later among the city dwellers and masses (Fatou 1985:563).

Ghana

In 1076, a group of Muslims known as the Almoravids, invaded Ghana, influencing it religiously as well as economically and politically. During the tenth and eleventh centuries, Islam was prevalent in this territory which included the areas of the present Senegal and Niger. Kumib Saleh was a chief trading city:

> By the beginning of the tenth century the Muslims influenced from the East was present. Kumbi Saleh had a native and an Arab section, and the people were gradually adhering to the religion of Islam The prosperity that came in the wake of Arabian infiltration increased the power of Ghana, and its influence was extended in all directions. In the eleventh century, when the king had become a Muslim, Ghana could boast of a large army and a lucrative trade across the desert (Franklin 1988:2).

Invading conquerors destroyed Ghana in the twelfth and thirteenth centuries.

Mali

In the year 1235, the kingdom of Mali began to emerge with prestige under the Keita dynasty. Sundiate Keita (1235-1270) was its first king, but without a doubt, Mansa-Mus (also called Gonga-Musa), who reigned from 1312-1337 was the greatest and most influential. According to historian John Hope Franklin, Mansa Musa's empire comprised much of what is now francophone Africa, and the best information of this period comes from the accounts of Musa's (and others') royal pilgrimages to Mecca.

> The kings, newly converted to the religion, were as ardent and pious as any Arabs of their day. As good Muslims, they looked forward to making the traditional pilgrimage to Mecca. . . . The historic pilgrimage of Mansa-Musa in 1324 exceeded all visits to Mecca . . . mosques were built where they were needed... he traveled to the holy places of Mecca and Medina . . .(1988:5).

He died in 1337, and Mali continued as a strong state until it declined in the mid-fifteenth century.

Songhay

Under the leadership of Sonni Ali (1464-1492), the town of Timbuktu, which Mansa-Musa and his successor Suleiman developed into the Islamic center of the West, was conquered in 1469. He was not a Muslim, and therefore met with great resistance. Songhay flourished under his political leadership. A year after his death, Askia Mohammad became Songhay's greatest ruler. He was an orthodox Muslim, and he used the laws of the Prophet Mohammad and the Qur'an to rule his country. He also served as a caliph of the Sudan.

> It was in the area of education that Askia made his most signficant reforms. Everywhere he established and encouraged schools. Gao, Walata, Timbuktu, and Jenne became intellectualizer centers where the most learned scholars of West Africa were concentrated and where scholars from Asia and Europe came for consultation and study. Scholars like El-Akit and Bagayogo, both juriconsults, were educated at Timbuktu. By the sixteenth and seventeenth centuries a distinctly Sudanese literature was emerging. At the University of Sankore black and white youths studied grammar, geography, law and literature, and surgery, whole in the mosques Askia and his subjects studied the religion of Islam in order to practice and promote it more effectively (Franklin 1988:6).

And concerning Nigeria, which by the fourteenth century was greatly Islamicized, it is written,

The nineteenth century saw the development of the "theocratic" states, with an emphasis on the uniqueness of Islam and its unwillingness to tolerate other religions. From the Wolof in Senegel to the Hausa in Nigeria and Cameroon, the Islamicization of the common people became rapid, its consolidation being helped by the protective policy of religious neutrality on the part of the colonial governments of France and Britain (Kane 1978:214).

Muslim traders and imams were responsible for much of the spread of Islam. Indications are that more research is needed in this historical area because the majority of the Africans brought to the Americas were taken from these territories of West Africa. While caution must be taken not to exaggerate the Islamic influence, we must note that it was significant. In most of western Africa and the former Congo, with the exception of Nigeria, it would appear that Africans holding differing religious beliefs co-existed together.

Islam in East Africa

The same appears to be true of the East Africa where Arab coastal settlements have been established since the seventh century. Traders settled in the areas of Somalia in the north, extending south to Zanzibar both influencing and being influenced by the traditional African culture. Later the Ahmadiyyah Mission, Pakistani missionaries, were also active in spreading their religious beliefs in this area, as a result of India prepartition (Swann, 1994).

The first impact was made by the Arab and Persian traders of the coastal fringe in the thirteenth and fourteenth centuries. This resulted in the founding of Swahili culture groups in East Africa but let the Bantu untouched. The second period coincided with the extension of the European trade and rule into the interior in the nineteenth century. One reason for the expansion was the fact that the Europeans recruited all their guides, servants, police and carriers from among the Muslims of the coast (Kane 1978:214).

Though not many American bound Africans were allegedly taken from East Africa, the impact of Muslims in this area was great as evidenced in the use of Swahili as a common language unifying many of the peoples of this region.

Islam in North America Before Columbus

Research pioneered by British linguist and anthropologist Ivan Van Sertima indicates how African Muslims from the West Coast of Africa, specifically from Mali, travelled as seafearers and were present in the ancient Americas. Considerable anthropological data indicates, among other things, that the ancient peoples of South and Central America worshipped gods deplicted with Negroid features (1976:138-179).

Leo Wiener of Harvard in 1920 published his <u>Africa and the Discovery of America</u>, which also held the view that Africans inhabited North and South America before Columbus. It is this work which provided the foundation for Sertima's research. He utilizes: (1) the cultural anthologies found nowhere else except in Americas and Africa, including African languages and the transportation of plants, cloth and animals from Africa to the Americas; (2) the diaries, letters and journals of the explorers themselves; (3) the Carbon 14 process which dates sculptures found in the Americas; (4) Arabic written documents, charts maps and other recorded tales given to the kings of Mali; and (5) dated skeletons found as recently as 1975 to substantiate theories of the African presence in the ancient Americas.

When reviews of Wiener's books are considered, it is noteworthy that the judgements pertaining to his research on Africa appears to reflect the racial ethos of the day. Weiner wrote *Africa and the Discovery of America* in 1920, and in 1924 he wrote *The Contemporary Drama of Russia.* The *Book Review Digest* contains reviews of the former book and author which include phrases such as "he is not always convincing, and is often dogmatic" and "worthless as a scholarly contribution" (1920:566), while Wiener's latter book is described as "rendering a valuable service," "a most compendible packet of information." and "here at last in a history of the Russian drama . . . a startling revaluation of accepted values" (1924:629). This would suggest a negative reaction to the subject matter rather than to the author's scholarship. W. E. B. Du Bois, on the other hand, describes Wiener and *Africa and the Discovery of America* in the following words:

Professor Wiener shows us the amazing interaction of Africa, America and Europe in the early days of the slave trade. . . . His book indicates the widest scholarship. . . . The conclusions of Mr. Wiener are striking: "When I began my scrutiny, I was firmly convinced, as is the universal belief, that tobacco, manioc, yams, . . .were blessings bestowed upon the world by the Indians. . . . But the most painful discovery was in the line of Indian religion. Here everything turned out to be topsy-turvey. In the first volume I show that the Negroes have had a far greater influence upon American civilization than has heretofore been suspected (1920:350).

Concerning Van Sertima who has sought to prove that Africans had contact in the Americas before Columbus, it is written, ". . . he has pursued it with good judgement and persuasive evidence drawn from a wide variety of sources. A fascinating case worth the attention it demands," wrote P. L. Adams in the *Atlantic Monthly* (1977:99). The book reviewer of the May 1977 issue of *Choice* has written ". . .the author's agument is presented in a clear, logical manner and is couched in much more reasonable terms than comparable books that purpost to show long-stance diffusion in ancient times. . . . Recommended for purchase by those libraries associated with with departments of anthropology or history" (*Book Review Digest* 1977:1359). In the two other entries in the Book Review Digest, the reviewers discounted the authors' knowledge of the subject matter: the *New York Times* (March 13, 1977) and the *Library Journal* (December 1, 1976).

Yvonne Y. Haddad, in an article entitled "The Muslim Experience in the United States," also affirms that Muslims from West Africa sailed across the ocean and established contact in the Americas before Columbus. According to Haddad, Columbus' library contained a copy of the work of the Arab geographer, Al-Idrisi. "This book, which describes the discovery of the East coast of the 'new continent' by eight Muslim explorers, is said to have inspired Columbus' own expedition" (*Link*, 1979).

Period of Enslavement

It is crucial to note that the first Africans who were brought to the English colonies were not brought here to serve as slaves, nor did all Africans and African

Americans serve as slaves. An in-depth research will verify that for a while religious freedom existed when the Dutch ship landed in Jamestown, Virginia, in 1617 with twenty Africans, indentured servants, on board with white indentured servants. "They entered as unfree persons in a society in which large numbers of people were similarly unfree. Their status was similar to that of many Indians, Englishmen, Scots and Irishmen. In 1661, Virginia passed the first law making Negroes formally and legally slaves for the duration of life" (Wesley 1969:62). Again, Wesley points out: "By 1790, there were approximately 13,000 Negroes in New England, of whom roughly three-fourths were free men. Vermont and Massachusetts had no slaves at all" (1969:111). In addition to the African Americans who earned and maintained their free persons status, many of the free African Americans gained freedom when they volunteered for military service in the struggle to break free from British colonial power during the American Revolution.

The masses of Africans in the context of North America, however, served as slaves making possible the development and maintenance of an economic system based on inexpensive labor. Molefi K. Asante and Mark T. Mattson observe that:

> No more tragic episode has ever been recorded in human history given its continuing impact on contemporary societies. In addition to the Africans taken from the continent, others were brutalized through warfare with the Europeans and subsequent warfare among Africans over the control of access to European goods. Long, forced marches from the interior to the coast, detention camp diseases, and the horrible Middle Passage across the Ocean to bondage, often killed one-third of the people captured by the enslavers. This brutish business depended upon force of arms, and Europeans ventured into Africa with their arms ready to snatch Africans from their villages. In addition to this practice, they turned to purchasing prisoners from African kings who were often lured by greed and intimidation into the transaction. However, the overwhelming majoritiy of Africans taken from the continent had to be taken by force and were often held in fortresses until slave ships came (1992:28).

The economic factors which motivated the European slave trade, and the fact that it was motivated and sustained by the Christian message continues to have ramifications that impact the current variables of economics and religion, as they exist among the dominant culture as well as within the African American sub-culture.

The Question of Religious Identity

What were the religious identifications of those African women, men and children who were captured and brought to North America in 1619 and throughout the period of enslavement which lasted until 1859 when the last ship, "The Wander" landed in Georgia with more than 300 persons aboard? This is a key question, yet a diffiuclt one to answer. The specific religious beliefs held by Africans forcibly brought to North America are unknown to us for obvious reasons. Considered as property instead of human beings, not much consideration was given to the personhood of the African. The prevailing attitudes held by those who called themselves "masters"allowed them to label the Africans as heathens without religious beliefs. A second reason why it is exceedingly difficult to find historical data to support evidence of a strong Islamic presence in early American history is because of the "de-Africanization" process which took place in route to the Americas. Portugal, Great Britain, Jamaica and the rest of the Caribbean were popular sites for Euro-centric indoctrination and de-Africanization processes to be introduced. However, according to worldview theory, these people held certain religious beliefs, and it is through these beliefs that the experience of enslavement had to be filtered, understood and interpreted.

Christian Roots

To be sure, some Africans were Christians and some were religious believers who worshipped in the traditional religions of Africa before the Middle Passage and the African diaspora. Historians (Latorette, Mbiti) inform us that in the sixteenth century, in several countries of Africa, African Christian communities already existed.

> In the area just south of the Congo in what was known as the kingdom of the Congo a native chief was baptized near the end of the fifteenth century. His son who succeeded him seems to have been earnestly Christian and under him a large proportion of his subjects were baptized. A son of this second generation Christian was consecrated bishop (1975: II 927).

However, the majority found Christianity during the period of enslavement. The Portuguese (Roman Catholic) Christians, under the leadership of Prince Henry, baptized the Africans as soon as possible, and in most instances, even before the Africans left their home villages.

> There, on that fateful day in 1444, Henry's men came upon the first large group of Africans. They tiptoed through the high grass and crept to the edge of the village and then, said a contemporary, "they looked towards the settlement and saw that the Moors, with their women and children, were already coming as quickly as they could out of their dwellings because they had caught sight of their enemies . . . ." The captives were promptly baptized and enslaved. Within ten years Portugal was importing one thousand Africans a year. A century later, Negroes outnumbered whites in some sections of Portugal (Bennett 1966:34-35).

Although some Africans' conversions among the Portuguese-African descendants did occur, limited success was obtained among the majority of the Africans until the late eighteenth century (Raboteau 1987:6). The "christenization of the heathen" had been used to rationalize and legitimatize the use of Africans as slaves. Realizing this, it is not surprising to discover that the first African settlers (indentured servants) in North America were named Anthony and Isabella. According to Wilmore, "perhaps fewer than six percent of the Africans who were brought to the British colonies in North America became Christians during the first one hundred and fifty years after their arrival in 1619" (1982:70).

However, the quotation above warrants a critical review, for it reveals two crucial truths that should not be ignored: (1) that these and other Africans were described as Moors, and (2) that Arab contact and influence (and thus religious affiliation) extended to the geographical areas from which many of the Africans were captured and sold. This data cannot be denied. Yet significant as it is, these facts have often been overlooked in African-American religious history as interpreted and presented throughout Christian and Euro-centric historic interpretations.

Islamic Roots

Recorded history indicates that the Muslims had deep and extensive contacts with Africans before the Christians, particularly on the west coast of Africa.

Evidence shows that the nature of the relationships was inclusive, extending from inter-tribal and interfaith marriages, to victims taken as spoils of war. Islam's perception as an inclusive religion that accommodated Africans in its original development, may have aided in its appeal.

In Africa, north of the Sahara Desert, the people defined as Arab and Berber by ethnicity, are primarily Islamic by faith. The Berbers are often referred to as Moors by some early historians. These Muslims propagated their faith as they entered sub-Sahara Africa by the desert trade routes. The rise of Islam found African people in all parts of the world; African merchants traded in India, China and Europe, and they lived in Japan, Venice and Arabia.

> When the Arabs exploded and carried Islam across North Africa and into Spain, Negroes went with them. As a religious ethic, Islam was unusually effective in cutting across racial lines. All Moslems, whatever their color, were brothers in the faith. "If a Negro slave is appointed to rule you," Mohammed said, "hear and obey him, though his head be like a dried grape." . . . In this climate, a man could be a slave today and a prime minister tomorrow. An extraordinarily large number of Negroes played heroic roles in the rise and spread of Islam--men like Mohammad Ahmad, the Sudanese Negro who claimed to be the Messiah; Abu' Hasan Ali, the black sultan of Morocco and Bilal, the friend of Mohammed. There were also numerous black generals, administrators, and poets. The abundant and detailed descriptions of inter-racial relations in the Arabian Nights and other Oriental literature proved that race was not a crucial factor in the Islamic world (Bennett 1966:12).

The significance of the name Bilal mentioned above was alluded to by Samuel Zwemer, a Christian missionary to Muslims who along with others, also noted that "the first one who led the call to prayer was Bilal, a Negro of Medina" (1909:12). As it will be shown in a later section, the name Bilal will take on greater significance as Islamic influences develop further within the context of the United States among African Americans. Among other significant, but little known facts about Muslim history in the United States are the following:

> Records also mention the 1717 arrival in the United States of Arabic speaking slaves who refrained from eating pork and believed in Allah and Muhammad. Other references point to the existence in 1790 of "sundry Moors" in South

Carolina. The state house of representatives voted to try them according to the laws of the citizens of South Carolina and not under the Negro codes, because they were subjects of the Emperor of Morocco, the first national leader to recognize the independence of the United States in 1787 (Haddad 1979:2).

The *National Anti-Slavery Standard* and the *Anti-Slavery Reporter*, from the years of 1859 to 1885, published a large number of newspaper and magazine interviews which substantiated the fact that numbers of the Africans brought to American were from present day Nigeria and the old Congo where Islamic influence was, if not substantial, at least known. Blassingame has compiled newspaper and magazine interviews which cover the years of 1827 through 1863, giving unquestionable evidence of Africans in North America who came from areas where Islam was practised. One in particular describes Dimmock Charlton (Tallen being his true name, born in 1799) a Kissi by tribe, related to the Malinke who are known to have practiced Islam. He was enslaved and brought to Georgia. The interviewer provides a description, that in spite of personal prejudices, provides us with a possible explanation as to how Tallen had been captured and "christianized" when:

> . . . a war broke out between his own and a neighboring tribe and his people were conquered, and among the prisoners who were captured and driven to the coast to be sold to the slavers. . . .Then came a voyage of three weeks--three weeks of horror. The little savage from the great 'fresh water' of Central Africa, who had never heard of civilization and had never been taught to believe in any other God than Fetish, took now his first step in that great scheme whereby, our Doctors of Divinity teach us, the Heavenly Father is to lead his race to the blessed knowledge of Christian light and life. He met the horrors of the 'Middle Passage'. He listened, day and night, to the groans of the dying; he suffered the agonies of thirst and suffocation. . . . (Blassingame 1977:326-327).

As more interest is shown in this aspect of inter-religious history in Africa before colonization, research will provide more data to indicate the nature of religious pluralism that existed and the role religion played in tribe wars. The position held on the role of Muslims as primary slave sellers of Africans and who eventually sold only those persons who were non-Muslims has been put forth, but needs further research. When I questioned one contemporary Muslim theologian regarding this matter, his response indicated that Allah does not hold the current generation responsible for acts committed by others ('Abdul Quadir Morris June 1:1992).

Religion and Worldview Change

The anthropological perspective instructs that all people have a worldview from which they see the totality of life. When it comes to the discussion of the Africans enslaved and brought to North and South America, this significant fact has often been overlooked or discredited as if these persons were merely blank pages in a book. Prior to the disruptive acts of the European slave trade which resulted in the removal from the continent of Africa between fifteen to fifty million Africans from 1482-1888, Africans already possessed an adequate worldview model and culture that served to meet their particular needs (Asante and Mattson 1992: 27).

Conflict and Crisis

Before their conflict with the enslavers, Africans had a healthy and holistic perception of themselves as human beings. They, like most ethnically defined groups saw themselves to be a superior people as revealed in folklore and art, a people blessed and protected by God in their own territory. Basil Davidson, among other eye witness historians, in describing Africans of this period, present us with healthy societies that adequately meet the needs of their people.

The impact of being captured, becoming the object involved in the world's largest forced migration, and then being sold into European slavery, forced Africans to develop an appropriate worldview response that included a religious understanding. Whatever their "heart" religion was, whether the traditional African religious belief system or that of Muslims or Christians, an appropriate personal worldview response had to be created in order to filter the thoughts, emotions, values and activities caused by such a crisis. The worldview of the African had to adjust to the concept of slavery based on dehumanization and the concept of Christianity as they experienced it as religion.

Charles Kraft's anthropological perspective would support this. He provides a figure that demonstrates the resistance of religion. According to Kraft, changes that are forced at the periphery of culture causes "ripples" of influence toward the worldview core of the culture (1984:362). The act of enslavement represented an attempt to make a large number of peripheral changes in the African worldview. The fact that it was done in the name of religion tended to result in a "rippling" of misleading information about God, religion, power and outsiders. This approach provided Africans new to the Eurocentric language, thought processes and ways of knowing and valuing life, with no assistance with the issue of worldview re-adjustment.

The tenacity of the African worldview in the minds of those enslaved, the enslavers preoccupation only toward producing cheap labor, and according to Kraft, the revolutionary (rapid) process of the abolition of slavery, resulted in the following:

> For even yet large numbers of blacks have not found it possible to develop habits, attitudes and skills that will enable them to function well in contemporary American society. Nor have whites in general learned to accept blacks as human beings. For the conceptual cores of both black and white worldviews have been only slightly altered. We have succeeded in the easy part--we have changed a peripheral custom or two. But, probably because of the rapidity of the peripheral changes, many of us have "holed up" in our traditional worldview (including the strong feelings of what the "place" of blacks and whites should be rather than seeking to change it in such a way that it supports the changes in the more peripheral areas of our culture (Kraft 1984:346-347).

His etic evaluation gives support to the multi-cultural theory: large numbers of Afrocentric people did not and have not found it possible to develop Eurocentric habits, attitudes and skills that would enable them to function well in a Eurocentric society. Therefore, in terms of the European slave trade, the goal related to the African woman and man, was to create disequilibrium and disruption. The first reaction was to cling to that worldview which is familiar and known, in spite of the superficial external alternation imposed by the Eurocentric worldview; second, to question it in light of experiential truth and present social and cultural realities which juxtaposed it; and thirdly, to unconsciously and consciously, make adjustments in light of the Eurocentric impositions. Though the majority of the outward, material

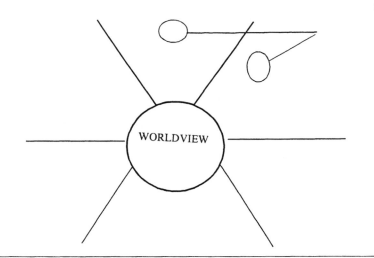

55

Figure 1
THE RIPPLING EFFECT OF THE INTERPRETATIONS OF
FORCED CHANGES ON THE WORLDVIEW OF A CULTURE
(Kraft 1984:362)

African culture was lost and eventually forgotten (according to some theorists), the African worldview core of thoughts and understandings of life were left intact, and provided some stability during this time of transition.

The Resiliency of Religion

There is debate as to how much of the religiosity of the African was retained throughout the period of enslavement. Wilmore, Raboteau, Herskovits and others support the theory that the area of religion offers the best insights to African retentions. Gayraud Wilmore has stated, "Although the African gods did not survive more than a brief period on American soil, the indigenous African worldview and traditional African spirituality did continue in the slave community" (1982:73). Haddad concluded that many of the Africans brought as slaves to the United States were Muslims, who were eventually forced to convert to Christianity by their enslavers (1979:6). However, the fact that almost a hundred years passed before enslavers felt compelled to provide any religious instruction for Africans in their care, meant that the original religious beliefs were allowed to be practiced and sustained, if not overtly, surely in secret.

The "tenacity of culture" is a phrase Henry Mitchell utilizes in *Black Beliefs: Folk Beliefs of Black America.* He remarks:

> To kill a culture you have to kill the bearers of the culture. That is to say, the life stance and worldview of a people are deeply engrained and not readily changed. . . . There is more and more evidence that slave mothers, and sometimes fathers, too, participated in the raising of their children. The passing on of a culture and worldview were inevitable, and the fact that slaves were in constant contact with new arrivals bearing African culture. . . (1975:37).

Mitchell describes what is the current consensus of most modern historians: that the African worldview influences existed among Africans and early Africans born in the United States for many decades, thus making it possible for some religious beliefs and practices to be maintained and continued for several generations in some locations. If the passing on of a "largely unconsciously" (Kraft 1979:53) culture and worldview were inevitable, so too was the passing on of unconscious religious views which are core to the African perceptions of reality.

Religious Options

The early churches in North America developed and expanded as did the exploration of the American frontier. Through time and a variety of circumstances, including the coming of European missionaries to the new colonies and the "Great Awakening," the churches began to slowly reform through spiritual emphasis, religious education and revival. One consequence of this resulted in a split within American Protestantism over the question of African Americans and the institution of slavery. Northern and southern divisions were formed, greatly influenced by these issues, within the major denominations of European heritage.

A later consequence was the birth of African-American denominations and churches that began to emerge at the turn of the nineteenth century. Life on the plantations for those who served as slaves was extremely difficult and since an African, or person of African descent, was considered "property" to the purchaser, life was lived cautiously. The types of sermons preached to the Africans and African Americans during this period of enslavement by Christians; the fact of forced illiteracy which prevented learning how to read the Bible; and the corrupt teachings that passed as biblical proclamation are records of history. As a result, the original African Americans and Africans who continued to be transported to America to labor as slaves had to use discernment in their approach toward religious beliefs and practices. Several options were available as to what to do with the Christian theology presented to them as a means of both evangelization and instilling subservient values.

Religious Option One: Total Acceptance

First of all, the Africans and African Americans who were exposed to Christian theology during this period of history could have accepted what was spoken to them unquestionably, though there is no indication that this was the case. In fact, this new religion, Americanized Christianity, contradicted at its core the African traditional religions and philosophies of life, particularly the concepts of humanity and community (Mbiti, 1971). As the slave trade continued to build momentum, the non-acceptance of European American Christianity often resulted in more than a few slave revolts inspired by Africans who identified themselves as Christians. The 1822 slave revolt of Denmark Vesey and that of the African-American Church in South Carolina in the same year stand as two examples.

The letters of the Rev. Frances Le Jau, written during an earlier period of 1706-1717 to the secretary of the Society for the Propagation of the Gospel would seem to confirm this.

> He reports of the difficulties of an Anglican minister in an outpost of the British empire often touched upon efforts to convert the Native American and African populations. A few slaves did become Christians, often against the wishes or will of planters who feared that baptism would lead to social revolution. . . . It is estimated that the black population of South Carolina in 1715 outnumbered the white by 10,500 to 6,250. Le Jau's converts therefore represented only a small fraction of the Carolinians of African descent (Sernett 1985:24).

There is also early historical evidence that some persons in slavery would describe themselves as religious, but refuse to identify or give a name to the god/God they worshipped. Consider this statement taken from the narrative of James Curry. After seeing the cruelty his mother faced in slavery as a young girl, and how each of her husbands was taken from her and her children, and sold to another planter, Curry described her in this manner. "She was a very good and tender mother. She never made a public profession of religion, but she always tried to do right, and she taught me to know my Maker, and that we should all die, and if we were good, we should be happy" (Blassingame 1986:130).

The authenticity of this family is supported in a "List of the Free Black Heads of Families in the First Census of the United States," and would thereby date this narrative about 1790. This mother, like many of African heritage in the United States, did know, and had experienced the presence and power of the biblical God in their lives; however, they could not relate it to the Christianity they were taught to experience (Haney 1990). This observation is a crucial one, for it describes a major historical reason why even today there is a growing tendency for more persons in the African-American community to feel that Christianity is inadequate and therefore to totally reject it--believing that it is not relevant to their experience of life.

Religious Option Two: Acceptance with Modifications

A second option available to the Africans and original African Americans was to accept the European American Christian evangelization that was forced upon them, however, with adjustments and modifications. Many Africans did go beyond the acceptance of Christianity as a survival strategy, and experienced a personal relationship with Jesus Christ as Lord and Savior in spite of the gospel's perverse presentation. Modifications of worldview concepts related to self, the nature of the divinity, and the nature of evil and sin were required within the realm of the religious, and thus life itself. Changes had to be made at the religious worldview level first that then permeated their entire psyche in order to accommodate the actual experience of European presented theology.

Two Types of Churches

This period in history gave rise to two kinds of churches: the observable church which the European planters could approve of, and the so called "hidden" or "invisible" church in which the African Americans did their own theologizing. Sernett's *Afro-American Religious History: A Documentary Witness* (1985) contains an autobiography of the Reverend Peter Randolph who worked as a slave and described vividly the plantation churches, both the visible and invisible church. This hidden church is the type that has become increasingly common throughout the world, particularly in those areas of restricted access, oppression and hostility. The seeds of the Christian theologies of African Americans called "black theology" were planted at this time in history among the invisible churches.

The majority of the historical African-American churches that would later become African-American denominations and congregations began to emerge during the period of enslavement. In addition, many of the Christian songs in North American called "spirituals," along with some folk and gospel songs, grew out of this invisible church. What these churches became is best summed up in these words: "What both the slave churches of the South--"the invisible institution"--and the free churches of the North developed was a religion suffused with a sublimated outrage that was balanced with a patient cheefulness and boundless confidence in the ultimate justice (morality) of God" (Mitchell 1975:55).

This same history reviewed from the perspective of a contemporary Muslim is revealing. Muslims with nationalist tendencies continue to question how it is that *so many* African Americans were drawn to Christianity in light of the intimate relationship between Christianity, the institution of slavery, and the dehumanization process that accompanied Christianity. While the Christian attributes the embracing of Christianity as the work of the Holy Spirit and of a Living God, to the Muslim this period of history was a clear reflection that the Europeans and their religion "were the works of the devil." The evidence of this is obvious in that it was in the name of the Christian God that (1) the African-American family was separated and destroyed continuously as individual family members were sold from one "Christian" plantation to another; (2) the matriarchal family structure was instituted; (3) the person of African descent in the United States was not only denied his or her sense of personhood and all that is insinuated in that denigration, but also denied knowledge of their true heritage; and (4) the only systematic economic leverage created was one that developed a caste system for the masses of African Americans. While this religious interpretation of history might be questionable, the social realities are factual and today their ramifications plague the United States.

The answer to questions as to how African Christians were able to discern the movement of God in spite of the human interpretations of his Word can best be provided by those men and women who embraced the biblical concept of God and God's message. It is only through the study of bibliographies of persons such as Frederick Douglass, Henry Bibbs, Lucy Craft Laney, Sojourner Truth, Henry Garnett Highland, and Jarena Lee who lived with the contradictions, and yet were able to discern between the true Christianity and the perverse interpretations, that more insight is gained.

As African Americans gained a better understanding of the new culture into which they had been forced, including the informal learning of a new language; the system of racism and injustice based on skin color continuously formulated in the United States; and the nature of the culturally bonded interpretations of Christianity that was presented to them, eight African-American Christian denominations and several separated churches were founded in the late seventeenth and eighteenth centuries. Further modifications, coupled with dissatisfaction and frustration with North American Christianity, led to the formation of many marginally Afrocentric Christian (and Islamic) sects and cults.

A Third Option: Favoring Indigenous Religious Beliefs

To reiterate, the first option of the African brought to North America was to accept the new understanding of God which was presented to him or her in a new country in the midst of brutal oppression inflicted in the name of the same new God and religion. The second option was to accept this new religion only with modifications and changes that would offer the African some kind of explanation for his or her life experiences. The third option to be considered here, was simply to reject totally the American Christian evangelization which was forced upon them. And many did and, along with it, rejected biblical Christianity. Within their African perception of reality "conceptualizations of what reality can or should be, what is to be regarded as actual, probable, possible and impossible," Christianity was viewed as a false religion (Kraft 1979:53). The African worldview held by the constantly arriving African women, men and children did not impede these efforts. Christianity, as it was presented and experienced, was often rejected by persons who had an already adequate concept of religion and had experienced its roles in their own lives. This rejection tended to be greatest when it opposed and contradicted their definition of Divine Creator and humanity, as well as failed to meet their basic religious and spiritual needs and expectations.

> First, there was a turning away from Christianity altogether. Many slaves reacted to eschatological preaching in disbelief when it became obvious that nothing was going to happen within the time period that made sense to them. We know that millions never became church members and many backslide from their "conversions," much to the astonishment and dismay of the missionaries. In their reports of evangelization efforts many missionaries speak of apostasy on the plantations as a common occurrence. Some slaves were never convinced that the white preachers were telling the truth. Others believed and were baptized, but it seems that many, perhaps the majority, drew back from their original commitment and either returned to the remnants of their ancestral religions or believed nothing (Wilmore 1982:80).

It is clear through their development and continuous practice, that syncretistic religions such as Vondu and Santeria, offered alternatives to persons who sought to worship. Sernett says: "Many slaves put their confidence not in pro-slavery preaching but in an alternative system of belief variously known as conjure, hoodooing or root doctoring . . . conjuring served as a counter-cultural protest to the worldview of the dominant society and met the needs in the slave quarters that Christianity did not" (1985:76). But what of those Africans brought to America who were Muslims? Were there persons who successfully resisted attempts to "christianize" them, and instead practiced their traditional Islamic beliefs and practices? The need to live cautiously, to conform and adapt in order to survive, does to some degree diminish some evidences of Islam as practiced on the plantations. This has also contributed to the demise of Islamic worshippers. Those under the watchful eyes of taskmasters would either give up practicing their faith, or continue to practice their faith in secret. Evidence indicated that some Muslims continued to practice their faith when they could and as long as they could, but other educated ones with access to sympathetic Europeans and European Americans attempted to return to their African homeland in order to live and worship as they were accustomed to do.

The Indigenous North American Muslims

The African-American Muslim is correctly referred to as the Indigenous Muslim of North America. The obvious reason is that the first people to practice Islam in this context were the Africans and African Americans. The other reason is that the largest indigenous sector of Americans who have become Muslims are from the African- American population.

> Undoubtedly, the Atlantic slave trade was the single most important vehicle for the pre-nineteenth century transportation of Muslims to the Americas. The peak of this economic enterprise was reached in the mid-eighteenth century, sources indicating that there was a small but continuous flow of African Muslims captives into the American colonies well into the nineteenth century. Unfortunately, we do not have enough information to estimate the number of Muslims enslaved in the United States. However, the known biographies, autobiographies, and the materials concerning their attempts to gain freedom seem to suggest that perhaps they numbered in the thousands. Given the general tendency of slave masters to record the "noble" or "royal" backgrounds of slaves, it is not surprising that we do not have accounts from more than a few Muslim captives who appear to have been recruited from lower social ranks. Therefore, one should be cautious in estimating their numbers, as the slave merchant's area of operations was sufficiently large and in the interior of West African to ensure the victimization of Mande, Wolof, Tuareg, Hause, Yoruba and other "ordinary" Islamized peoples. Contemporary research indicates that the majority of them were transported to Brazil; nevertheless, significant numbers, though small in proportion, existed in the Caribbean and the United States (Haddad 1984:196).

Persons brought from Africa to serve as slaves, and who spoke the "formal" Arabic language (as opposed to the pigeon or vernacular Arabic of the local villages), and who had contact with an English or American person who was capable of recognizing the Arabic sounds or letter, had a good chance of becoming noticed, and in some cases received special attention.

African Muslim Scholars

Educated European Americans who came into personal contact with the Arabic-speaking Muslims and recognized the Arabic language, seemed to have been impressed, and occasionally took a personal interest in them. There are several interesting stories told of African slaves in Maryland in the 1700s, one who was found praying five times a day, bowing in the direction of Mecca. Job, son of Solomon, may be representative of them. He was born about 1701 in the kingdom of Futa near the Gambia River. He was captured and sold into slavery in approximately 1730. Job worked in Maryland on a tobacco plantation, escaped and was jailed. Abolitionists arranged for his freedom and passage to England. He wrote out, from memory, three copies of the Qur'an enroute to England, and while there, he translated a number of Arabic inscriptions for the Royal Society. He returned to Fula in 1735 (estimated date). Information regarding the majority of these Muslims is however, unknown to us today. Historian Carter G. Woodson also describes another Muslim who, early in United States history, was discovered to be an orthodox Muslim and an Arabic scholar (Woodson 1992:70), though no date was furnished.

The "Typical" Muslim

The typical Muslims, however, tried to observe the Islamic customs the best they could. In spite of the use of the original vernacular in the following quotation, one still is able to obtain the sense of reverence and religious commitment held by this Muslim female.

"Muh gran come from Africa," remarked Rosa Grant of Possum Point, Georgia. "Huh membuh when I wuz a chile seein muh grn Ryna pray. Ebry mawnin at sun-up she kneel on duh flo in uh ruhm an bow obuh antech uh head tuh duh floe tree time. Den she say a prayuh. I dohn membuh jis wut she say, but one wud she say use tuh make us chillun laugh. I membuh it was "ashanegad". wen she finish prayin she say 'Ameen, ameen, ameen'" (Raboteau 1978:46).

Similarly, Katie Brown of Sapelo Island, Georgia, was a descendent of Belali, and made this observation.

> . . . Belali an he wife Phoebe pray on duh bed," Katie recounted. "Dey wuz bery puticluh bout duh timed dey pray and dey berry regluh bout duh hour. Wen duh sun come up, wen it straight obuh head an wen it st, das dah time day pray. Dey bow tuh duh sun and hab lill mat tuh kneel on. Duh beads is on a long string. Belali, he pull bead an he say, "Belambi, Hakabara, Mahamadu," Phoebe she say, "Ameen, Ameen" (1978:46).

Raboteau contines:

> Charles Lylee visting Hopeton Plantation on St. Simon's Island, Georgia, before 1845, encounted "Old Tom, head driver for the plantation, a Foulah who had remained a strict Muslim, though his children and grandchildren had "changed the Koran for the Bible" (1978:46).

Because of the plantation owner's initial lack of concern for matters of religion, there was opportunity for limited freedom of worship of Muslims in the beginning, especially in the South Carolina and George areas. According to Lincoln and Mamiya, "The influence of varieties of Islam among blacks in the United States has had a long history, stemming f rom the African Muslims who were brought to North America as slaves and who constituted as much as 20% of the slave population on some large southern plantations" (1990:389). A captive Moor named Abduhl Rahhahman (born in the city of "Tomuctoo", approximately 1762 and enslaved in Mississippi) provides us a glimpse into his life through both a biography and an interview. Blassingame refers to the vivid, descriptive autobiography written by Rahhahman who had been in slavery for forty years when the 1828 interview occurred (1986:682-686). The details mentioned in Rahhahman's autobiography (as well as that of other Muslims) are confirmed in the "African Repository, III" (February and May 1828).

Omar Ibn Said

Several historians describe the life and person of Omar Ibn Said (also known as Uncle Moreau) which leads to the conclusion that he was perhaps a most popular Muslims because of his eventual conversion to Christianity. He was interviewed at the age of 89, between 1856 and 1863. He was born in West Africa along the Senegel River about 1780, and learned to read the Qur'an and to recite Muslim prayers as a child. Omar Ibn Said was from an educated family, and in addition to teaching youth from the Qur'an, he became an Arabic scholar for ten years. He later became a trader before he was enslaved. He and two other of his tribesmen landed in Charleston, South Carolina in 1807. He was sold to several cruel plantation owners, and each time he escaped. It was while in jail near Fayetteville, North Carolina that he filled the jail walls with Arabic writings, and attracted the attention of many, including a sympathetic General James Owen of Bladen County. Omar Ibn Said, in an autobiography in Arabic, in 1831 wrote:

> Before I came to the Christian country, my religion was the religion of Mohamaad, the Apostle of God-- may God have mercy upon him and give him peace! I walked to the mosque before day-break, washed my face and head and hands and feet. I prayed at nooon, prayed in the afternoon, prayed at sunset, prayed in the evening. I gave alms every year. . . . I went on pilgrimage to Mecca. . . .When I left my country I was thirty-seven years old: I have been in the country of the Christians twenty-four years (Raboteau 1978:47).

At that time, Omar Ib Said was a strict Muslim who, according to his own testimony, kept the fast of Ramadan and other Islamic rituals. However, although an English translation of the Qur'an was provided him, he eventually abandoned the Islamic religion and began to embrace Jesus as the Christ. He was baptized by a Presbyterian minister, Rev. Snodgrass, and became a member of First Presbyterian Church, Wilmington, North Carolina. He was greatly affected by the great revival of 1858 (Blassingame 1986:473).

Fragmented recordings of other African Muslims are available, though without much supporting facts. Another Muslim was known to have been sent back to Africa as early as 1733 with the assistance of General Oglethorpe. And another un-named Muslim was reportedly "ransomed" and sent to Liberia in 1828. After 1855 there seems to be little, if any, descriptions of Muslims who openly practiced their faith. Thus, while we do not have access to an abundance of scholarship, there are some eyewitness accounts of the Muslims' interpretations of their religious life. We do have available observable behaviors from which we can surmise certain understandings which will assist in this analysis of the religious history of African Americans. The use of Arabic, persons praying five times a day in the prostate position, the recitation of the Qur'an, and the refusal to eat pork and to participate in the consumption of alcoholic beverages were observable practices that were easily notable and recordable.

According to Charles E. Silberman, several accounts of African Muslims brought to America to serve as slaves were collected and preserved by three ethnologists--Theodore Dwight (nephew of one of the presidents of Yale University, and cousin of another who served as recording secretary of the American Ethnological Society), William Brown Hodgson, and James Hamilton Couper.

> Dwight attacked the notion of Negro inferiority insisting upon the high level of both Moslem and pagan Negro civilization in Africa, and telling the stories of a number of Moslem slaves he had met. "Among the victims of the slave trade among us", he wrote, "have been men of learning and pure and exalted characters, who have been treated like beasts of the field by those who claimed a purer religion (1964:80).

It becomes obvious that some Muslims practiced a strenuous understanding of Islamic religious obligations early in their history. Why some chose to remain Muslim is not actually known. Whether they did so to escape from the unnatural hardships of the world through another theology, or in order to create within themselves a life style that was in itself a protest against the prevailing society, we don't know. Perhaps the elements of a legalistic interpretation of the religious life, and the need for a radical renewal of faith in God in the midst of oppression and suffering continued to strengthen the Muslim believer.

We must lament the fact that we do not have available the actual samples of the Qur'anic verses that were memorized and the Arabic language that was spoken daily, the songs that were sung, or the oral traditions that were handed down. What matters, though, is that there is an authentic acknowledgment of the multi-religious nature of the African American experience from its origin. Global mission history has taught the Church, often at a high cost, of the failures of refusing to take seriously not only other religious understandings, but also how God is able to work in and through them.

In summary, it needs to be emphasized that the Africans already possessed an adequate worldview model and culture that served to meet their particular worldview needs, prior to the periods of enslavement and colonization. During the Middle Passage and the period of enslavement, the African worldview core of thought and understandings of life were left intact, though most of the outward forms and materials of the culture were lost. Several scholars, including Wilmore, Raboteau, Herskovits and W. E. Du Bois insist that by looking at that area of the worldview called religion, that we can best see some of the African retentions. "Although the African gods did not survive more than a brief period on American soil, the indigenous African world view and traditional African spirituality did continue in the slave community," observes Wilmore (1982:73).

There were very few factors, if any, that influenced newly arrived Africans to favor the acceptance of Eurocentric Christianity for approximately the first hundred years on this continent. The result was that these persons maintained and drew strength from the religious interpretation of their indigenous culture and world view; not that which was imposed upon them by force. In fact, the lack of factors that would influence acceptance of a new worldview change and a new religious understanding (such as security, morale, borrowing of traditions, openness to new ideas, respect of the source culture, and the differing of basic premises of source and worldviews) simply did not exist. Therefore the African and African-American's experience of life in the United States would cause them to hold tenaciously to their traditional understandings of God and religion, rather than to accept the new one which was the cause of catastrophic disruption of their lives.

African American Missionary Attitudes Toward Islam

After the mid-nineteenth century, there is little information available on African-American persons who advocated or practiced Islam. Either the Muslims had been pressured to convert to Christianity by the plantation owners and they gradually lost interest in Islamic practices, or they practiced their faith in secret, leaving no recorded evidences. Voices of Muslim leadership and their messages, and other evidences of Islamic beliefs and practices are simply not available, and it is unfortunate that this particular aspect of history may be lost to us forever.

It is not until fifty years later, during the early twentieth century that we find substantial evidence that Islamic teachings and related religious knowledge was proclaimed, taught and practiced among African Americans with consistency. The factual evidences of Islamic survivals that were available during the preceding period take a different form during the current period under study. From the period following Emancipation through the Reconstruction phase, it was primarily the African-American missionary movement in Africa which influenced and informed the majority of opinions regarding Islam and Muslims. The missionary arm of the emergent African-American denominations and congregations which stretched wide to Africa, was aided not only by a sense of divine call from God, but also from both the general church and some segments of society as possible response to the Emancipation Proclamation.

Institutions such as the Freedman's Board and the American Colonization Society, and individual African Americans who sought to foster pan-Africanism, unknowingly, helped to place African Americans in direct contact with Muslims and the religion of Islam. The majority of African Americans who came in contact with Muslims held similar views of disdain, loathing and a sense of superiority toward them common to the majority of Christians living within the United States. And yet there were exceptions, and the influence of the exceptions on some, especially

Christians, was great. Not only did the influence come from individual African Americans serving overseas, but also from African students who began to study in primarily African-American colleges and universities in the United States who helped to share opinions and attitudes toward Islam in Africa.

After the Civil War, many European Americans and a few African Americans supported the idea of sending African Americans back to Africa as a possible solution to the problem created by granting freedom to persons of African heritage. The founding of Liberia, Africa (1822) and the desire of the United States for a colony for African Americans set the groundwork. The American Colonization Society (1817) created and assisted in the creation of several strategies to serve their purposes, including the strategy of engaging African Americans in global mission by putting them in contact with Africans on the continent of Africa. James Costen, in a 1989 lecture at Austin Seminary, has provided us with an accurate description of how one denomination, the Presbyterian Church, advanced this notion of mass emigration of African Americans to Africa as early as 1759.

The Freedmen's Aid Society (1866) and later Gammon Methodist Seminary (organized in 1883 for the training of African-American church workers), and special projects such as the Steward Missionary Foundation (1894), were developed for the sole purpose of training African-American missionaries for Africa. The Student Volunteer Movement (1888) which was organized with over 20,000 volunteers for foreign missions included African Americans being sent to Africa (only) to convert "the heathen."

> White missionaries trooped to black campuses to speak about Africa. In an address to the student body of Atlanta University in 1888, for example, a white missionary began his lecture with the standard Biblical prophesy that 'Ethiopia shall soon stretch out her hands unto God.' He claimed that God has ordained slavery as the mechanism for raising a new African elect into civilization and Christianity. Once blacks had been civilized in America, he reasoned, God caused slavery to be ended and Africa to be opened so that their destiny to 'cover Africa with homes and schools and churches and Christian States'; God gave them authority to take the continent 'for their work and reward' (Williams 1982:6-7).

The Theory of Providential Design

The "theory of Providential design," alluded to in the above quotation, makes claim that it was God's design that African Americans should have experienced slavery in the United States in order to participate in the evangelization of Africa. It was the accepted norm adopted by more African-American and (European American) Christians and missionaries without question. A comprehensive listing of African- American missionaries who served the various denominations in Liberia, Sierra Leone, and in Western, Central and Southern Africa (1877-1900) is provided by Williams (1982:184-194).

When these missionaries came in contact with the religion of Islam on the continent of Africa, their attitudes, except for a small minority, were basically the same as their white American and European missionary counterparts. They saw Islam as a religion to be condemned as severely inferior to Christianity.

> Baptist John Coles felt that Islam was even worse, "if possible, than heathenism". Similarly, a writer in the A.M.E. Voices of Missions concluded that while paganisn "marks the lowest stratum of ignorance and superstition", Islam was even more baneful because it destroyed "the remaining vestige of humanity" in Africa. H. B. Parks also took a belligerent attitude toward "Mohammedanism", calling it a "great wall of darkness" against which the missionary army has been hurling itself (Williams 1982:114).

Missionary Alfred Ridgel

The Rev. Alfred Ridgel who worked in Liberia with the A.M.E. Church denounced Muslims for several reasons, these included the Qur'anic references to untruths related to Jesus, the Islamic tolerance of polygamy, the Islamic tolerance for the whole African way of life, and its "convictions and its missionary impulse." According to Ridgel, ". . . Every Christian should be on the alert and spare no pains to urge incessant war against . . . an evil that threatens our very existence in Africa. . . . Let us pray Almighty God to forever blot Mohammedanism out to existence" (Williams 1982: 11:12). In spite of several significant factors including the difficulty in obtaining the financial support needed for the work of the African-American missionaries, health problems encountered in the field, many resulting in death, and conflicts between the African nationals that in some instances prevented the missionaries progress, no doubt the willingness of these missionaries to work among the people and to learn the Arabic language was impressive.

<u>Edward Wilmot Blyden: An Advocate of Islam</u>

Edward Wilmot Blyden, born in 1832 in the West Indies, was an exceptional person who served as a missionary, as well as a British ambassador to Liberia. As an outstanding leader and scholar, he influenced African-American Christians through his writings and speeches during the years of 1860 throughout the 1890s, more perhaps than any other missionary sent from the United States. A.M.E. Bishop Benjamin Arnett stated that Blyden had an intellectual status "attained by no other Negro in the world" (Williams 1982:13). According to Williams:

> He was exposed to Islamic nations of interior West Africa, and after an 1866 visit to Egypt and Syria, Blyden became increasingly respectful of the followers of Mohammed...his greatest contribution occurred after the 1887 publication of his book, *Christianity, Islam and the Negro Race*. He followed that with several articles in the *A.M.E. Church Review*. Finally, in 1886 Blyden resigned from the Presbyterian ministry to become a 'minister of truth.' The Presbyterian Mission Board was so disillusioned with their use of black missionaries that they did not appoint another one to Liberia until 1895 (1982:13).

In Blyden's own words:

> I must uphold the Mohammedanism not for its peculiar teachings--but so far as it agrees, not with European teachings, but with the teachings of Christ--and so far as it tends to build up my race in numerical strength, in self-respect and physical health--all of which the method of Christians tend to undermine . . . I prefer what is good for my people in the method of its propagators to what is evil in the methods of Christian teachers (Williams 1982:115).

Blyden's theology eventually led to a universal deism, and he became instrumental in the development of a reform movement in Liberia. However, before he broke ties with the missionary efforts of the church, his missional theory of cultural relativism based on respect for the indigenous culture, and the practice of urging missionaries to learn the native language as soon as possible and to bond with the people, created a following of individuals who were greatly influenced by him. The A.M.E. missionary J. R. Frederick, working in Sierra Leone, admired Blyden, and yet while holding on to his Christian theology of mission, utilized some of Blyden's methods of empathy with Islam. As a result, it is reported that he was responsible for the conversion of a local African king from Islam to Christianity (Williams 1982:116).

> Thomas A. Johns, a Liberian student at Lincoln University and a follower of Blyden wrote a series of letters to the *Washington Bee*, complaining about Christian attempts to wipe our traditional cultures and substitute Western customs, in contrast to Islamic missionaries who respected the local values. Africans were, he asserted, honest, loyal, and benevolent, and they should be honored by black Americans rather than condemned (Williams 1982:116).

When Blyden was speaking at the A.M.E. Church conference in 1889, he was heard by Bishop Benjamin Arnett, Bishop Daniel Payne and Bishop Henry Turner. After listening to Blyden, they were convinced that the African-American Christians had a clear mission and calling in Africa. He had helped to plant a new vision which immediately took the A.M.E. Church in the 1880s in the forefront of missionary activities with a new zeal.

Bishop Henry Turner: Islam, a Bridge to Christianity

In addition to being born a freed person in 1834, and a pastor of the largest African-American church at the time, Henry Turner was appointed in 1863 by President Lincoln to serve as the first African-American chaplain in the United States. Turner, however, "became disillusioned with the United States and turned toward African emigration and missions as the only hope for black people" (Williams 1982:48-49). He began to see the needs of black people in America, Europe and Africa uniting not only for Christian purposes but also for economic development and intellectual reasons. He became Bishop for Africa of the A.M.E. Church in 1893, and in that same year, he was instrumental in getting a course on "Africa" taught at Wilberforce University. Bishop Turner, while not totally accepting Islam, did hold admiration for the Muslim teachers he had contact with in Sierra Leone, and respected their self-pride and their strict moral standards.

He saw the influences of Islam as God's plan of preparation for the redemption of Africa by Christianity. . . .'The Mohammedan religion is the morning star to the sun of Christianity. . .God save the Mohammedans, is my prayer, til the Christian Church is ready to do her whole duty.' Thus, for Turner, Islam was not to be condemned, because he was confident that it would ultimately aid in the Christianization of Africa (Williams 1982:116-117).

As bishop, Turner influenced many church leaders toward a new interest and support for the continent of Africa. In conclusion, it must be noticed that though the influences of key leaders such as Blyden, Frederick, and Turner were great both on the African continent and within the United States, the majority of the African-American church workers in Africa continued to condemn Islam, and engaged in Christian missions aimed wholeheartedly at winning Africa for Christ.

World View Issues for Christian Mission and Witness

As a result of the peculiar developmental of race relations in North America, there has emerged basically four African-American philosophical schools of thought: the emigrationalist (Marcus Garvey, Edward Blyden), the assimilationist or melting pot theorist (Booker T. Washington, Frederick Douglass), the cultural nationalist or cultural pluralist (Martin Luther King, Jr., El-Hajj Malcolm "X" Shabazz), and the political nationalist (Louis Farrakhan, Cornel West). This heterogeneity within the African-American community (including the mosque and church) must be kept in mind as consideration is given to the nature of the church within a religiously plural society.

Due to the close identification between culture and Christianity, the historical challenge of the African-American churches, led by the Spirit of God, was defined early on in history as having to search beyond Americanized Christianity for a more authentic, biblical understanding of Christian community, love and justice in a pluralistic environment. As confirmed by Rita Dixon (1992), William Pannell (1992), James Cone (1986) and other theologians throughout the centuries, "an essential characteristic of Black Evangelism is that evangelism must be concerned about the progress of the whole person--the spiritual, the social, the economic, the intellectual and the emotional development of the full person" (Dixon 1992:33). The relationship between social environment and worldview is more important in the formulation of religious beliefs than we realize. This is certainly evidenced in the birth and nourishment of two distinct African-American Christian communities, and in a small but growing population of African Americans who perceive Christianity as being irrelevant to the African-American experience. Among the various issues that have already emerged in this history that Christians need to consider as they engage in mission and witness are primarily four: racial identity, perceptions of religious truth, community consciousness, and the desire to be part of a universal community. These are recurring themes which will be explained in-depth in the proceeding chapters.

CHAPTER 3

SIGNIFICANT ISLAMIC MOVEMENTS IN THE UNITED STATES

Clifton E. Marsh has authored a book entitled *From Black Muslims to Muslims: The Transition from Separatism to Islam, 1930-1980* (1984) in which he traces the development of the Nation of Islam (1930-1974) to the World Community of American Muslim Society in the West (1975-1980), observing that this transformation is consistent with the Max Weber analysis of social movement development. Marsh identifies the three stages and related leadership associated with the transformation in the following manner: the formation stage (organization founded by Wali Fard Muhammad), the formalization state (development of ideology and institutions by Elijah Muhammad), and the traditionalistic (the change from separatism to Islam by Warith D. Muhammad). In this chapter, key persons involved in the leadership of this transformation will be discussed with an emphasis on missiological behavior.

However, four additional persons will be considered briefly, due to their Islamic influence within the African-American community. They are Noble Drew Ali, Louis Farrakhan, and Malcolm X. In a succeeding chapter, Warith D. Muhammad's leadership will be analyzed separately. Under the dynamic leadership of these men, both domestic and international missionary involvements have prompted African Americans to claim Islamic identification as Muslims. The two forms of Islam, popular and formal, are active within the African-American community, with each conforming to the appropriate definitions and descriptions, according to Islamic scholars such as Musk, Woodberry, Speight, and Denny.

The conversion to Islam by African Americans was evident by the end of the nineteenth century. While the names of those who made the Islamic presentation are not known to us, the fact remains that Islamic knowledge was shared intentionally within the African-American community. Neither is it known how much, if any, of this Islamic awareness was directly or indirectly affiliated with the activities of the American Islamic Propaganda movement or its founder Muhammed Webb, the first European American who preached and established Muslim "circles" in several east coast cities at approximately the same period of time. However, what is known is that there was an introduction of Islamic philosophy and religious knowledge to a young man born Timothy Drew (1886-1929) in North Carolina, who significantly influenced large numbers of persons toward Islam.

The Moorish American Science Temple

In 1913, Noble Drew Ali (the former Timothy Drew) founded the Moorish-American Science Temple in Newark, New Jersey. Just as the European slave trade (through its geographical expansion) was the primary and first structure which enabled people of African descent to follow Islamic beliefs on the continent of North America, Noble Drew and his movement became the second major means of dissimulating Islamic beliefs and teachings. As a result of the Moorish-American Science Temple, Islamic influences were disseminated, though impartially, and places of worship for "Moors" (Black worshippers of Allah) emerged. With a growing following, he later founded other temples in Detroit and Philadelphia. The message was clearly pronounced.

> Blacks were 'Asiatics.' He also insisted that 'for a people to amount to anything, it is necessary to have a name (nation) and a land.' He called on all Blacks to refuse any affiliation (such as Blacks, colored, Ethiopians or Negroes) save that of Asiatics, Moorish or Moors. While Christianity was the religion of the White man, Islam was the religion of the Asiatics, and each nation should have its own religion (Haddad 1979:6).

This movement became popular in major urban areas such as Detroit, Pittsburgh, Chicago and in some southern cities as well. According to Yvonne Yazbeck Haddad:

. . . Noble Drew Ali took as his starting point the desperate situation of people of African descent in American society, and the hope that identification with a movement in which the potential for contribution is recognized could foster a transformating pride in the community. His was an eclectic amalgamation of Eastern philosophies in which Drew Ali was part of a spiritual heritage including such figures as Buddha, Confucius, Zoroaster, Jesus and Muhammad. (1984:265).

Noble Drew Ali and His Philosophy of Ministry

The faith of this movement was based on a version of the Qur'an, a call for African Americans to return to Islamic teachings, and an observance of the Islamic rites of Friday worship and daily prayers. Noble Drew Ali's undergirding philosophy was based on the premise that Christianity is the religion of Europeans, and that Islam is the natural religion for Asians, in which group he included Americans of African heritage. *The Holy Koran of the Moorish Science Temple of America* was the sacred book of the movement, and it contained pictures of Ali and King Ibn Saud of Saudi Arabia, though the organizations charter was granted by Egypt (Akbar Muhammad 1984:199; Haddad 1984:199). With the covering of "Islam," Eastern philosophical thought, as well as early nationalistic racial ideas of the day began to characterize the Moorish Temple.

The idea of an Islamic nation (or state) was central to his thinking. While Drew taught that African Americans were the descendants of the Moabites and Canaanites (Haddah, Haines and Findly 1984:199), he believed that the religion of Islam could be a way of uniting an oppressed people. Before he died in 1929, his teachings were widely accepted, compiled and disseminated. As a result, thousands of African Americans had converted to Moorish Science Temple.

The Lost-Found Nation of Islam in the Wilderness of North America

The Nation of Islam (correctly named the Lost-Found Nation of Islam in the Wilderness of North America) represents the third significant dispensation or movement of Islamic development in the African-American community. The founder has been known by several names including Wallace D. Fard, W. D. Fard,

Wallace Fard Muhammad, and W. F. Muhammad. Using an Islamic perspective during the years of 1930-1933, Fard sought to re-educate African Americans concerning their true heritage (as Muslims) and their economic plight.

Wallace D. Fard

The Nation of Islam was founded in Detroit in 1930 by an immigrant whose ancestry is unknown, who was fluent in several European and Middle Eastern languages, and who was known by several names: Wallace Fard Muhammad, Wallace Farrad and W. D. Fard. Allegedly, he was born in Mecca, Saudi Arabia and came to the United States in order to "free African Americans from their mental bondage and to reunite them with their brothers in the Muslim world" (Akhar Muhammad 1984:201). W. D. Muhammad in an article entitled, "Self-Government in the New World," described both Fard Muhammad's motivation and mission. Concerning this motivation, he has written:

> Master Fard saw that the church was a failure in the Bilalian (Black) community. In the early 1930s, the Bilalian church community was mostly a community of dead, so-called Negroes. Most of church people were hating their own identity, and they didn't even know it. . . . This is the condition in which Master Fard Muhammad found us in the early 1930s. He observed that the so-called Orthodox Muslims had come here and tried to reach us, but they had failed. They invited us to Islam, to Allah, and to the Holy Qur'an. . .but only a very few of us listened to them. . . . Master Fard Muhammad discovered the real problem and then he designed a skillful plan to bring home the prize. . . .When he saw that our problem was that we were already too spiritual (too wrapped up in the Bible), he devised a plan. . . . Master Fard Muhammad discovered that what was absent in the dead Bilalian community was material- -we were totally ignorant to material worth. So he began to study scripture, and he designed his plan step by step after the plan of Almighty God (Sernett 1985:414).

Sernett reveals not only what Fard thought of African Americans, but also his perspective on the ineffectiveness of the church:

> Master Fard offered friendship because he knew that the only friend we identified with was the friend of 'Jesus.' We identified with that friend because our suffering resembled his suffering. Master Fard began to take our minds off that Jesus because he realized that until we could see our own suffering, we would never be able to be serious about doing something to remove that suffering--so

he began to tell us about our own suffering. The church had made the mistake of telling us about the suffering of the Hebrew boys in the fiery furnace and the suffering of the Jews under Pharaoh. They made the mistake of telling us about what was happening 'over yonder across Jordan' instead of bringing our minds home to see what was happening to us right here in America (1985:416).

Lincoln (1973) enables us to develop significant insights into how Fard was successful in initiating his new religious movement and the strategies he employed. The macro-societal factors which continued to deny equal citizenship and discourage the human psyche were in the founder's favor. The sociological and psychological affects that resulted from being treated as second class citizens in the country they helped to develop and create; the continuous migration from the caste system that was developing in the South and the injustices encountered there, not infrequently carried out by pseudo-Christian sects, such as the Ku Klux Klan (1919), which then, as today, continues to go forward with the cross before it. The presence of churches with similar separatist and racist theologies which were found in the North as well, all contributed to a sense of hopelessness that accompanied the African American. In addition, the appeal of the Universal Negro Improvement Association (Marcus Garvey, founder and leader, who was in turn influenced by a Sudanese-Egyptian Muslim scholar), all seem to have prepared the way for the preaching of "Allah and Prophet Muhammad" with some acceptance.

The Missionary Strategist

Identified as a peddler selling a variety of goods, Fard would meet people, house to house, who would welcome him inside and listen to his message. He was able to identify the cultural felt needs of African Americans and relate them globally to the Black people of Africa, as the motherland of all the civilizations. Whereas others, such as Garvey had stressed the relationship of all Black people to the geographical location of Africa, Fard went even further and related Black people (around the globe) to their "natural" religion, that of Islam. His religious teaching mission, and his moral, social, and health concerns were presented as a holistic faith and very much relevant to the contemporary life challenges facing African

Americans. Some listeners were attracted to the messenger as well as to his message, and soon his followers grew in number and were organized.

Religiously, Fard used what was known and available to his hearers, the *Holy Bible*, as a textbook, a teaching tool, in order to teach about the so-called true religion--not Christianity, but Islam. Just as the early Christians used Judaism to prepare the way for the Christian faith, so did Fard utilize the Bible. The Bible served as a pre-Islamic evangelistic tool-- carefully interpreted it in such as way as to introduce the Qur'an as the final revelation of God. Along with Fard's increasingly strong attacks on the European race, the challenge to reject Christianity and to make a decision for Islam was presented. As a result, the overwhelming Muslim membership consisted of former Christians who felt that Islam, as it was presented, was more relevant to their life situation.

Eventually W. D. Fard was elevated to the status of a divinity among his followers. He was considered to be an incarnation of God who had come to lead his people out of the wilderness, the long awaited "Messiah" of the Christians and the "Mahdi" of the Muslims. He allegedly disappeared mysteriously in 1934. What is significant is that successful usage of certain missiological principles and strategies by Fard helped to create and sustain an Islamic environment ready to receive a new interpretation of life. Factors of contextualization, cultural anthropology, perceived theological revelations and breakthroughs, as well as a concern for urban geographic expansion usually associated with church growth, are present in the history of this movement also.

The Leadership of Elijah Muhammad

Before his disappearance, Fard and his teachings had a profound influence on one man in particular, Elijah Poole (1897-1975). Poole was a Christian, a son of a Baptist preacher, and was later a Baptist preacher for a brief period of time. He moved from Georgia to Detroit in 1923. It was there that he became acquainted with Fard, and for three and a half years (1931-1934) Elijah Muhammad worked under and was mentored by Fard. For the next forty years, under the leadership of Elijah

Muhammad in Chicago, the Nation of Islam reached its greatest heights in terms of numerical growth, expansion and influence. The contribution Elijah Muhammad made to the Nation of Islam is summed up in the following:

1. A program of total commitment by the convert (including a separation from previous habits and associations).

2. Devotion to the studying of the new faith based in part on the Qur'an.

3. A return to the original divine order of a male-dominated society, which included denying certain rights to women.

4. The development of self-love and self-pride based on a superior knowledge and sense of heritage.

5. An emphasis on moral living and ethical conduct that prohibited gambling, drinking and the eating of some foods such as pork.

6. Integration into a caring community of "brotherhood" that provided the follower with a sense of belonging, of support and sustenance against a hostile world.

7. A sense of national and international (pro-Arab) identity that gave purpose to live.

8. A practical knowledge of acquisition of wealth through hard work.

9. The development of a paramilitary organization within the movement, which espoused pacifism and prohibited voting in political elections.

According to Bennett, to indicate their distaste for the traditions of the period of enslavement in the United States, the so-called Black Muslims abandoned their "slave-given names" and adopted the letter "X" (1966:323). The "X" is proof of the renunciation of certain aspects of Euro-American life as well as a sign of a new religio-social identification. It is because Elijah Muhammad upheld the philosophy of pro-Blackness and advanced the ideology of an African-American state (similar to the present Nation of Israel), and depreciated Whiteness (including the development of myths to indicate the origin of their "evilness"), that his followers soon were known as the "Black Muslims." He is described by one writer in the following manner:

> . . .Elijah Muhammad built a paramilitary movement, proclaiming himself as the supreme authority. His community of Blacks took a stand against Jews and Whites. His pro-Arab proclivities, following the Koran, denied rights to women, espoused pacifism, and prohibited gambling, drinking, and other vices. His program of austerity prohibited voting in political elections. His program of austerity prohibited gambling, drinking, and other vices. He advocated a separate state for his people to be called The Black Nation of Islam (Albert Shulman, 1981).

According to Akbar Muhammad, three factors are primarily responsible for the tremendous growth of the Nation of Islam (NOI) during the 1950s and 1960s. First was the greater visibility of the Nation as a result of its growth and purchase of property throughout the nation. Second, the doctrinal disputes between the African-American organizations which favored a position of integration and accommodation, and growing conversations with Arab organizations on the other hand increased the visibility. And third is the growing international interest in orthodox Islam within the United States.

> Because of its numerical strength, its popular appeal amongst African Americans as an outspoken expression of many of their socioeconomic grievances, and its alleged Islamic character, the Nation of Islam was viewed as a possible ally of the Muslim world. But its doctrines were not in accord with generally accepted Islamic beliefs. Several attempts were made to ameliorate the basic divergent tenets of the movement. In view of the widespread opposition in this country, but the generally milder and sympathetic attitude of foreign Muslims, Elijah Muhammad decided in favor of numerous suggestions that he visit some Muslims countries (1984:205).

An additional factor of influence came from the result of the conversion of Malcolm X. More will be said about his impact later.

Elijah Muhammad claims the Qur'an as his chief authority (Shulman, 1981). He was recognized as an important Muslim leader in the United States when he made the traditional Muslim pilgrimage to Mecca in 1959. He was well received throughout his travels to Muslim countries as the leader of the Muslim community in the United States. However, in spite of the travel to countries such as Turkey, Egypt, Syria, Jordan, the Sudan, Ethiopia, Saudi Arabia, and Pakistan, and the exposure to orthodoxy, as well as the warm receptions he received, Elijah Muhammad was less than impressed with the poverty, and social and economic conditions he witnessed during his travels in those countries. It was under the leadership of Elijah Muhammad, who later became known as the divine messenger to African Americans, that Fard Muhammad was deified as Allah. In *Message to the Blackman in America*, he is often quoted as saying "Almighty God, Allah, who appeared in the person of Master Fard Muhammad . . .chose me to teach you" (Elijah Muhammad 1965:242).

Perceptions of the Nation of Islam

While the Nation of Islam has undergone drastic changes within the past decades, and is continuing to do so under the leadership of Louis Farrakhan, the "old" Nation of Islam which developed, formed and led by Elijah Muhammad for more than forty years, has been defined in several ways from the perspective of outsiders. C. Eric Lincoln has called the "Black Muslims" a social protest movement symptomatic of the anxieties and unrest which characterized the contemporary work situation (1961, 1971:211).

James H. Laue, building upon Anthony Wallace's formulation of a "revitalization movement," defines them as a contemporary revitalization movement aimed at constructing "a more satisfying culture" for Black Americans who are "quickly learning the methods of adaptation for survival, of toning down their rhetoric in order to attract more sympathy from Black intellectuals and less hostility from the 'host' White population" (1971:211). Though these observations were written before the death of Malcolm X, both writers are able to identify emic themes that continue to be central to the movement throughout its institutionalization. These include a religious-historical identity, which is clearly stated in this quote:

The White man has robbed you of your name, your language, your culture, and your religion Muslims were told (by Muhammad). Through this treacherous stripping of the "so called American Negro" of his heritage, the White man has succeeded in subjugating the Black man-whose real language is Arabic, whose real religion is Islam and whose original homeland is the Nile valley in Northern Africa (Laue 1971:231).

It also includes a holistic program of self improvement which has caused the following observation to be made by Laue: their (i.e., the Black Muslims) "puritanical ethical prescriptions place them in the mainstream of the dominant American middle-class value system" (1971:231). They also place a high value on morality as the solution to societal evils, in addition to self discipline, and a work ethic leading toward economic development.

The Impact of Malcolm X's Leadership

The most articulate, educated and charismatic leader of the Nation of Islam was Malcolm X. While much has been written about his life and though most persons are familiar with his life related to racism in America, less is known about the religious side of the man who eventually embraced Sunni Islam and became Al-Hajj Malik Shabazz, as well as his Islamic influence. Whatever his religious identity was at any given period in his adult life, his view of Allah, whether as a Black Muslim or Sunni Muslim, was related to social justice and proclamation--there was no dichotomy. James Cone describes Malcolm's qualities of leadership as courageous, intelligent, integrity, dedicated and "committed to the continued development of (his) mind through a disciplined program of study" (1992:298). U. S. Representative Maxine Waters said of him:

> What Malcolm did was to help empower Black men to speak up, to challenge Whites in ways that were not done before...These guys could stick their chests out because Malcolm was articulate, he was a brother who'd been in prison, and on the streets, and he knew what the real deal was ("The Meaning of Malcolm X" in *Newsweek*, November 16, 1992).

Often identified as the most articulate Black Muslim by both insiders and outsiders alike, Malcolm is attributed with being directly responsible for the expansion of the Nation of Islam movement during the 1950s.

Malcolm's Leadership Style

Malcolm, before he became chief aide to Elijah Muhammad, was minister of Temple #7 in Harlem, New York. He founded and organized several mosques (then called temples), across the nation including the Los Angeles mosque #27 (considered an emeritus mosque) 1957. Marsh (1984), Lee (1988), and C. Eric Lincoln (1991) all observe that while Elijah Muhammad had the attention of the average African-American, it was Malcolm who attracted the intelligencia among African Americans.

> Malcolm was an indefatigable organizer and speaker. Whereas Muhammad speaks almost exclusively to the Black masses, Malcolm frequently appeared at colleges and universities, and he was a popular radio and television discussant. He also visited temples in every part of the country with the regular frequency of a salesman. He organized new temples, pumped spirit and encouragement into the missions or newly founded cell groups, conducted rallies and fund-raising campaigns, and served as Muhammad's general trouble-shooter and spokesman (Lincoln 1991:206).

In addition to founding and organizing mosques, Malcolm's influence through a national newspaper created by him was also great. Through the organizations newspaper, *Muhammed Speaks* (created in 1959), Malcolm presented the teachings of Elijah Muhammad which were already carried in several other papers including the Los Angeles *Herald Dispatch*, as well as doctrinal issues, political stances and practical skills.

Malcolm's articulate and effective role as spokesperson for the Nation of Islam, handed picked and mentored by Elijah Muhammad, took him across the country and in several Muslim countries dedicated to the building up of the Nation of Islam. It was not until 1963 that Malcolm was suspended as Minister of Temple #7 in New York. The reason given was that he had disobeyed a directive from Elijah Muhammad, and had commented on the assassination of President John F. Kennedy (Marsh 1993:84). In the following year, 1964, Malcolm officially left the Nation of Islam in March to establish the Muslims Mosques, Inc., and the Organization of Afro-American Unity. Two months later he made the *hajj* to Mecca, and in July, spoke at the Organization of African Unity in Cairo. It was following the *hajj* then that he converted to orthodox Islam and changed his name to El Hajj Malik El-Shabazz. He died one year later, February 21, 1965.

Conversion to Sunni Islam

Recently, much has been communicated to the public concerning the pilgrimage of Malcolm X to Mecca (1964) and his experience of the worldwide Islamic community which marked the true conversion of this man from the NOI to the American Muslim Society. The religious personage of Malcolm, and his spirituality, especially that of the "post-hajj" Malcolm, is often lost to the general populace. However, in their attempts to proselytize and engage in some *daw'ah* activities among African Americans, the Muslim community, especially the Muslim Youth Council (headquartered in Washington, D.C.) has emphasized the conversion of Malcolm to orthodox Islam from the Nation of Islam, and its significance.

> Malcolm represents a leader which all communities look up to as dynamic, intelligent, and most importantly revitalizing. The Muslims of today, from all parts of the world see Malcolm as a man who not only had strong convictions and beliefs, but was not afraid to voice them and stand up to a system which expects conformity to a certain way of thinking. ...When we remember Malcolm X, we cannot ignore that he did change from seeing race as a dividing issue to his final testimony, which was as a Muslim who believed in a religion which spells out clearly that all humankind is created and judged equally (Brochure published by the Muslim Youth Council).

C. Eric Lincoln recalls that as early as 1959, Malcolm had made special trips to Egypt, the United Arab Republic, and other Muslim countries and was received as a Muslim (1991:246). It was not, however, until 1964 when Malcolm performed the pilgrimage to Mecca, until his death the following year, that his words, thoughts and impressions of Mecca and orthodox Islam were articulated and shared. They reflect not only his change in religious perspective, but also a change in philosophy. Concerning his religious beliefs, it is written:

> Malcolm's religious beliefs were directly related to his activist political ideology: God aids those who get involved and do their utmost to change their circumstances. . . . He must have thought himself able to obtain the support of members of the Nation, foreign and African-American Sunni Muslims. His

defection from the Nation, his establishment of both the Muslim Mosque Incorporated and the Organization of Afro-American Unity were reflective of his ideological position. . . . His travels in Muslim and African countries in 1964-- again, a period of intense nationalism--demonstrated to many Muslims and non-Muslims that Islam and political activism are not necessarily antithetical. Malcolm was welcomed officially in the mutually antagonistic countries of Saudi Arabia and Egypt. From Saudi Arabia he obtained a 'religious license'; from Egypt he received 'a religious and political character.' With such credentials he was accepted *theologically* by the majority of American Muslims--immigrants and African-American--many of whom applauded, though often softly, his political pronouncements (Akbar Muhammad 1984:207-8).

Malcolm's autobiography, and the numerous biographies and critiques of his life continue to influence many--lay persons as well as religious scholars, Christian as well as non-Christian. There are several compilations of works by Malcolm X, in addition to books and articles about him that trace his religious and spiritual development. Where his religious journey would have ultimately concluded, we do not know. He was murdered in 1965 and every year since then, celebrations and commemorative services have been held in his honor. Colleges, universities, schools, streets, clubs, organizations, days, festivals and scholarships have been named in his honor across the nation. The author Ellis has concluded, concerning Malcolm X:

> We lost him while he was in a state of 'becoming,' and it was the becoming itself that made Malcolm X "our living Black manhood". True humanity is to be in a perpetual state of becoming. This manifestation of becoming, like the ongoing quest for freedom and dignity was what made the contribution of Malcolm X so valuable to our historic quest, and we can be thankful for it (Ellis 1983:117).

Although Malcolm has been dead for more than twenty-eight years, his past leadership role among African Americans and his current hero status (see *Newsweek* article, "The Meaning of Malcolm X", November 16, 1992), has elevated his influence, both political and religious. national and global. As is often true with persons who have reached the hero status (for instance, John F. Kennedy), it is as if Malcolm's influence as a Muslim speaks louder now that it did when he was alive. It is therefore not surprising to read a book such as *Islam and Black Muslim Roots in Azania*, edited by Yussuf Nazeer, and to read of the global influence of Malcolm, the Muslim (1986:49) today.

<u>Warith D. Muhammad: The Inheritor of the Nation of Islam</u>

While the leadership of Warith D. Muhammad will be presented later, it is important to recognized that when Elijah Muhammad died in 1975, his son Warith Deen Muhammad succeeded him as the supreme minister of the Nation of Islam. Immediately, however, Warith Muhammad's leadership, within a rapid period of time, discarded many of the previous policies of the Nation. As far as the original doctrines were concerned, they too underwent radical changes. W. D. Muhammad first reversed the major goals of his father by teaching racial brotherhood and religious toleration. European Americans were no longer viewed as devils and could (and do) join the movement. He even recognized Jews and Christians as spiritual brothers (Shulman, 1981).

Secondly, W. D. Muhammad made radical changes within the organization and structure of the Nation of Islam. He disbanded the Fruit of Islam, the paramilitary arm. He eliminated racist and separatist teachings and re-interpreted other doctrine for consistency with orthodox (Sunni) Islam. The rigid disciplinary rules and dress code instituted by his father were also discontinued. And he also discarded the belief in the divinity of Fard Muhammad, and in Elijah Muhammad, his father, as "the Messenger." The movement continued to realign itself more and more into line with the historic Islamic faith. Haddad states:

> Until 1975, when the leadership of the World Community of Islam in the West was assumed by Wallace (Warith) Deen Muhammad, the community was perceived as an American sectarian religion that contained Islamic trappings but lacked validity. Its doctrines, its worship as well as its racist assertions were seen as un-Islamic. Since 1975, the movement has been accepted as one within the fold of Islam. Its tenets have evolved to agree with the teachings of the Qur'an. Doctrines defining God as Black and dismissing Whites as devils have been changed with the explanation that the former ideas were necessary transitional beliefs because of the brainwashing the Blacks underwent as slaves (Haddad 1979:6).

Dr. Muhammad Abdul-Rauf, former director of the Islamic Center in Washington, D.C., during an interview spoke of the large conversion of African Americans to Islam, noting that, ". . . one of the most significant changes occurred during a big ceremony two summers ago in New York City, when Muslims declared that the doctrine of White against Black was no longer acceptable. Muslims subsequently began accepting Whites as members" (*National Courier*, March 4, 1977). Willoughby, the interviewer also noted, ". . .With the denunciation that Elijah Muhammad was a prophet, and with other realignments by the Black Muslims, Abdul-Rauf appealed to the historic Moslem faithful to accept the Black Muslims as bonafide Moslems" (*National Courier*, March 4, 1977).

In addition, the "American Muslims" as the followers of orthodoxy in the United States are called, and W. D. Muhammad have been recognized internationally and supported by the Islamic world community in many ways. The provision of scholarships granted to African-American Muslim teachers and Muslim university students to Middle Eastern schools, invitations for international visits to Muslim countries, and the invitation to participate in global Islamic discussions and planning sessions are available. Some large urban African-American communities have become recipients of substantial financial contributions to enable and encourage the planting of mosques and Islamic centers. In addition, as leader of the Muslim community in the United States, W. D. Muhammad has been accepted by the World Mission Council of Imam administrators, and has been given the responsibility of certifying all Muslim Americans who make the pilgrimage to Mecca.

Much more will be discussed about W. D. Muhammad and his leadership in the following chapter. It is important however, to mention him and the direction he took the Nation of Islam historically because the reactions of the dedicated members of the Nation of Islam were varied. Some re-assessed their religious and social positions and were drawn toward orthodoxy with W. D. Muhammad. These were the majority, and they have personally brought themselves more and more into line with the teachings of orthodoxy. What many Muslim scholars fail to realize is that of the many African Americans who became strongly interested in Islam prior to the 1960s Civil Rights Movement, many grew to resent the Black Muslim movement, as a result of several factors, including the conversion of Malcolm X to orthodox Islam, and the promises of integration and assimilation. However, instead of throwing out the proverbial "baby with the bath water," they sought and discovered the core faith of Islam. True, though some followers still continued to uphold the teachings of Elijah Muhammad, many came to realize that the teachings of the Prophet Muhammad of the Qur'an, contradicted the teachings of Elijah Muhammad.

Louis Farrakhan: Leader of the "New" Nation of Islam

In 1977, Minister Louis Farrakhan, known as "the National Representative of the Honorable Elijah Muhammad, Messenger to us all," reacted strongly and negatively to the new direction in which Warith D. Muhammad was taking the "Black Muslims." After "trying on" orthodoxy for two years, he began to re-organize the Nation of Islam. Under the leadership of Farrakhan, the NOI movement was revived and adapted in the original direction that Elijah Muhammad and its founder Master Fard Muhammad had initiated.

According to Bevins (1992:51), the role of the trained theologian, in the anthropological model, in this instance Minister Louis Farrakhan, is that of "reflector and thematizer," the one who is able to provide the questions from which an indigenous popular Islam emerges. An example can be seen in a series of taped lectures in which Louis Farrakhan asks these questions (McFadden 1986:121):

1. Is it in the interest of a slave master to preach to the slave the truth about God?

2. Is it in the interest of God to use the slave master as a vehicle through which his truth would come to the slave?

3. How can God trust the slave master?

4. Why should the slave even trust the slave master in the first place to bring him the knowledge of God?

5. Should not the slave be extraordinarily suspicious?

It is this type of rhetorical discourse that represents his deliberate and determined efforts to assist members in contextualizing theology. It has never been his goal to become "orthodox." Farrakhan's questions are of the teaching "rhetorical" type. However, one is led to ask if the members of the NOI are really free to think for themselves.

There is an increasingly small number of members who are known as Black Muslims who still uphold the teachings of Elijah Muhammad and receive much media attention. Primarily because though their nationalistic appeal is great, and their spiritual appeal is weak, as the members of the Nation of Islam come to realize that their teachings of the prophet Muhammad (the founder of Islam) contradict the teachings of Louis Farrakhan and Elijah Muhammad, they tend to seek God in orthodox Islam.

Through the use of the primarily anthropological contextualization model, the overall goal of the Nation of Islam has become the penetration of its traditional ethnocentric message into and integration with, the African-American community, as a single system of beliefs, values and behaviors. According to McFadden, among the three goals established for the movement's membership in 1986 were (1) to generate five million dollars in revenue; (2) to raise the spiritual level of the movement's followers; and (3) to increase the members' understanding and knowledge of Master Fard Muhammad. These goals continue to be identified for the membership through the movement's local ministers who are responsible for accomplishing them.

The danger identified in the anthropological model, that of cultural romanticism, has already befallen upon the Nation of Islam, and has forced the Nation to reconsider some of its key premises in light of social change, and the need to be interdependent and globally conscious (1992:53). In response, the Nation of Islam has adapted its message to appeal to *all* oppressed and disinherited peoples both within and without the United States. Native American Indians, as well as Hispanics have identified with the "new" Nation of Islam, and its mission and ministries throughout the Caribbean and in parts of Africa continue, though its numerical strength is not known.

Translation Model of Contextualization

In Farrakhan's insistence of reviving the message of Elijah Muhammad as divine and unchanging, and in light of the fact that Orthodox Islam has been firmly planted in the African-American community (and rejected by the Nation of Islam), the Nation of Islam has been challenged as to how to adapt the "former message" to fit current social change. The translation model comes into view in that it emphasizes the communication of a Muslim religious identity as well as a cultural identity within the context of a divine message that has been translated from the "old" to the "new" Nation of Islam. It also provides a means of helping the Muslims of the Nation of Islam to be faithful to an "essential" perceived Islamicist related content (Bevins 1991:30).

As the main leader and spokesperson of the largest Nation of Islam organization, Louis Farrakhan is astute and aware of the importance of deep structures of language. He is an eloquent speaker who is cognitive of the fact that words carry much more than meanings: they are the vehicles of all sorts of emotional and cultural connotations as well. Rather than relate to a particular theology, the more general human categories of life and life experience become the standard by which the leaders of the Nation of Islam articulate their theology.

Farrakhan demonstrates this not only in the way he utilizes the Bible to translate the meanings of familiar Christian doctrines into a (proto-Islamic) context, (thus making doctrines appear in a different formulation), but also in his ability to translate Islamic doctrines into "dynamically equivalent" messages to suit the Nation of Islam's needs. The Qur'an is approached as a particular message which is wrapped in foreign (Arabic) cultural trappings, a product of socially and culturally conditioned experience. However, a significant problem is identified related to the translation model--what exactly is the "core" of Islamic belief that must be accepted? If it is simply the *shahadah* (the Islamic confession in Allah and Muhammad as God's prophet), then the integrity of the Qur'an is diminished considerably, as it is in the Nation of Islam, even though it (the Qur'an) is referred to often. Farrakhan is quoted as saying:

> the effects of the changes...in addition to the information I gained about our people abroad, caused me to reassess the Honorable Elijah Muhammad, his teaching and program for Black people. My articulation of this caused Eman [*sic.*] W. D. Muhammad to announce to the entire Muslim body that I was no longer a person with whom the Muslims (WCIW) should associate, listen to, or even be given the Muslim greeting. I naturally took this to mean that I was excommunicated from the World Community of Islam (Akbar Muhammad quoting from *Black Books Bulletin*, 1984:209).

The focus of this model of contextualization is primarily on the cultural identity of a people, and their reflection and ways of articulating the faith within a particular context. Secondary importance is given to the religious text of the Qu'ran, or Islamic tradition. With the initial emphasis on starting to do theology where people's actual faith is, and by focusing on the human experience in history and culture, a key presupposition is that people in culture are the best theologians. Since the very beginnings of the Nation of Islam which are traceable to Fard Muhammad who would go door-to-door talking to people and raising theological questions, the emphasis has been there--on local people doing theology.

Mission and Theology

The rejection of formal Islam has, however, not hampered the international connections that have existed with the Nation of Islam and Arab Nations for at least fifteen years. Millions of dollars are given each year to the Black Muslim movement from Islamic countries overseas. Farrakhan maintains, of the Arab states, that their interest (friendship and financial aid) is based principally on their belief in the propagation of their religion and has said, regarding the potential of receiving financial support from various Muslim countries, "We expect, by the Grace of Allah, large sums of money to come from the Arab world. . . .If I were not a Muslim I don't know whether they would be as eager to help me because what they're interested in is really the propagation of Islam" (1986:199).

And regarding the Nation of Islam belief in Elijah Muhammad as the last messenger, which clearly conflicts with the orthodox beliefs in the Arab prophet Muhammad, he maintains that on this issue "he takes the position that support from the Arab nations is more important than whether or not they accept Master Fard Muhammad as God and Elijah Muhammad as the Mahdi. He maintains that the movement's success within the United States will prove the true identities of both men" (McFadden 1986:200).

Since it has never been the goal of the leaders of the Nation of Islam to become "orthodox," I believe that as a nationalistic-religious movement, the Nation will continue to exist because it unapologetically meets some important key felt needs. At the same time, and in spite of the latest efforts at revitalizing the Nation of Islam, it is the opinion of McFadden, Marsh, and my opinion that as a religious movement, the Nation will also have a long and difficult history, particularly as the members grow older and seek spiritual truth beyond themselves.

The NOI Muslims believe strongly in the Bible, but believe and emphasize strongly that it has been corrupted. They do not believe in Christianity, nor traditional interpretations of it (Luzbetek 1991:373). It is concerning Christianity that Farrakhan is most adamant. Farrakhan attributes the fear of Whites by African Americans to the visual representation of Jesus that was given to people of African descent during the period of the enslavement. He claims that through Eurocentric interpretations of Scripture, African Americans and non-White peoples throughout the world have been victimized and retarded in their efforts to improve their lives. He reports:

> You know White people came to Africa with the Bible and the so-called message of Jesus Christ. When it ended up we had the Bible and Jesus and they had the land and the mineral wealth. They came here to my brother, the American Indian and now the Indian is on a reservation. He got the Bible. He got Jesus. He got the reservation. In Mexico, Central and South America, look at the people. They live in abject poverty, squalor, filth, and disease. They got the Bible. They got Jesus Christ. White folks got the country (McFadden 1986:115).

The Nation of Islam, unlike the church, has kept before it the goals and aspirations of the African-American community since Emancipation and Reconstruction days. These have been, and continue to be: economic development, racial pride and self-help (Meier, 1988). Both Robert Schreiter (1985:13-15) and Louis Luzbetak (1991:64-66) would refer to this as a theoretical ethnocentric model, because of their focus on cultural identity and continuity. Albany Louis Effa (1992:25) identifies the anthropological model as the preferred model of the majority of contemporary African theologians because of its commitment to the human person in culture, and the concerns and questions from human experience which are also taken seriously. Certainly, this has been a primary model utilized by African-American theologians in addition to the praxis model. Robert E. Hood in *Must God Remain Greek? Afro Cultures and God Talk* (1990) demonstrates this and Bevins (1991) exemplifies this in his chapter on the anthropological model.

<u>The Influence of Other Historical Islamicist Missions</u>

While the Nation of Islam was developing and organizing itself to become one of the largest and most influential socio-religious movements within the African-American community, the presence of other Islamic and Islamicist movements were also growing and influencing members of the community. Three such movement are mentioned here to indicate the variety of Muslims upon the scene, in addition to the influences of the Shi'ite Muslims.

The Ahmadiyya Movement

The Islamic Ahmadiyya movement, an Indian reformist movement (1908) also had success among African Americans (Posten 1990, Akbar Muhammad 1984), as a result of their missionary efforts beginning in the 1920s. The founder was Ghulum Ahmad who was believed to be a reincarnation of Buddha, Jesus and the Prophet Muhammad. He taught and preached an Islamic identified theology, and presented a religio-social set of beliefs which appealed to many African Americans, and as a result, some converted to Islam through the Ahmadiyya movement.

Although the numbers of persons who converted is not available, it is a fact that more African Americans responded than European Americans. Larry Posten makes note that the sending of missionaries " . . . proved to be an effective innovation . . . there were some 500 converts by the year 1959. Thirty percent (30%) of these were Orientals, 5-10% of 'Muslim' extraction and the remainder mostly Negroes. No more than 5-10% were White" (1990:273). The Ahmadiyyahs, according to C. Eric Lincoln, are now generally accepted as a legitimate part of Islam, and they have an increasing number of African-American adherents within the United States.

The Islamic Mission of America, Inc.

Another group operable at the same time as Noble Drew Ali's and Ghulan Ahmad's movements were flourishing, was the Islamic Mission of America, Inc. founded by Shaikh Daoud Admed Faisal, an African Caribbean. The Islamic Mission of America was actively spreading Islamic-based teachings among African Americans. This particular Muslim organization, according to Haddad, began in 1924 when Shaikh Faisal

> began teaching Sunni ("orthodox") Islam and Arabic amongst African Americans, thousands of whom embraced the religion. Twenty years later he is reported to have "established the Islamic Mission of 'America' as a non-governmental member of the United Nations and attended the UN sessions on a regular basis trying to insure that Islam was represented in a correct manner. Undoubtedly, his followers were amongst the Harlem Muslims described by Roi Ottley in 1943 (Haddad, Haines and Findly 1979:200).

And again, the authors write, "Shaikh Faisal, who seems to have had little or no academic training in Islam, was a passionate defender of orthodox Islam. He felt obliged to correct, in person or through his writings, the divergent doctrines of other leaders, including Elijah Muhammad" (201). His concern for the teaching of formal Islam among thousands of African Americans resulted in many who rejected Christianity and turned to Islam (A. Muhammad 1984:200).

The Hanafi Muslims

There is reported another group of Muslims called the Hanafis that need to be appropriately mentioned, though their numerical strength became greater at a later period. According to Haddad, Haines and Findly (1984:210), this movement is named for Abu Hanifa, "a prominent jurist and theologian who died in 767." It began in the United States by a man named Ernest Timothy McGhee who was born in 1921, but who later renamed himself Hamaas Abdul Khaalis. He led a movement in Chicago consisting of those persons who held to the teachings of the Sunni observance. According to Shulman, Khaalis ". . .preached peace and harmony until five of his children and a grandchild were murdered by his rivals. His sect has a membership of about 1,000 and attracts middle-class Blacks and a number of athletes" (Shulman 1981:121).

The Hanafi movement is significant in that it serves as an illustration of foreign Muslim intervention in conflicts between the U.S. government and American Muslims. Khaalis, a former national secretary in the Nation of Islam, later left the organization, and criticized its leader, Elijah Muhammad. As a result, the Washington office of the Hanafi movement was attacked and several Hanafis, including some of Khaalis' family members, were murdered. Accordingly,

> Khaalis decided to extract personal revenge. In 1977, he and some of his followers seized, for various reasons, the Washington headquarters of B'nai B'rith, the Islamic Center, and the District Building. During the three-day occupation, he made some interesting demands: (1) cessation of the New York showing of the film "Muhammad, Messenger of God", which though partly produced with Libyan and other Arab Muslim money, was considered sacrilegious by many in the international Muslim community; (2) deliverance to him of those who killed the Hanafis and Malik Shabazz, as well as two sons of Elijah Muhammad, Warith Deen and Herbert (Jabir), and Muhammad Ali, the former heavy weight boxing champion. The incident, in which 139 hostages were taken and reported killed, ended after the ambassadors of Egypt, Pakistan, and Iran met with Abdul Khaalis (Haddad, Haines and Findly 1984:210).

In the dissertation entitled, "Islamic Da'wah in North America and the Dynamics of Conversion to Islam in Western Societies" (1990), Larry Posten makes mention of two additional Islamic movements operating with some degree of success among African Americans. Concerning the Shi'ite organization, Islamic Societies of Georgia and Virginia, he quotes from Yasin T. Al-Jibouri, a contributor to Muslim intellectual life in America:

> Duel to the zeal of the Society's founders and the literature they circulated, several Sunnis did, indeed, find Shi'ism the answers they had sought since embracing Islam. They became Shi'ites and before too long began disseminating the faith to others. Entire families, mostly Black, became Shi'ite, and their number slowly but steadily grew (1990:250).

Posten proceeds to describe how Al-Jibouri claimed that by 1977, 55,770 copies of Shi'ite literature was distributed "mostly to Afro-Americans who could not afford to buy such literature," and how a "great number of theological questions which were raised by the converts could not be answered by any of the American Shi'ites with which Al-Jibouri was in contact", and consequently an Iraqi-trained Shi'ite was sent to the USA (1990:250-251). And concerning the Muslim World League he states: "Ahmad Sakr reported in 1977 that the Muslim World League was involved in 'carrying the message of Islam to our Afro-American brothers who are unfortunately in prisons.' . . . It implies that the League even at that time thought of Black Americans as a strategic element in American society. . . " (1990:303).

It would be extremely helpful to know the exact numerical strength of the various followers of Islamic beliefs, in light of the various movements. Recalling that history is an interpretation of events made usually by those in the majority, it is no surprise that the religious groups mentioned here, in addition to other African-American religious communions (Christian and non-Christian) were not included in the United States Census of Religious Bodies until the mid-twentieth century.

Summary

What each of these groups operating among African Americans have had in common are a commitment to the African-American community, the use of the Qur'an, a call to turn to Islamic teachings and practices, and a desire to worship God. Yet, it is only in recent years as the movement has changed from "Black Muslim" to "orthodox/orthopraxy Muslim" and from a proto-type Islam to "orthodox/orthopraxy Islam" has occurred, that the African-American churches have begun to sense the crucial, unique, urgent and unprecedented missionary challenge which Islam has created. Having now had almost a quarter of a decade of history, it is appropriate in the next chapter to analyze orthodox religious beliefs and practices as they influence the life of Muslims in Los Angeles County.

It is important, however, not to lose sight of the fact that each of the movements identified above has had a leader who has identified with Islamic tendencies and has interpreted his work within an Islamic identified mission. While knowledge of these theoretical understandings of theological discourse are very helpful within Christian dialogue in a religiously plural world, it should be noted that it has been primarily through the evidential (inductive, factual experiences) and existential (actual experience) realities that Muslims have formulated their beliefs and attitudes toward both Islam and Christianity. For instance, the importance of the present human experience in theologizing by African Americans can be seen in the example of the Nation of Islam which is not concerned with rejection by orthodox Muslims in the United States. Elijah Muhammad has admitted that some of the teachings and practices of the Nation were clearly at variance with orthodox Islam. His response was based on a justification of different interpretations within the unity of Islam. Muhammad would argue that African Americans had been the victims of "a harsh and cynical oppression, and the Islamic faith in its pure orthodox form is not appropriate to their needs" (Lincoln 1991:243). The importance of this dialogue lies in the fact that it indicates the significance of the present human experience in theologizing.

It is also significant at this juncture to acknowledge the lack of official response to the Muslims by one of greatest Christian leaders of the century, Martin Luther King, Jr. In 1991, James Cone published *Martin and Malcolm and America: A Dream or Nightmare*. Cone provided a comparative analysis of two well-known 20th-century leaders who represented two of the largest African-American faiths practiced today. Cone reflects on the struggles of freedom and justice that were prevalent during the 1960s, and the call for social change that both Martin Luther King, Jr. and Malcolm X issued stemming from their various faith stances. Cone describes the philosophy that influenced them: "integration, King, and "Black nationalism", Malcolm. Cone writes of King, "More than any other American of his time, King embodied the best in the Christian religion" (1991:150). And of Malcolm, he wrote, "Malcolm X identified the fight for justice as the central religious act" (1991:164). The author is correct in observing that neither man could be understood without the particulars related to his faith at work in the social dimension of life--the Nation of Islam, and later Sunni Islam for Malcolm, and the African-American Baptist Christianity for Martin.

Most significant, however, is that Martin Luther King, Jr., considered a prophet and saint by many within the African-American community, did not include the Muslims or Islam in his ecumenism or interfaith dialogue. In his famous "I Have A Dream" speech (1963), he spoke of Jews, Gentiles, Protestants, Catholics, Whites and African Americans that would one day join hands in freedom and cooperation. Neither Islam nor Muslims were included in King's speech. This lack of reference to Muslims was intentional, according to historian Sandy D. Martin in *The Journal of Religious Thought*, because of both his lack of familiarity with Sunni Muslims and his disdain for the NOI whose strategies contradicted his own (Spring 1992: 44-45, volume 488). Had King included the Muslims in his ecumenical dialogue and methods, he would have done a favor by acknowledging not only their presence as a religious community, but also their concern for freedom and personhood within the United States.

It is also important to notice the strategy of Islamic leadership historically. The author of *The Black Muslims in America* (1973) makes the following observation:

Black leadership in America--politicians, intellectuals and businessmen--has been uniformily dedicated to the principle of cooperation with the White man in any attempt to relieve the Black American's condition without exacerbating it by unnecessarily increasing the level of White fear and White hostility. Muhammad's harangues on 'the truth about the White man' are therefore considered dangerous and destructive, regardless of their truth or falsity. ... The strategy of Black leadership has characteristically been to avoid embarrassing the White man, even at the cost of some delay in attaining a desired end. This has not been just a matter of strategy. The Black American has clung tenaciously to his belief in the American Creed and the Christian ideal, and he had wanted to believe in the White man's essential integrity (Lincoln 1973:143).

However, the Islamic strategy of leadership in the African-American community has contradicted this pacifist stance, in the name of "religious truth," and has always appealed to African-American persons who felt and experienced the injustices as an outcome of the close relationship existing between American society and Americanized Christianity.

CHAPTER 4

THE LEADERSHIP OF IMAM WARITH DEEM MUHAMMAD

This chapter incorporates the research findings directed toward comprehending the leader and missional leadership primarily responsible for the phenomenal growth of Islam among African Americans. It is through Imam W. D. Muhammad that a dynamic Islamic witness has sprung from the indigenous roots of the United States culture which is most effective and authentic in converting predominately African Americans to Islam. Known as the *Mujjaddid*, meaning "renewer," according to Haddad, Haines and Findly (1984:209)), it is under his leadership that the overwhelming majority of Muslims who are African American, estimated at 65%- 85% of all Muslims in America, have embraced Islam within the past quarter of a century. These persons recently brought to the Islamic faith by Warith D. Muhammad represent what has been acknowledged by many as the "the greatest feat in recent Islamic history." "Probably the most spectacular phase in the history of Islam in the U.S. was the conversion of Black Muslims to true Islam after pilgrimages to Mecca and visits to other Muslims countries by such leaders as Malcolm X" (Waugh 1983:95). What was obvious to some such as Waugh more than a decade ago, and what is mainly unknown today, is that this transformation is primarily the result of the work and commitment of one person who has felt dedicated to this unique mission of converting the Black Muslims (popular Islam) into orthodox Muslims (formal Islam). C. Eric Lincoln has attributed W. D. Muhammad for making Islam "in a relatively short period of time, the major religion in America after Christianity" (1989:351).

The implications of such a feat are enormous, for they transcend at the outset the mere matter of ready-made corps of new adherents, although a hundred thousand or so new additions to any religion is in itself a signal achievement. But beyond mere statistics, the presence of a prominently visible, orthodox Muslim community in the United States would have political, social, and economic implications, which might in time reverberate far beyond the realm of the spirit" (1989:350).

In addition to assuming leadership of the Nation of Islam with the sole intent to bring it into line with orthodox Islam, W. D. Muhammad is said to have done more for the propagation of orthodox Islam than any *mujjaddid* in modern times. He has also impacted the African-American community through the creation of a nationwide quality educational system under his mother's name, the Sister Clara Muhammad Schools. Within his roles as the official spokesperson and religious leader of American Muslim Society, he has traveled extensively speaking, teaching, writing and imparting orthodox Islamic beliefs and knowledge as "the Muslim spokesman for Human Salvation."

Leadership Traits

Born on October 30, 1933 in Detroit, he was named Wallace D. Muhammad, a name allegedly given to him by the founder of the Nation of Islam, Wallace D. Fard, as a sign of consecration to a special mission. He was the seventh child born to Elijah and Clara Muhammad. He grew up steeped in the doctrines and practical involvements of the Nation of Islam. The majority of his formal education was gained at the Islamic University (primary and secondary school), located in Chicago, which did much to waken his desire to gain more Qur'anic knowledge.

The very day following the death of Elijah Muhammad, W. D. Muhammad began to move the Nation of Islam in a totally different direction. Ten years later, he was accepted fully into the Sunni Islamic community, and has emerged as a key leader of the Muslims in North America. W. D. Muhammad became independent from his predecessors in two primary ways. The first is evident in his thoughts which were dedicated to incorporating Sunni Islam, and second as evident in his methods, which focused on learning the Qur'an, and the importance of the Arabic language. Unlike his father who claimed the Qur'an to be his chief authority, it is the sole authority of W. D. Muhammad.

In the *American Journal of Islamic Social Sciences*, vol.2, no.2, 1985:248, Zafar Isaq Ansari provides a significant biographical sketch of portions of the life of W. D. Muhammad. He grew up under a domineering father and loving mother who taught him to study the Qur'an, and that as a Muslim, he was part of a world community. Ansari also portrays him as one who manipulated the principles of mass psychology to achieve the objectives of his movement. He later changed his name to Warith Deen Muhammad, as a sign of his complete identification with orthodoxy. Iman Muhammad, a conservative patriotic citizen who votes Republican, is the first imam ever to give the invocation before the United States Senate. Today he is a world leader, who is committed to developing pan-Islamic relationships as the Muslim community in American is developed and strengthened.

Recognized Leadership Skills

Warith D. Muhammad is the national leader, "the imam," who has the primary responsibility of representing the national American Muslim community, both immigrant and indigenous American Muslims. Having sought orthodoxy whole-heartedly since the 1960's, he has received some of his lifelong Islamicist education in Egypt (along with his brother Akbar), and is a well trained student of the Qur'anic and Islamic studies. According to Ansari Zafar,

> If we keep in mind the relationship of Wallace and the leader of the movement along with the former's native intelligence, his relatively good educational background and some of his leadership qualities, it becomes obvious that Wallace had solid bases on which to build his leadership. From an ordinary member, Wallace gradually rose to prominence as a lieutenant in the Fruit of Islam, and in 1958 to Minister of the Nation's Temple of the major metropolitan city of Philadelphia. Wallace Muhammad was not yet thirty when his influence in the Nation was perhaps second to none except Malcolm X and Raymond Sharrieff, the Supreme Captain of the Fruit of Islam. His knowledge of Arabic and several years education in Qur'anic teachings invested him with a high degree of prestige (Ansari Zanfar 1985:259).

Warith D. Muhammad has been awarded the "Gold Medal of Recognition " by the Ministry of Waqfs (religious endowments) by Muhammad Hosni Mubarack, president of Egypt, as well as the Walter Reuther Humanitarian Award. With his knowledge of the Qur'an and the Bible, Iman W. D. Muhammad has revived patriotism in America, human dignity and family values, and because of this, he has been awarded numerous humanitarian awards, citations and proclamations. His name and work have been entered into the congressional *Book of Records*. Perhaps the highlight of the recent years was his invitation to deliver the prayer at President Clinton's inauguration.

With a deep sense of mission and commitment, his leadership skills have accumulated in his ability to identify, articulate, and address the deep felt concerns and needs of African Americans from a religious perspective. In an essay entitled "The African Americans' Punishable Crime," he speaks of the "big" crime committed by African Americans.

> The more the freedom, the worse the behavior. We forgot the high and noble aspirations of those who suffered slavery and Jim Crow, those who worked for our sake and for our future. We forgot the high principles and great moral and civil aspirations and strayed to have fun on the weekends. We treated those sacrifices and that suffering as though it was for us to have fun weekends in these big cities of America. Don't you know a people putting aside the high moral value and obedience to Allah (God) which was the thing that invited Allah to help, now in their laxed morals they invite punishment. There has to be something to appeal to the many and invite the many to excellent productive behavior. Al-Islam is here (in America) to lift from us the curse (1991:106).

This is but one evidence of his cunning ability to identify key concerns and to pose them into a challenge. The core of his leadership skills are dedicated to the mission of calling African Americans to return to Islam, their 'true nature."

The Leadership Motivation

Growing up in the Nation of Islam, Muhammad was exposed to orthodox Islam as a student at the University of Islam, a primary and secondary school which taught Black Muslim indoctrination, math, world civilization, history and Arabic. As a student, he was greatly influenced by his Arabic language teachers. The first was a Palestinian Muslim who was employed to teach the Arabic language at the University; the second was a man called Kamil of Egyptian and African American ethnicity; and the third teacher was Jamil Diab, a Palestinian Muslim. In an interview with Ansari, W. D. Muhammad described him as:

A very sincere person, sincere in his faith, a very sincere and firm believer, rational believer in the teachings of the Holy Prophet.....I had a lot of private conversations with him. He never made me think he was trying to undermine my father. But in a wise way, a very clever way, what he did was that he tried to show us that...the Qur'an is a book that presents the best logic (1985:256).

Early in his life, W. D. Muhammad began to see his personal destiny involved with Islamic renewal. Zafar Ishaq Ansari, who is a professor of the Department of Islamic and Arabic Studies, Dhahran, Saudi Arabia, has made the following observation.

But since 1963, relations between Wallace and the Nation of Islam were known to be strained. During these twelve years he had been in and out of the movement several times. . . . It was well known to the leadership of the movement and also to the rank and file, that Wallace disagreed with the theology of his father. And hence it came as a surprise at the Saviors Day meeting when the National Secretary announced. . . (1985:247).

When still a young man and active as a lieutenant in the Nation of Islam, it was Esien-Udom who first commented that he had been picked by Elijah Muhammad to succeed him (1971:81-82).

As alluded to in the quotation above, W. D. Muhammad was separated from the Nation of Islam three times (*Muslim Journal*, January 29, 1993 and Cone 1993:189). He has written:

The first time that I was separated from the "Nation", it was because someone said I was saying things about the concept of God that was not approved in the Nation of Islam. For we were told that Fard was Allah in the person, the man who taught my father. So I was rejected when this (complaint) was forced on my father. And I say "forced" on my father, because my father knew that my mind was developing differently and he never bothered me (*Muslim Journal*, January 29, 1993).

According to him, it was his father who conditioned him to differ with the theology of the Nation of Islam. "The Honorable Elijah Muhammad conditioned me to question that theology. Those who were in the Nation of Islam for a long time know that he said, 'Brother and sister, doesn't just look at the surface. Look under the surface. Study it. There are answers that Allah wants us to get' " (*Muslim Journal*, January 29, 1993).

During 1965- 1969, W. D. Muhammad was excommunicated from the Nation of Islam for not accepting the image of God given to Fard Muhammad. He was accepted back into the organization in 1969, but did not regain his "Minister" status until 1974.

Leader Behavior

W. D. Muhammad exemplifies Islamic thought and behavior toward spiritual, physical and political needs being met through Qur'anic understandings. He is able to communicate Islamic perspectives and views effectively through the use of modern technology. Unlike the immigrant Muslim community which is recently discovering the power of media, W. D. Muhammad's utilization of it contributes greatly to his success as an influential leader. Each Tuesday, he flies to Chicago from his home in Little Rock, Arkansas to tape his weekly television show about the Muslim world which is aired across the nation. According to the *Muslim Journal Newspaper*, Islamic programs which feature his lectures have been established on Islamic programs on Public Access Cable TV Networks (*Muslim Journal*). The *Muslim Journal Newspaper*, published weekly, is "based on the Qur'an, Hadith of Prophet Muhammad (PBUH) and the promotion of Iman W. Deen Muhammad's Ministry" (editorial policy, every edition). In addition, he writes a column for the weekly *Muslim Journal*, gives lessons of Islamic vocabulary and culture; and travels across the country as the "Muslim American Spokesman for Human Salvation."

Task Orientation

At a recent event sponsored by the Johns Hopkins University and the Baltimore Jewish Council in which the ministry of Iman Muhammad was welcomed,

Imam Abdulmalik notes that "Ninety-nine point nine percent of those people who followed Elijah Muhammad for forty years are today followers of W. D. Muhammad" (*Muslim Journal*, December 3, 1993:23). Because the majority of African-American Muslims are from the traditional Nation of Islam movement and entered Sunni Islam in 1975, it is important to the leadership that the traditional values of Islam are embedded in their consciousness. Consequently, unlike the immigrant Muslims for whom the traditional values of Islam have had a greater hold on their consciousness, and who must now concern themselves with adapting to Western culture and a reappropriation of Islamic standards within the American society, Muslims of the American Muslim Society must struggle to find ways in which to bring their people "up" to what they see as the higher religious and worldview of Islam internationally.

W. D. Muhammad recognized that to do this would mean acknowledging a more active focus on the religious and spiritual aspects of Islam, and its commitment to truth, reasoning, intellect and personal understanding, and less on the traditional cultural expressions of Islam. The scope of his formal authority allows him to address these issues and concerns effectively. Because Islam is not official in the United States, legal and political constraints do exist. W.D. Muhammad has demonstrated the patience, skills, and savvy needed to accomplish his task.

Cross-cultural Muslim missionaries (in the role of advocates) and local imams (as innovators) use their powers of persuasion and their resources to help alter false attitudes towards Muslims, as well as to influence the general public leadership to bring about change in the roles and status of Islam. These efforts resulted in a number of significant reforms including a strong support of Saudi Arabia and United States, which has resulted in the Saudis donating most of $8.5 million to build a mosque for South Central Los Angeles, and five other major mosques across the country.

The Change

"A transition from what was then into what is now real (rational) and true" (*Muslim Journal*, January 29, 1993) is how the Muslims explain the move from the Nation of Islam to orthodox Islam. As the religious leader, it was an important task to move the Nation of Islam organization to a new understanding of self, and into a new religious paradigm. Internal and external changes were made, with constant reminders "to remember the change," In a speech made in Los Angeles on November 21, 1992, W. D. Muhammad stated: "The real purpose of the Nation of Islam was to give us enough faith in our own original creation to make us have faith in our ability to think for ourselves, to think independently. I can be a factor for that change, because I refuse to give up the habit and practice of thinking for myself" (*Muslim Journal*, Feb. 5, 1993).

Earlier, the Muslims under W. D. Muhammad, were referred to as Bilalians. Later Muhammad again changed the name of the movement a second time, no longer calling itself the American Muslim Mission.

> It's just the final step in the process of bringing our membership into the international Muslim community and to conform to where there's a normal Islamic life- just normal Islamic life. The hangover from yesterday of 'Black Nationalist' influence is something that we have to get rid of because it was in conflict with the open society and democratic order of an Islamic community (1991:82).

This fact that the Islamic impact among African Americans was first referred to as "Bilalian," and later changed to "the World Islamic Community in the West," followed by "the American Muslim Mission," later "Muslims in America," and now known as "The Muslim Society," are indications of W. D. Muhammad's initial lean toward relevant contextualization.

Daw'ah

Daw'ah refers to the concept of Muslim missionary outreach. In discerning the spread of Islam, Gudel has made a brief but significant observation in "Islam's

Worldwide Revival" (1985). Noting that there are mosque and Islamic groups in virtually every major American city, the author states:

> The Muslim Student Association is probably the most active Islamic organization in America. Their stated objectives are: . . . producing and disseminating Islamic knowledge, establishing Islamic institutions, providing daily requirement, initiating *daw'ah* (the propagation of the faith), recruiting and training personnel, (and) promoting and nourishing the unity of Muslims (1985:22).

Gudel indicates that the funding of Islamic outreaches in the United States may be most evident in the large gifts and grants given to numerous American universities, including one million dollars given to endow the King Faisal Chair for Arab and Islamic Studies at the University of Southern California from the government of Saudi Arabia (1985:21). W.D. Muhammad participates in this effort by promoting concern for "the establishment of the human nature and the human person" (1991:59). His message to African Americans is on placing the highest value on the human intellectual ability for it represents the progress of the human person as created by Allah.

Related to the problem of morality, and concerning the personal responsibility of Muslims related to *daw'ah* , W. D. Muhammad has written:

> So our duty is to go to people who are behaving as though crazy, behaving like animals that have gone insane. Our duty is to go to people who disrespect things that should be respected and are abusing and destroying themselves, ignoring their obligations to their families and communities and neighborhoods. We are to go to those people and invite them to come back to human conscious behavior and see the human being in his true worth. We are to invite them to realize that everyone has that great posession; every child is born in the world with that great possession (1991:77).

Muslims are encouraged not to begin immediately by speaking of the Prophet Muhammad to non-Muslims, but instead should appeal to the human intellect within the person.

> Go to them and say, 'You have already in you what is need to make you better than the people you are associating with. You already have with you in your possession the equipment that you need to rise up from this low level and

compete with the people that you are now dependent upon. . . . But most importantly, you were created an intellect with great intelligence. If you respect yourself as a creature of intelligence, you will have all the other changes you need coming as a result' (1991:77).

Then, according to W. D. Muhammad, it should be the witness of the Muslim to the Qur'anic teachings, in words, personal behavior and deeds that should attract people to Allah.

Cross-Cultural Missions in the United States

Gudel indicates that the funding of Islamic outreaches in the United States may be most evident in the large gifts and grants given to numerous American universities, including one million dollars given to endow the King Faisal Chair for Arab and Islamic Studies at the University of Southern California from the government of Saudi Arabia (1985:21). This is a significant observation because it explains some of the success that contemporary Muslims have in their efforts to propagate their faith. Various international Islamic missions are active in African-American communities in the United States because of the leadership of W. D. Muhammad and his emphasis on "unity among all Muslims." As it has previously been mentioned, the donation of 8.5 million dollars to build a mosque for South Central Los Angeles, and five others across the country, is a testimony to the commitment that the world Islamic community has in the United States among its indigenous people.

Cross-Cultural Missions/Overseas Missions

There is no such thing as the secularization of society in Islam, which means that *daw'ah* is concerned with all aspects of life. W. D. Muhammad appeals to contributions for *ansar* and *daw'ah* which supports and allows outreach ministry. As one who lived through the Civil Rights movement, this concern for mission is also seen at the center of his social justice. W. D. Muhammad appeals to generosity, a sense of responsibility and he condemns short cuts.

As a result, the Muslims of America under the leadership of W. D. Muhammad have established and supported Islamic missions outside of the United States. In the Bahamas, Barbados, Belize, Bermuda, Canada, Guyana, Jamaica, and Trinidad, masjids are active promoting the Islamic cause among the pluralism in these settings (Marsh 1984:134-135).

Group Maintenance Behavior

Group maintenance behavior refers to the ability of W. D. Muhammad to provide support and guidance to those under his leadership. It is primarily through the development of a particular organizational style and in the development of other Muslim leaders that behavior is formed and maintained.

Organizational Style

According to Maulana Karenga, the transformation of the Nation of Islam was dependent on several factors including criticism of Elijah Muhammad, the rejection of early Muslim beliefs concerning European Americans, "and the introduction of a strong Americanism and orthodox Islam" (1989:296). An additional contributing factor was the leadership style and problems of succession of Imam Wallace Muhammad who succeeded his father.

> Wallace's leadership style leaned toward decentralization and orthodox Islam even before his father's death. Once at the helm, he reshaped the Nation. Also his problems of succession were ones of establishing his authority, creating a new image of the NOI, and winning new converts and allies. So, he disavowed his father's divine authority and his God; disbanded the paramilitary arm, the Fruit of Islam; eliminated a possible challenge; and changed the military, or coercive, image of the NOI. He changed the doctrine of the NOI from religion Black nationalism to Americanism and orthodox Islam, winning new converts and allies who once opposed the race and earth-focused religious doctrine of his father (Karenga 1989:296).

No longer the head of the orthodox Islamic community, W.D. Muhammad resigned in order to become the "national spokesman" and presently a council of imams provide general guidance and direction. The local mosques have been organized similar to churches, with distinct religious purposes. According to Speight, "As a religious minority, Muslims feel tremendous pressure to evolve such an institutional mentality by changing the role of prayer leader and teacher to correspond to the role of the Christian minister; by acquiring substantial buildings for their activities and starting to depend on these buildings and activities to symbolize their identity; and in general, by narrowing the scope of their religious expression to the times of worship" (1989:78).

Leader Development

Education empowers people, and if Muslims are to have a voice in the world community, then they must take the idea of acquiring an Islamic education seriously. Constantly, W. D. Muhammad is reminding the Muslims of this obligation as recorded in the *hadith*. Several quotes he makes, representative of his emphasis on education included, "Muslims, male and females, must seek knowledge from the cradle to the grave"..."the ink of the scholar is more precious than the blood of the martyr", . . .and, also from the Qur'an is a constant reminder that the scholars will have a place next to the prophets in paradise (*Muslim Journal*, Nov. 27,1992:3). Islamic schools, retreats, classes, seminars and other opportunities, including study abroad in an Islamic country, are made available to imams and other leaders. Incentives include awards, diplomas, trips to Mecca, and creative means of public recognition.

Representative Behavior

In this section, the beliefs, practices and behaviors that govern W. D. Muhammad will be considered. As leader, his behavior is considered representative and therefore reflects what is possible, permissible, and worth modeling.

Theological Understandings

W. D. Muhammad is thoroughly Muslim in his theological understanding of Islamic law and tradition. The five pillars of Islam define the most important acts of worship, and provide the framework of a spiritual life. Each one of the pillars is performed with the awareness that it fulfills the divine and perfect will of God. Islam is perceived as the continuation of God's divine message which God revealed to all

God's Prophets. W. D. Muhammad often quotes:

> Say: We believe in God and that which was revealed to us, and that which was revealed to Abraham and Ishmael and Isaac and Jacob, and the tribes; to Moses and Jesus and the other prophets by their Lord. We make no distinctions among any of them, and to God we have surrendered ourselves (Qur'an 2:137).

The Qur'an, according to him, contains the message which was revealed to Prophet

Muhammad, and in the final and complete revelation of God. The Qur'an, along with

the *hadith* (the teachings and practices of the Prophet) and the various Schools of

Law, form the religion of Islam, the teaching and guidance of God. Within these

three levels of authority (the Qur'an, the *hadith*, and the various legal schools of

interpretation) are found all guidance necessary to create a society and social

institutions that reflect Islamic values and commitments.

Qur'an

The authority of the Qur'an is assumed by W. D. Muhammad, and is

unquestionable (while the Bible is presented as erroneous). The Qur'an is viewed as

the divine response to the prophet Muhammad to the historical situation of that day.

The task of the Muslim is to interpret the Qur'an for today. This often means

changing today's situation to meet the Qur'anic view. Take notice of the creative, yet

thought-provoking approach often taken by W. D. Muhammad as indicated in "A

Message of Concern," in which he has written against the Afrocentric notion, stating:

> What would happen if people would sit in churches throughout the world for centuries with the image of an African-American man as savior of the world before them? What would this do to the mind of the world's children?
>
> What would happen to the world's children put under a figure of a particular race presented, pitiable, and in pain "the Savior of all men"?
>
> Qur'an, Sura, verse 64: 'Say, Oh people of the Book! Come to common terms as between us and you: that we worship none but God, that we associate no partner with Him, that we erect not from among ourselves lords and patrons other than God. If then they turn back, say ye bear witness that we (at least) are Muslims (bowing to God's Will).'

> Civilized nations should want that their religions be also civilized. False worship is the worse form of oppression. We are no gods. We are only men, 'mortals from the mortals, He (Allah) created.' Qur'an.

This message has been included in many editions of the *Muslim Journal*.

The Role of Human Responsibility

The Qur'anic view of humankind, in which men and women are the highest creation of God, is central to W. D. Muhammad's message. God created them with a free-will, to make choices concerning life. In the Qur'an God has given women and men the right guidance for life, and in the Prophet Muhammad is provided the perfect example of faithfulness. The true Muslim, then, is the person who accepts freely and willingly the power of God and seeks to reorganize his/her life according to the teachings of Islam through submission to God.

Orthopraxy defined as "right practice," is the best term to use when speaking about the responsibility of Muslims before God. Frederick Mathewson Denny makes a crucial comparison when he states, "Christianity stresses doctrinal clarity and understanding by means of creeds, dogmas, and theologies. Islam and Judaism, on the other hand, view religion as a way of life and ritual patterning of that life under God's lordship" (1985:98).

This orthopraxis also contains an understanding of love toward God. Often Christians who have worked with Muslims conclude that the Islamic religion is void of the concept of God's love; however, the concept is presence, though weak compared to the Christian understanding of divine love. According to *The Achievement of Love: The Spiritual Dimensions of Islam*, Islam does contain the idea of love and demonstrates that love is present in Islamic faith, though as a prerequisite to faith, not as a result of faith.

> Because in most other activities, the results are obtained by the following sequence: Acquiring knowledge, then understanding that knowledge, then putting it into practice, after which the results are obtained. But in *Tasawwuf* (the path of love), the practice comes first, then the results are obtained, after which comes the understanding of this path. This is so because the emotions and

states of love and "nearness" cannot be understood before they are experienced (1987:50).

According to Woodberry, the word used in the above quotation, *Tasawwuf*, means "sufism," not the path of love, though love may be a significant part of the way (March, 1994). So while the knowledge of a God who loves unconditionally is absent, and the Islamic concept is admittedly weak, Muslims do have an understanding of God's love from which to begin a witness to the biblical understanding of the love of God. This emphasis is represented not only in the Islam that these Muslims have embraced, but is also known from the core message found in the Christianity, but which was usually rejected early in one's personal life.

Idolatry

Idolatry is in the concept of one God with three natures (i.e., "the Trinity"). W. D. Muhammad's commitment to this is seen in relations to the notion of *shirk*, which denies the unity of God, and in the reminder that prayers must be in all praises to God alone, without distortion or corruption. The oneness of Allah is constantly stressed. The entire focus of Islam is on the worship of the One God called *Allah* in Arabic who is omnipotent, omniscient, and sovereign and who makes humankind aware of the universe and their place in it.

> He is the Creator of heaven and the earth. How should He have a son when He had no consort? He created all things and has knowledge of all things. Such is God, your Lord. There is no god but Him, the Creator of all things. Therefore serve Him. He is the Guardian of all things. No mortal eyes can see Him, though He sees all eyes. He is benignant and all-knowing (Qur'an 6:101,102).

Beliefs without Actions

W. D. Muhammad states that Allah is love, but that message is insufficient in and by itself. Belief in this God must be expressed in action and works. Faith alone is not enough to please God, but must be made evident in behaviors and actions. Listen again to the words of the Qur'an.

> But of all creatures those that embrace the Faith and do good works are the noblest. Their reward, in their Lord's presence, shall be the gardens of Eden,

gardens watered by running streams, where they dwell for ever. God is well please with them, and they are well pleased with Him. Thus shall the God-fearing be rewarded (Qur'an 98:8).

This theme of justification by works governs every Muslim. And the nature of God is considered to be such that God is unapproachable by sinful human beings. It was the Muslim scholar and philosopher Ibn Sina (Avicenna) who first systematically developed the doctrine that all reality is divided into two categories, "that which is necessary (God), and that which is contingent (creation)" (Tingle 1985:8). God is perfect and holy, and communicates his will through the Qur'an only. Allah is a God of judgment as well as a God of mercy.

The Umma

Because God is viewed as one, the Creator and Nourisher of all, humanity is perceived to be one family. Each person relates directly to God through faith in God, and good actions, without any intercessor. This is most obvious during the time of the *hajj when* people of all races and nations present a picture of true unity. W. D. Muhammad is the first imam in the United States to take more than 300 persons on the pilgrimage. Within the Qur'an, there is no notion of a chosen people; or of a hierarchy of clergy and laity; or, the any concept of the incarnation. While the universality of the prophet Muhammad's message is emphasized, and the *hajj* is given as evidence of unity, Darius Swann, retired missiology professor at the Interdenominational Theological Center, Atlanta, Georgia, questions this. "Beyond the *hajj*, does the Islamic tenet of the unity of the faithful hold up in a society operating powerfully against it, i.e., found on racism and discrimination, economic privilege, etc.?", he asks (February, 1994).

Leadership Style

According to Imam Abdul Karim Hasan of Masjid Bilal (Los Angeles), the growing acceptance of Islam among African-American converts can be directly attributed to the personal visits in each area of the country by the national Muslim leader, "who has accepted speaking engagements in just about every week of the year" (*The Los Angeles Sentinel*, November 18-24, 1993:1). In addition to speaking engagements, appearances on weekly television and radio broadcast programs have enabled W. D. Muhammad to effectively share the concepts of the Islamic faith, to clarify misconceptions, and to provide a vision of what can be accomplished through the embracing of Islam. His style of leadership can be characterized as personable, educational and intense.

Ecumenism

In *The Islamic Impact* (1984), Akbar Muhammad has written an article entitled "Muslims in the United States: An Overview of Organizations, Doctrines and Problems," in which he describes the accomplishments of W. D. Muhammad as they relate to his ability to relate to non-Muslims.

> Imam Muhammad has received the acclaim of the national and international Muslim community and enjoys cordial relations with the U.S. government and Christian groups. He has been hosted by a number of foreign Muslim governments and organizations, including at least one in the People's Republic of China. The former hostile position of the Nation toward the United States government, and Christians and Jewish groups has given way to a concililatory attitude toward all. . . a delegation from President Ronald Reagan assured the Imam that his government welcomed good relations with him. . . . He recently initiated a drive to get ten million signatures on a "Petition for a dialogue between Imam Warith Deem Muhammad and Pope John Paul II regarding Racial Divinities in Religion." In accord with Islamic doctrine he is opposed to any representation of God. Additionally, he is contemptuous of the Christian "Caucasian image of God that makes Bilalians think inferior and act inferior, and that makes Caucasians equally artificial" (1984:209).

Though W. D. Muhammad is involved personally in ecumenical activities and encourages local imams to do the same, one must be clear on his stance toward Christianity and Christians. While he does affirm that Christians and Muslims worship the same God "and there is only One God," he affirms the religion of Al'Islam and the Qur'an are "destined to be our Savior" (1991:102) He observes:

> The church has given us some kind of real uniform life, a lifestyle and a behavior that have kept us in good shape with human sense and human feelings. But the church role in the African American grows weaker and weaker as we become

freer and freer. It grows weaker and weaker as an influence to keep good behavior in us (1991:103).

Regarding Christianity, W. D. Muhammad further states:

Religion, when it is accepted only in blind faith, can only carry a people until they come in contact with a truly free people that have to compete with. To have long lived achievements, the need is for a vision that gives us its spirit. . . . Most are not Christians of vision. . . .they have not been able to turn on enough of our people to bring about a healthy situation in this country for Christian African Americans. . . . I believe the main thing that makes establishment of the 'Blackman' so difficult is that Christianity an image-centered religion is unnatural for us and counter productive for us. . . .Some people in Detroit and Chicago changed the 'White' Jesus to a 'Black' Jesus, but this did not change their defeating circumstances (1991:109).

In this regards, in an ecumenical effort, W. D. Muhammad has requested that African- American clergy join him in the effort to get rid of images, Black and White, of God.

It is also worth noting that W. D. Muhammad encourages Muslims to join in the efforts of moral people, wherever they are. In an interview with Marsh, W. D. Muhammad is quoted as saying:

I am a religious man, and a religious leader. I try to represent the religion the way the prophets represented religion. I think that it is being true to the religion. The prophets Moses, Jesus and Muhammad were all champions of the moral life of the people. You have people losing faith in the future of employment, business opportunities, giving up and accepting crime, welfare or just idleness. That's a major moral problem. We have to respond as religious leaders, Christians, Jews, Muslims; we have to respond just as the prophets would respond (1984:123).

Muslim Organizations

Several significant Muslim organizations are seeking to make a tremendous impact in all areas of Muslim and non-Muslim community life. At the National Islamic Convention held in Detroit (September 3-6, 1993), the National Muslim Business Association addressed several significant areas of business and finance, while recognizing that:

The potential for the Muslim Business Association system is enormous and its upward mobility is long overdue. It serves as a viable alternative financial institution founded upon the concepts and principles of Al-Islam, which can only enhance strong leadership and expertise in America's financial arena. It is a pioneering effort into the 21st century in establishing a solid Islamic way of business life in America.

Lest we forget, this is the legacy that made Muslim converts in countries where there were none. By demonstrating the exhibiting moral and ethical values, businessmen were impressed with the attitude, skill, honesty, and integrity of the Muslim businessman. Hence, native people accepted the entire Islamic way of life (*Muslim Journal*, Dec. 3, 1993:5).

Among the many active Muslim organizations are the Institute of Islamic Information which sponsors the annual Daw'ah Conference which met November 27-29, 1992 in Chicago under the banner of "Daw'ah: Working Together," and the Muslim Education Association which is located on the campus of the Muslims Teacher's College (Randolph, Virginia).

The perpetuation of Islam as a system of thoughts and actions related to all of life is the first strategy of contextual theology. Islam is presented as a way of life that has a "constitution of moral and spiritual rules that can never be changed, regardless of time, place or age. It is perceived as a system that can be applied and implemented by all people without any fear of failure. It is a guaranteed agent of success" (*The Minaret*). Secondly, institutions have been established to serve and teach Islam as both a (religious) law, as well as a (social) structuring of behavior. Islam parochial schools are key to the continuation of Islamic values, and as persons lose hope in the public schools, Islamic schools appear to be an attractive alternative.

Organizations and associations are also key, for they encourage persons to respond Islamically to key questions such as: "How well do I know myself? How genuine is the religious experience I am trying to interpret? How well does my language express this experience? How free of bias am I? Do I feel comfortable with a particular expression of my religious experience? Why or why not? Do I really understand what I am trying to articulate?". It is Bevins who identifies these transcendental types of questions which are asked, over against the contemporary type questions that African-American Christians tend to ask themselves: "How can I express the reign of God in an African-American way?" or "How can I show how African-American culture both reflect and challenge Christian values?" (adapted, Bevins 1992:98-99). The difference between these two sets of questions is revealing: the first set tries to evaluate one's own authenticity as a religious and cultural subject, while the latter questions are concerned with identifying relevant theological themes.

Just as organizations are numerous and important within the African-American community serving various key functions, so also are organizations important to maintain the Islamic identification and agenda. Their main goal is to promote Islamic education in both public schools (from elementary grades to the university level), as well as in the mosques and Islamic centers. It is a firm belief that in addition to *daw'ah,* a strong emphasis on Islamic education and knowledge is the key both to the future of Islam in this country as well as the key to attracting the interest of non-Muslims to Islam. One cannot help but notice the sense of *daw'ah* that motivates and accompanies such practices in reality.

Exogenous Situational Variables

How well W. D. Muhammad is able to meet his long range goals of bringing the entire Nation of Islam into Sunni Islam, and to firmly establish orthodoxy through an active Muslim community of African Americans is dependent on several key situational variables that are worth noting. There are four in particular: African- American and religious orthodoxy, the Nation of Islam, the immigrant Muslim community, and women and gender issues.

African Americans and Religious Orthodoxy

C. Eric Lincoln has raised a crucial concern. He suggests, "Since Blacks have had more than sufficient reasons to question 'orthodox' interpretations of any faith in the long travail that is the Black experience, they have learned to rely on feeling-- the direct experience of the divine--rather than on the official formulas and prescriptions of the experts" (1989:350). Given that reality, will African Americans embrace Islam and the reforms made by W. D. Muhammad, he asked. Present indications are that many African Americans are seeking a viable religion experience, and that Islam has been embraced by many. The desire to belong to a world religious community, something greater than the local setting, is also important.

The Revived Nation of Islam

A major responsibility of W. D. Muhammad is to put the leadership of the American Muslim Society and the current leadership of the Nation of Islam (i.e., Farrakhan) into proper historical and contemporary perspective. Imam Muhammad's declaration is this: that Farrakhan's message won't help African Americans.

> We need to come to a religion that respects our human decency, that respects our appreciation for intellectual behavior and intellectual life, rational life. . . .We need common good rational sense. With that, we'll start to have the condition internally to deal with weaknesses within us and outside of us. Drugs, gangs, destruction of property, all this we can deal with if we have the internal strength. . . .But that internal strength is not going to come from emotionalism, blind faith or just rushing to some idea that appeals to your blackness or appeals to your oppressed life and gives you an escape from the stress of oppression. . . .Our religion speaks to pride, the Koran speaks to the pride of all colors. God says we should respect each other (*Los Angeles Sentinel*, June 10, 1993:A-2).

Many Americans remain confused about the development of the Nation of Islam and how it differs from formal Islam, and much time must be spent by both national and local leaders to make clear the distinctions. As alluded to in the previous chapter, the Nation of Islam is in transition, and is seeking to establish a firm future under uncertain circumstances. Whether Farrakhan will be successful in this endeavor, or in the end, pledge his allegiance to Sunni Islam, has yet to be seen. In the *Atlanta Voice*, Farrakhan has stated in several ways that "he is evolving from his separatist attitudes of the 1980s and wants to build ties between religions" (May 22-28,1993).

Immigrant Muslims and Unity

The immigrant Muslim community is heterogeneous, with many divisions. The various places of origins of these Muslims and their theological (Qur'anic) understanding, and their national and ideological differences, tend to divide Muslims in this country. There are reportedly 73 different Islamic religious bodies active in the United States. As we move toward the year 2000, a key goal is to work toward unity among the various Islamic bodies.

Once immigrant and African-American Muslims are able to dispel their stereotypes and prejudices toward one another, their common purposes and goals of establishing Islam firmly on the North American continent will bring them together in unity. There are signs of encouragement in this direction on both the local and national levels. Positive indicators are evident in the work and mission of W. D. Muhammad as he is recognized and supported by the larger Islamic community. In areas such as Los Angeles, the Islamic Center and the masjids cooperate in many significant areas of outreach and common ministry.

Women and Gender Issues

A final exogenous situational variable which will effect the work and ministry of W. D. Muhammad is how he officially addresses issues of concern to women. African-American women tend to reject Islam based on what is perceived to be the subordinate place given to women in general, because of the emphasis on "the natural identity of the role of women as mother".in the religion. While he has encouraged his followers to advance women in the life of the mosque, there are few indications that this has occurred in any significant way. While female Muslims in the United States applaud the visibility of Muslim women such as Fatima Ahmad Ibrahim of the Sudan and the active leadership role she plays in national affairs in that country, there is no counterpart in the United States (*Muslim Journal*, November, 1992). While the Nation of Islam has at least five female ministers, such as Minister Ava Muhammad, an articulate lawyer and religious leader, the American Muslim Society does not have a leadership role for women within the religious sphere of life.

At a time in history when more African-American women are enrolled in seminaries across the country more than ever before, and when women such as U. S. Senator Carol Moseley Braun (the first African-American female senator) are actively providing leadership in the governing of this country, W. D. Muhammad has not been able to be progressive in his official placement of women in leadership roles within Islam. Unless Islam is able to change its perception of discrimination against women (such as permission given to men for polygamy and to men to beat their wives, etc.), the absence of African-American women converting to Islam in large numbers will continue.

Muslim Women and Leadership

In a recent article entitled "Contributions of Women in Building Muslim Society," the Islamic author makes the case that there were a few women companions of the Prophet who contributed to the case of Islam "through their intelligence and professional skills" (Shahnawaz 1993:41), and who qualify as maintaining positions of leadership.

> There were many women jurists in the early Islamic history. In jurisprudence, 'Aisha had few equals and Umm Salam also gave many legal rulings. Others are Safia, Hafasa, Umm Habiba, Juwairiya, Maimuna, Fatima, Zahra, Umm Sharik, Umm 'Atyah, Asma bint Abur Baker, Haila bint Qanif, Khaulah bint Tuwait, Umm al-Darada, Atikah bint Zaid, Sahalah bint Suhail, Fatima bint Qais, Zainabah bint Abi Salamah, Umm Aiman, and Umm Yusf. A noted medieval Muslim scholar, Imam Badr al-Din Kashani, explained the rationale for appointing a woman judge (Qadi): 'where is ability to give testimony, there is also ability of *Qada* (ruling).' According to Tabari, a woman can be an absolute judge in every matter (Shahnawaz 1993:43).

Of all the illustrations provided by the author of the various occupations held by women companions of the Prophet, that of Islamic jurists most involve leadership in matters concerning religious belief and practice as understood by the western mind. In spite of this, immigrant Muslim women do participate in the life of the mosque and Islamic centers in ways which would not be available to them in their home countries, such as engaging in the planning and development of new mosques, teaching religion classes and involvement in community activities. These activities, as Haddad notes, are being "seriously curtailed".

> Particularly in mosques where leadership is assumed by imams who have been educated at al-Azhar University in Cairo or in Saudi Arabia, women often find their freedoms limited and their opportunities for full participation diminished. In some instances newly arrived imams are working in cooperation with revivalist Muslims in their mosques to have women behind curtains or in

separate rooms than worshipping with the men. Many of the second- and third-generation immigrants, however, are upset by these reactionary moves, and feel strongly that any attempt to keep women from full participation in the religious and social life of the community is un-Islamic (1983:262).

This environment does, however, encourage women to assume leadership roles in areas related to maintaining family values and preparing Islamic leadership for the future (*The Minaret*, November/December 1992). Each masjid has its own Sister Classes and each Islamic center, its women's association that relate to the needs of women Muslims, and encourages children and family events. For example, the Southern California Muslim community sponsored in 1992 its second annual American Muslim Achievement Awards, this year focusing on Muslim women, and its first Muslim Women's League symposium on issues related to family law.

On the national level, the International Union of Muslim Women (headquartered in Garden Grove, California), is an example of the leadership of Muslim women, actively demonstrated to support women of Bosnia-Herzegovina, Somalia, South Africa, Sudan and occupied Palestine. Another example is seen in persons such as Leila Diab, a member of the North American Coordinating Committee on the Question of Palestine, United Nations, who works to empower women in their local struggles to raise their voices.

> International Women's Day recognized the significant contributions of women's participation in widening the gap for peace, promoting the empowerment of the unorganized and the poor and marginalized woman throughout the world.
> The importance of women's ability to create an alternative educational development movement based on the principles of self-determination, cultural and economic achievements, irrespective of their decaying social environment, is significantly distinguishable by the fruits of their strength, commitment and faith in humanity (*Muslim Journal*, March 26, 1993:3).

Because Muslims in North America represent the most educated community of Muslims in the world, women are often called up to represent and speak on behalf of those who cannot speak for themselves. Clearly, one significant future goal includes enabling dialogue between Christian womanist theologians and African-American Muslim religious leaders.

CHAPTER 5

THE PRESENT AS HISTORY: FOCUS ON SUNNI MUSLIMS

In *Muslims and Christians on the Emmaus Road: Crucial Issues in Witness Among Muslims* (1989), several important current trends affecting Christian mission among Muslims worldwide are evident in Los Angeles County. The contemporary religio-social factors which include the evolution of folk Islam into formal Islam, the effects of urbanization, the need for holistic ministry among the poor, and Islamic contextualization have each come together to present one of the greatest challenges facing the African-American churches' mission and witness. In this chapter the issues above will be considered from both the local and national perspectives, describing Muslims who seek to witness faithfully to Islam. A description of the Los Angeles context will provide the framework for examining the religious life of the Muslim.

The Los Angeles Context

Situated on the Pacific coast of the southwestern United States is the nation's third largest state, California. Statistics indicate that one out of every ten Americans live in California. Three out of four Californians live in urban areas located within 20 miles of the ocean, and three out of five live in the metropolitan areas of San Francisco and Los Angeles (Sachs 1986:45). Large communities of African Americans are due to "restrictive covenants," laws of the state which forced African Americans to live in certain designated geographical areas, such as Altadena and Compton, particularly from 1918-1953. The focus of our attention is on the Los Angeles County area.

Los Angeles County accounts for approximately one-third of the total population of the entire state, and is itself larger than forty-two of the fifty states.

According to the *Los Angeles County Almanac* (1992), its 1990 population was recorded at 8,863,164. The city of Los Angeles is the second largest city in the USA, with 3,485,398 residents. The median age is 31.4 years, and the ethnicity breakdown, according to the *County Almanac* is as follows:

White	53.2
Black	9.9
Latino	21.6
Asian	4.6
Other	10.0

The African-American Migration

Although fifteen of the original forty-four individuals who founded today's Los Angeles were African Americans, the African-American influence, as it has been recorded, remained relatively insignificant until approximately the 1930s. In 1880, there were 188 African Americans in all of Los Angeles County, and by 1920 there were an estimated 19,000 African Americans. They consisted of less than 3% of the population (Pearlstone 1990:128). For African Americans, the pattern of migration has been primarily from the rural south to urban Los Angeles throughout the mid-twentieth century. A major component of the city's population growth was the upsurge in the number of African Americans after World War II, when defense industries on the west coast offered new opportunities. It is reported that within a five-year period (1940-45) the African-American population of Los Angeles County increased from 75,000 to 150,000.

> The migration of large numbers of African Americans to the North and West raised anew the difficult question of how Blacks and Whites could live together peacefully in communities where the patterns of race relations were not clearly defined . . . the lack of housing, the presence of race baiters and demagogues, the problem of organizing the newly arrived workers and the impotence of local governments created an ideal atmosphere for the emergence of racial violence... (Sachs 1986:68).

Between 1960 and 1970, the number of African Americans increased from 335,000 to 504,000 as they settled or remained in the city while Whites moved into the surrounding suburbs. Many Californian African Americans are middle-class professional and business people. An exemplary case is that of the city of Inglewood. In 1980, the city of Inglewood was 55% African-American, had an African-American mayor, and the highest individual income and educational level for African Americans in any large city in the United States. Coincidentally, one of the most active Islamic Adult Center's which focuses on Muslim information dissemination and education exists here.

Another community, View Park, in Baldwin Hills, is described by the *Los Angeles Times* as one of the relatively few neighborhoods in the United States that is both solidly African-American and solidly upper middle-class (Pearlstone 1990:131). Many, however, are also crowded into the poverty-stricken Watts district. "The majority of Blacks have been and continue to be poor; many were originally drawn to Watts because the land was inexpensive and considered undesirable by the White community. When the African-American population became so substantial that Whites feared that a Black town with a Black mayor would emerge, Watts was annexed" (Pearlstone 1988:130).

Between 1970 and 1980, the percentage of African Americans fell from 17.9 to 17% in the city of Los Angeles, primarily do to the high cost of living. The unemployment rate during the 1970s and 1980s ranged from 7% to 9.9%. African Americans constitute a smaller portion of California's population than of the nation as a whole: less than 8% in 1980.

Islam Within the Greater Los Angeles Context

Muslims compose approximately 25%-35% of the world's population, and 1.6% of the United States population. The actual estimated numbers of Muslims range from 4 to 7 million in number. Islam is fast becoming the second largest religion, replacing Judaism (*National Catholic Reporter*, Feb. 8, 1991:53). According to Dawad Assad, secretary general of the Council of Masjids in the USA, an estimated 10% of all Muslims live in California (*Los Angeles Times,* Jan.2, 1991). The greater Los Angeles area contains a young, growing, and active Muslim community with many mosque and Islamic centers providing unique religious and social services to both the Muslim population as well as the general community at large.

Presently, immigrant Muslims in the United States represent the most educated Muslims (per capita) is all the world. In *Islamic Values in the United States* (1987), Haddad conducted a study which indicated the amount of acculturation that was indicated with the contemporary Muslim community. The study was very revealing in that it showed how the immigrant Muslims' practice of Islamic rituals, including dietary and other practices, changed within the USA over a period of time. It is unfortunate that Muslims on the West coast were not included in this study.

The Islamic Centers

While most Muslims tend, like Christians, to group themselves according to their ethnic backgrounds (Albanians, Arabs, Bangladeshi, Filipinos, Indonesians, Iranians, Nigerians, Pacific Islanders, Somalians, Tatars, Turks and other South Asians, and African Americans), the Islamic Center of Southern California prides itself on its ethnic diversity in worship, work and witness. In fact, in *The Muslim Community in North America* (1983), fourteen mosques/centers identified by Kettani are termed "model," and one is located in Los Angeles. Founded in 1978, the Islamic Center of Southern California is known for its ethnic diversity, and is supportive of African Americans in terms of understanding and appreciating Islam as an inclusive religion. It is considered to be one of the most politically active in the country also. Among other things, it is concerned with support for State Senator Art Torres of Los Angeles in his bid for a seat on the Los Angeles County Board of Supervisors; the monitoring of media coverage of Middle East events and of American Muslims since the terrorist attempt on the New York Trade Center (1992); and learning how to effectively influence the American political system.

The initial years of the Islamic centers witnessed a rapid development due primarily to a sense of commitment, hard work, and a spirit of cooperation. Various activities continue to be launched in response to articulated felt needs. As different problems emerge, the centers seek to address them from a Qur'anic understanding that is sensitive to the various ethnocultural groups. While internal problems do arise, the tendency is for the broader visions and model of Islamic unity to prevail.

Byron L. Haines and Frank L. Cooley (1987) have identified over six hundred mosques or Islamic centers in the United States, and Yvonne Haddad (1986:5) has identified 59 such mosques/masjids and centers in the state of California. These figures, which are now obsolete, represent more Muslim associations on university campuses (10), mosques/centers associations (32), and masjids (17) in California, than any other state except New York. These are some of the major masjids/mosques and/or centers I have personally identified as playing the most significant role--that of religious community--in the lives of the present generation of Muslim African Americans.

1. Muslim Student Association of Greater Los Angeles
2. Muslim Community Service Center (3341 Leimert Boulevard.)
3. Institute of Islamic Studies (3420 W. Jefferson Boulevard)
4. Islamic Center of Southern California (434 S. Vermont Avenue)
5. Islamic Council of California (3406 W. Jefferson Boulevard)
6. Islamic Society of California (781 Bolinas Road/Fairfax)
7. Jafaria Islamic Center
8. Masjid Bilal Ibn Rabath (5450 Crenshaw Boulevard)
9. Masjid Felix Bilal
10. Masjidus Salaam and Islamic Center (2900 Florence Avenue)
11. Masjid Ar-Rasul (11211 S. Central Avenue)
12. Masjid Bilal (4016 S. Central Avenue)
13. Masjid Aomu'min (1635 S. St. Andrews Place)
14. Masjid Taawhid (Altadena)

In addition, to programs sponsored by the mosques, there are many Muslim worship practices that take place in homes, since membership at a mosque is not required. There are also three major bookstores which contain materials and resources of concern to and about Muslims. One in particular, the Daw'ah Bookstore, is a name which reminds Muslims again of the Islamic missionary thrust.

The Islamic Centers located in the Los Angeles area offer a variety of programs for the Muslim community. Most offer daily prayers, *Jum'aa* congregational prayers, Sunday Sister's classes, Sunday School for Islamic studies, and lectures series such as "What is Islam?" and "The Difference Between the Nation of Islam Muslims and Orthodox American Muslim Society Muslims." Fundamentals of the Islamic faith classes, *Salat* (prayer and worship training classes), and Qur'anic and Arabic classes are also offered weekly. One of the greatest strengths of the mosque/center is that it is both "of" the community and "in" the community, that is, involved in all aspects of life in its immediate community, ranging from the feeding of the poor, to the visitation and ministry to those in prisons. Guest lecturers and speakers from other Arabic countries often provide interesting and challenging issues on many concerns of interest to the community at large. This has contributed to their continued effectiveness, particularly among people who are disenfranchised and are in need of empowerment. Popular forms of missionary outreach throughout the nation include strategies such as cafes/bakeries/restaurants that cater to healthy eating, in a friendly, communal atmosphere which allows Muslims to share and propagate their faith in a variety of ways are present. For the Qur'an makes clear the responsibility of the Muslim to: "Call men to the path of your Lord with wisdom and kindly exhortation. Reason with them in the most courteous manner. Your Lord knows those who stray from His path and those who are rightly guided" (Qur'an 16:125).

International Students

The number of Muslim students on university and college campuses is growing. There are approximately 1000-1500 international students from 25 Islamic countries in the greater Los Angeles area. The majority are affliated with the Islamic Society of North America (ISNA), and are preparing to work for the establishment of Islamic governments and societies in their home countries. The ISNA is also dedicated to the propogation of Islam, concentrating on students, particularly African- American converts at the university level. Several of these persons within the Los Angeles area have embraced Islam and have become active believers and/or imams, serving the purpose of Islam both abroad and at home. Also, Muslim alumni who remain in this country are encouraged to establish and organize mosques wherever they are located.

A Mutually Supportive Relationship

In spite of what has been presented here, there are often questions raised as to how far the immigrant Muslim community has accepted the African-American Muslim community. As mentioned previously, one of the most admirable values of Islam is that it is perceived to be relatively free from racial prejudice when compared to the history of the relationship between Christianity and African Americans. While African Americans tend to worship in the masjids/mosques that are within their local geographical communities, one can frequently see Muslim African Americans, majority men, at the primarily immigrant Islamic Center. The Center has been very supportive and understanding of the plight of African Americans, perhaps because immigrant Muslims too are often discriminated against.

A recent trip to the Center was quite revealing related to this question of acceptance of African-American Muslims by the immigrant Muslim community. Outside the Islamic Center, several African-American men were outside in discussion. Inside the center, I was greeted by a Middle Eastern Muslim, who led me to an African Muslim who informed the Egyptian imam that I was there to see him. One of the informational brochures given me was a brochure emphasizing "Malcolm X, The Muslim," and it described his spiritual journey that led him to discover orthodox Islam. On the cover was a photo of El Hajj Malcolm Shabazz, at Mecca, praying with his hands in the proper Islamic position.

After meeting with the Dr. Mispah, one of the many imams on duty daily, I spent time in the bookstore talking with the European American Muslim woman in charge. Veiled, she was reading a copy of the *Autobiography of Malcolm X*. After browsing through the bookstore, noticing the Islamic and Qur'anic materials available in both English and Spanish, and for both children and adults, several resources were purchased that day. However, there were three in particular which have importance germane to the issue concerning relations between African-American Muslims and immigrant Muslims.

The first purchase was a copy of *Muslims in North America: Problems and Prospects* by a North American Muslim scholar, Dr. Ilas Ba-Yunus, published by the Muslim Student Association, 1977. Well circulated among the national Muslim community, it identifies four problems peculiar to Muslims on this continent. They are defined as: (1) the conflict of Islamic ideology and American values that are encountered in the socialization process of Muslim children; (2) fewer jobs in the future in light of diminishing resources and the growing population; (3) the problems of limited Muslim marriage partners for the upcoming generation; and (4) the problem of the need to support African-American Muslims.

Slightly different but more pressing is the problem of those who have willfully accepted Islam lately. A very large portion of new Muslims in this society is of those who have been the objects of discrimination because of their color or race. We Muslims are more fortunate in the sense that we are color blind in our social relationships. It is the duty of the larger Muslim population to give support to their new brethren who are being discriminated against by the Whites because of their being Black and who are now further discriminated against by other Blacks for their being Muslims. Those who become Muslims lately have done so in order to solve their spiritual and also social problems and not for the sake of adding more to their already heavy baggage of difficulties. I am sure that, Insha Allah, they shall remain steadfast in Islam despite the growing discrimination because of their becoming Muslims. But, what is going to happen to their children? Then, our new brother has not just one but two problems. One is that of their continued low social-educational-economic status because of racial discrimination and the other is the problem of their children which they share with other Muslims in this society (March 1977:10-11).

Written in 1977, this is an indication of how the attitude of acceptance and unity has been perpetuated.

The second resource is a book entitled *Bilal Ibn Rabah: From Darkness to Light* (second edition, 1992). Translated from Arabic by Sara Sleen in London, it is the detailed life story of the first *mezzin* and friend of the Prophet Muhammed, who was an African. This is the same person for whom Warith D. Muhammad, first named the new movement he initiated toward American Muslim Society (i.e., "The Bilalian Muslims"), and who an early American missionary to Muslims, Samuel Zwemer remarked, "The first one who led the call to prayer was Bilal, a Negro of Medina" (1909:12). One should not underestimate the implications of this relevant fact, particularly when compared to other religions which have often been presented as anti-African American, or which have developed theological understandings which are negative toward people of African descent.

And the third was a copy of the *New York Minaret*, a weekly newspaper published for Muslims primarily of Pakistan and Indian descent. It included information concerning Warith D. Muhammad, the African-American Muslims, and schedules of some of their future activities and events. For example, the paper announced that on February 18-21, 1993, the third annual American Muslims National Leadership Conference would be held at the Howard Inn, Washington, DC. The theme was "America 1993 and Beyond," and conference speakers included Senator Jay Rockefeller, Dr. Mahoud Abu Saud, a congressman, and other key speakers. Workshops dealing with issues such as Muslims and democracy, leadership, medi and national health care were offered. Unless one recognized the location of this conference, on the Howard University campus, perhaps the single largest African-American institution of higher learning, the significance of inter-cultural Islamic activities and connections will be overlooked.

These are small but rather significant evidences that Warith D. Muhammad and the American Muslims have warmly found a place not only in the Islamic community (*umma*), but also with the Muslim community in Los Angeles. The

Islamic Center of Southern California, and the presence of mosques that are currently under construction in Watts and Los Angeles, are indicators of the worldwide encouragement and support given to the development of a strong Muslim African American community.

The Muslim As a Religious Believer

The typical African-American Muslim adult is a first-generation Muslim (male) who converted to Islam from the Nation of Islam (1975), and has studied the American Muslim Society for about fifteen years--some continuous, most off and on. It is not uncommon to meet second-generation Muslims also. The attraction and success Islam has for and among African American men has been contributed to a number of factors. C. Eric Lincoln and Lawrence H. Mamiya have identified several: the legacy of Malcolm X; the macho image projected by Muslims; the Qu'ranic attitude of self defense over against the Christian counsel to turn the other cheek; the number of African-American sports heroes and role models who have converted to Islam and assumed Muslim names; and the active street and prison ministries carried out by the Muslims.

> Finally many Black men have been attracted to Islamic alternatives because the Muslims have been very active in working in prisons and on the streets where they are, a ministry which is not pronounced in most Black Christian churches (1992:391).

And they also make the important observation:

> The phenomenon of more Black males preferring Islam while more Black females adhere to traditional Christianity is not as bizarre as it sounds. It is already clear that in Islam the historic Black church denominations will be faced with a far more serious and more powerful competitor for the souls of Black folk than the White churches ever were. When is the question, not whether (1992: 391).

Today these Muslims are among the baby boomers' generation, and because of the value that Islam places on the family from Qur'anic teachings, they are raising their children as Muslims, committed to orthodox Islam. The second generation of Muslims in America, according to a special report in the *Los Angeles Times* entitled

"Islam Rising," is "middle class, politically savvy and diverse" (April 6, 1993). As more men continue to be drawn to Islam, women for a variety of reasons, are viewing Islam as a viable religious option also.

Many of the Muslims interviewed are persons who understand well the teachings and practices of the faith of Islam, and who seek to live a truly devoted life. Though they may or may not attend mosque classes regularly, many attend *Jama'a*, and most insist that Islam is a simple religion and that it is not difficult to practice Islam in America. They all take pride in identifying themselves as Muslims. And they are aware of the fact that the question of "Who am I?" is for the practicing believer of any religious faith, a social and political question, as well as a religious one.

The Muslim Characteristics

Figure 2 is a presentation of the typical stages that a person must relate to and make decisions as they go through the process of developing a Muslim identity. As is the case with any religious group, it must be acknowledged that there are a wide range of responses within the Islamic faith. As one is in process of making the decision whether or not to embrace an Islamic identity, he or she is immediately encouraged to become active in a variety of classes geared toward Islamic nurture (stage one). These classes have three major learning focuses: the *shahaddah* spoken in Arabic, learning the basic Islamic beliefs related to personal, familial and communal life, and the significant religious beliefs and practices of Muslims.

It is during the second stage that a personal choice is made whether to proceed as a practicing Muslim or not. If the new Muslim has strong and encouraging contacts, the pressure to conform as an observant Muslim is great. The third stage represents the Muslim who has become actively involved in embracing and practicing the central religious beliefs and practices of Sunni Muslims. These Muslims are actively nourished in their faith as much by the imams and Islamic teachers as by volunteer spiritual leaders. The process of being in community contributes to the development of a keener sense of Islamic identity.

STAGES OF CONSCIOUS DECISION MAKING

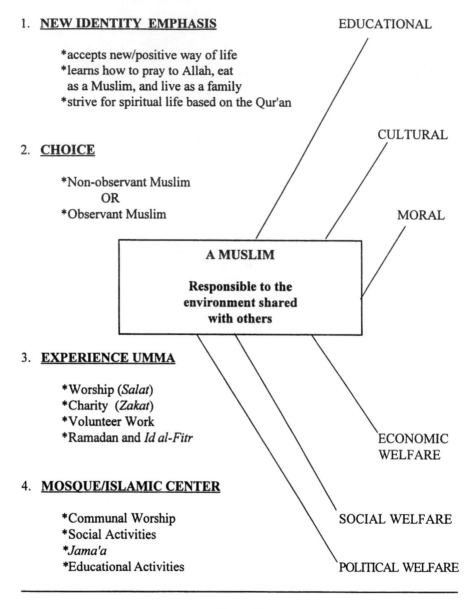

1. **NEW IDENTITY EMPHASIS**   EDUCATIONAL

   *accepts new/positive way of life
   *learns how to pray to Allah, eat
    as a Muslim, and live as a family
   *strive for spiritual life based on the Qur'an

   CULTURAL

2. **CHOICE**

   *Non-observant Muslim
        OR
   *Observant Muslim   MORAL

   A MUSLIM

   **Responsible to the
   environment shared
   with others**

3. **EXPERIENCE UMMA**

   *Worship (*Salat*)
   *Charity (*Zakat*)
   *Volunteer Work
   *Ramadan and *Id al-Fitr*   ECONOMIC
                                WELFARE

4. **MOSQUE/ISLAMIC CENTER**

   *Communal Worship   SOCIAL WELFARE
   *Social Activities
   Jama'a
   *Educational Activities   POLITICAL WELFARE

Figure 2
THE AFRICAN AMERICAN MUSLIM

Stage four represents participation and involvement in the local mosque and wider Islamic community that is indicative of one who actively identifies himself or herself as an avowed Muslim, and who seeks to live responsibly within the African-American community in which he or she lives. The result is an Islamic understanding of God and life that influences and impacts all areas of life. This process helps to explain why there are Muslim believers who revealed that prayer is important to them spiritually, and are faithful in their prayers five times a day, some in Arabic. Many have or are presently studying the Arabic language in an attempt to study the Qur'an; their fluidity with the language varies, depending on how long they have been students of Islam.

The typical Muslim I interviewed may be characterized by a sense of sincerity, integrity and personal religious commitment. The majority of them frequently worship in neighborhood mosques within the African-American community and struggle to transform their community while determining their place in history. The self identity of Muslims interviewed is underscored in the desire to learn Arabic, observe the Ramandan fast, and make the *hajj* to Mecca.

Key World View Themes

Participant observations led to a more systematic procedure called "domain analysis"--an examination focused specifically on the premise that people construct different conceptions of the world based on those basic assumptions and images that provide a more or less coherent way of thinking about the world. These are most observable when the universal characteristics of life such as ethnoscience, time, space, and relationships with others are examined. From each, we observe that a worldview is not a random assortment, but rather is a causality system. A worldview, according to Kearney (1984), is both reflection and reflection of reality (it is not reality, but an approximation of reality), and must include the dynamics of language and culture--for language produces basic presuppositions. Given the emphasis that Muslims place on the Arabic language and in their worship and prayer, requires that special attention is given to this aspect and the way it affects the Muslim's view of culture.

This domain analysis is helpful as it concerns itself with issues and theme differentiations which exist cross-culturally, as well as internal paradoxes and systems of differences within the same society or among sub-groups. This lends insight into the dynamics of cultural/sub-cultural differences. We are encouraged to affirm the validity of theologies, realizing that each theology is an understanding of divine revelation within a particular historical and cultural context. The epistemological question is a significant one for it points to the fact that each culture learns and processes knowledge in different ways, neither being better, but simply different. In order to achieve one major purpose of this study, which is to discover what accounts for the contemporary growth in the number of African Americans who are turning to the Islamic faith as an expression of their religious beliefs, certain bodies of knowledge must be identified. The informational needs are identified and presented in the Appendix.

This analysis employed in studying the African-American Muslim culture is based on ethnography, particularly that of taxonomic and componential analysis. They have aided in the discernment that though African-American Muslims are utilizing essentially the same kinds of outreach activities and programs used by African-American Christians, these symbols have been given a new interpretation to accompany the Islamic message. By viewing culture as a system, this indicated a "concern for cause and effect and the value of ideas, things, concerns, etc., are all part of what society must handle" Shaw (1988:107). This resulted in a clearer analysis of the context. Though the kinds of religious activities (Christian and Muslim) in the African-American community are basically the same in structure, a major difference lies both in the way each faith is contextualized, and the faith content.

By means of a variety of Islamic materials, groups and organizations, local mosques/masjids, local and national networks, Muslims throughout Los Angeles are allowing Islamic behaviors and actions to significantly influence their lifestyles.

Their activities range from identification with mosque-related activities, distributing Islamic literature, fund-raising and building local schools and worship activities, and the meaning of such involvements were discovered through the interview process. It did not take long to discover that most of these activities are carried out with a strong sense of *daw'ah,* a word used by Muslims to refer to their missionary outreach and invitation to non-Muslims with the hope that they might embrace Islam. This missionary outreach is not carried out as a distinct or separate entity, but rather is inherent in all that Muslims do as Muslims. I recognize that this is one reason why my interest and desire to know more about Muslims was so well received. This information, presented in Figure 3, laid the groundwork for domain and taxonomical analysis.

What follows is a synopsis of the primary theological themes which appear to be important to the Muslim worldview of life. These themes are isolated for clarification purposes only, and are significant in that they help describe a contemporary religious movement within a religiously plural society that has effectively contextualized itself within a nation, and among a particular people. Together these themes allow us some insight into a dynamic movement which is directing the lives of thousands of individuals, women, men and children.

Spirituality

When questioned as to why African Americans are converting to Islam, a key response had to do with the spirituality perceived in Islam. Even before the 1950s, there were devout African-American Muslims who were drawn to Islam through a variety of associations such as with evangelical Muslim groups such as the Ahmadiyyas, Muslim recruitments at colleges and universities, the Marcus Garvey movement, and with associations with international Muslims. What many academicians fail to realize is that of the many African Americans who became strongly interested in Islam during the Civil Rights era of the 1960s, many grew to resent the "Black Power" movement; they sought and discovered the core of the faith of Islam.

144

DOMAIN	SEMANTIC RELATION	STRUCTURAL QUESTION
1. Kinds of Muslims	x is a kind of y	What are the kinds of Muslims in Los Angeles?
2. Reasons for becoming Muslim	x is a reason for y	What are reasons for becoming a Muslim?
3. Parts of an Islamic attraction	x is a part of y	What are the reasons people are attracted to Islam?
4. Aspects of Muslim practices	x is an aspect of y	What are the practices of a Muslim lifestyle?
5. Ways to view Christianity	x is a way to y	What are the ways Muslims view Christianity?
6. Ways to view Jesus Christ	x is a way to y	What are the ways Muslims view Jesus?
7. Kinds of attitudes toward women	x is a kind of y	What are Muslim attitudes toward women?

Figure 3

TAXONOMICAL ANALYSIS

Most Muslims (Sunni) are concerned with the correct Islamic faith and correct Islamic practices within the North American context. While the influence from the immigrant community can be viewed as a cultural move toward Islamic liberality (Haddad, Maher Hathout, Hassan Hathout), in the case concerning African-American Muslims, the focus of their move is toward orthodoxy. Related to the faith, these Muslims profess faith in one God, who created and rules the world; in the Qur'an as the sacred and last holy Scripture; and in the major and minor prophets, including prophet Jesus, and in the prophet Muhammad as his last messenger; and they believe in predestination, the Day of Judgment, and in angels, both good and bad. As Muslims they pray five times a day facing toward the *Kaa'ba* (the House), give alms or charity (to help not only Muslims in need, but poor people from the immediate community), and they make the *hajj*, which is a pilgrimage to Mecca, at least once in a lifetime. For those who have already made this pilgrimage, the *hajj* is described as a "high and holy spiritual blessing."

Now, recall this statement made in the introductory section of this study by Halima. It is an articulation I heard frequently, but not as well expressed as it is here.

> When I discovered Islam I was very moved. I loved the focus on the family and the interconnectedness of all things. My religious perspective permeates all facets of my life. The Five Pillars of Islam give me strength. The foundation of Islamic belief, the first pillar, states that there is no God but God. Knowing that helps me to put all my problems into perspective (*Essence*, December 1992:55).

This is how another Muslim expressed his faith journey.

> Matthew, Mark, Luke and John each had different perspectives and understandings of Jesus that didn't make sense. The Book of Revelation needed explaining and there were so many different understandings. . . . Christianity did not connect with reality. I was present at Saviors Day in 1975. I was invited to the mosque by a Nation of Islam member. I wanted a Qur'an, but it was on the back table and by the time I got there, it was gone. This happened twice. The third time, I snatched the Qur'an from the table early, went into the worship service, and paid for it afterwards. I didn't go back to the mosque, but I read over three years, the whole Qur'an.

As this particular man shared his journey, he felt that the truth of Allah was always there, but that the church and the Nation of Islam were blinding him from the truth of God in the Qur'an.

While there is no doubt that some African Americans are drawn to Islam for a variety of reasons, including as a "cultural statement" or "in recognition of spiritual ties to Africa"; or because the Christian "church was representing more of a barrier to African American progress than Islam," Muslims have spiritual reasons for being attracted to Islam. It is emphasis on "One God"; its emphasis on discipline, morality, and conservative values; "Islam, a religion of mercy for all people"; "it conforms to the truth about God that I have been seeking, and the fact that it is a simple (over against) a contradictory faith"--all speak to issues of spirituality and the desire to worship God aright. These are persons who try to govern their human practices as defined by what they perceive as Qur'anic truths they have discovered. Submission, or "surrendering oneself" completely is at the core of their worship of Allah.

Racial Identity and Pride

One of the most admirable values of Islam is that it is perceived to be relatively free from racial prejudices when compared to the Christianity practiced in the United States since the 1700s. While this cannot be proved worldwide, the USA must be treated as a special case in many ways. The mere fact that racial issues today are seldom discussed or acknowledged when most Muslims speak of their attraction to Islam, in itself, speaks clearly. Islam within the North American context has historically claimed to be the true religion of the "Black man" (in fact, of every person). (This is a misquote from the Qur'an which actually states that all people, in truth, are Muslims.) In 1975 when Warith D. Muhammad dismantled the Nation of Islam and moved toward orthodoxy, he originally called this newly created Islamic movement "Bilalian Muslims." This was a reference to Bilal ibn Rabah, the African (one time Ethiopian slave and friend to the Prophet Muhammad) in Mecca who was not only the first appointed muezzin in Islam, but who, according to Samuel Zwemer, is also revered throughout the Muslim world. That was later changed, however.

Perhaps if immigrant and African-American Muslims are able to dispel their stereotypes and prejudices toward one another, their common purposes and goals of establishing Islam firmly on the North American continent will began to connect and intersect. It was Warith D. Muhammad who gave the inaugural prayer for President Clinton, and it is he who is recognized in and supported by the Islamic world community in many and significant ways, indicators of the acceptance of Islam in the United States. He has undoubtedly contributed to a positive racial identity among African Americans for the Muslim community, as well as for Muslims worldwide.

W. D. Muhammad is an active participant in the Islamic world discussions where key decisions are formulated, particularly those affecting the Muslim community in North America. He has become the recipient of substantial financial contributions to enable and encourage the growth of Islam in the United States. A new mosque is currently being constructed in both Los Angeles near the USC campus, and in the city of Compton, which is heavily Hispanic and African American, and will no doubt seek to reach both populations of the community. (The Islamic Center, Los Angeles, sells the Qur'anic materials in Spanish, as well as English and Arabic.) Another example of the racial pride that has accompanied Islam is seen in the contemporary popularity of Malcolm X who later became known as Malik El Shabazz, and later converted to the American Muslim Society from the Nation of Islam. Because he spent an unspecified amount of time in Los Angeles and the surrounding areas, and was the founder of mosque #27 in Los Angeles, Malcolm's influence here is great. He founded many of the original mosques (temples as they were called then), and was responsible for attracting a "different" type of individual toward Islam. Under his mentorship and guidance, mosques were later founded throughout Southern California, including, San Diego, Bakersfield, Long Beach and Compton, in addition to others near the Los Angeles area.

Religious Truth

Because of what Islam means to Muslims, the religious and spiritual nature of "truth" is identified solely through and in the Qur'an. According to the Muslim philosophy I heard expressed, in spite of the fact that African Americans have had their ancient African history (pre-American history) denied and miscued, and have been mis-educated, it is Allah who is responsible for the current "awakening" and growth of Islam among African Americans because it represents "truth."

An Arabic-speaking international student, while studying in the United States, became interested in the phenomenon of religious conversions from Christianity to Islam, primarily because of the fact of the similarities presented in both religions, both claiming to possess the ultimate truth. He discovered that it was not the similarities, but rather the differences between the two religions that lead to the conversions to Islam. The hypothesis of the study, which states that religious conversion from Christianity to Islam was based on a person's conception of truth, was a valid one. He writes:

> All of the respondents said that Islam does satisfy their search for the truth as they conceptualized it. . . . Each one of the respondents was given the change to come up with his/her own definition to the concept of 'the Truth.' The majority defined it as that which conforms with reality. Others said that truth is that which does not change over time. A third group said that truth is the Word of God as revealed to mankind, and the rest defined the truth as belief in One God. It does not matter what each of the respondents said about the definition of the truth. What does matter is that they all believe that Islam does satisfy their conception of the truth. . . (Hedaithy 1985:28-29).

This clearly is supported in my findings.

Community Consciousness

As we have seen and will continue to see, Muslims continue to identify not only *with* the African-American community, but *within* it. This has contributed to their continued effectiveness and attractiveness, particularly among a people who tend to be disenfranchised and are in need of human dignity, support and empowerment. Unlike some churches which choose to relocate or sell their church buildings when the neighborhood changes, the mosque values its identification within the community and remains. It seeks to further address the social, religious, and political needs of the community, again informed by Qur'anic-based understandings. While the local mosque has served as the center of worship, systematic observation has shown that the mosque is also the center for many outreach activities and ministries by Muslims. A myriad of community concerns have been addressed by them, sometimes in conjunction with the larger African-American community, a function that was at one time a priority to African-American churches. These include community services--basic and necessary activities such as voter registration, college preparation classes, African-American and Islamic study programs, prison services, drug abuse, gang counseling and intervention.

Muslims are involved in a variety of kinds of activities throughout the African-American community. One of the more popular forms of outreach, in addition to drop-in centers, is in the form of a cafe or restaurant. Throughout the nation, sponsored by Sunni Muslims as well as members of the Nation of Islam, are many such cafes, bakeries, and restaurants which cater to Islamic dietary requirements, but also help to create a sense of community within community. I have often frequented the Muslim mosques, bookstores, and cafes, and have discovered them to be, in theological terms, a place of belonging and sanctuary, where the concern for community and holistic living (religion, health, politics, etc.) are communicated and experienced.

The Desire for a Universal Community

In light of Christianity's intimate relationship with global colonization, slavery, Western imperialism, racism and classism, the Islamic appeal to brotherhood of all people cannot be denied. Muslims realize this and utilize this knowledge as part of their outreach strategy. A typical brochure distributed by the Muslim Students Association entitled "Islam at a Glance," contains these words:

> A major problem which modern man faces is that of racism. The materially advanced nations can send man to the moon but they cannot stop man from hating and fighting his fellow man. Islam, over the last 1400 years, has shown in practice how racism can be ended. Every year, during the *Hajj* the Islamic miracle of real brotherhood of all races and nations can be seen in action.

The perception of Islam, whether real or imaginary, as a multi-ethnic brotherhood, is strong. It is usually considered or compared against a low form of Christianity that one has experienced negatively. It is also presented with an appeal to an idealized Islamic history. For instance, what evidence is given for the observation that African Muslims participated in the first link in the horrible chain of the European slave trade?

A contemporary analysis of the African-American worldview realities would support the values of spirituality, cooperation, community, sharing, group support, interdependence, social responsibility, and a holistic life perspective. These values (as well as well as the ability to function bi-culturally within both the African-American and European American populations) have been observed, and are affirmed by Theodore Walker (1992), Kochman (1981), Clarence Walker (1992), White and Parham (1984), Wimberly and Wimberly (1986), Abraham (1990) and Crockett (1991).

For some, Islam as it is perceived presently within the North American context, appears to complement values affirmed in the African-American worldview more so than those evidenced in much of the actual encounter with Christianity, both within and outside of the African-American community. The distinctions which resulted in the formation of African-American denominations and churches historically, are affirmed. It would appear that the African-American worldview and significant factors (social, cultural, historical and political), have been studied and given contextual considerations by Muslims who are concerned with the missionary nature of their faith *(daw'ah)* within the United States context, and who also are seeking to engage in relevant missional approaches. I believe that what is known about Christian mission models (Luzbetek 1991:84) is also true concerning Islamic mission models: that though they vary in mission approaches, strategies, and motivations, various major categories can be identified, dependent on whether their dominant feature is described as ethnocentric, accommodational, or contextual.

This process affirms that the Muslim worldview is understood on its own merit, for it reveals a complicated yet different and intelligent way of viewing reality. It is complicated because in significant philosophical and ideological ways, Islam, as it is perceived within the North American context, challenges significantly the contemporary role of morality. The new values and conventions embraced by converts to Islam resonate with the traditional African-American concerns for morality, the equality of all people, and moderation for both personal and communal well being. By focusing on how changing one's habits and perspectives can lead to a new self-understanding, we have seen how the best human actions are perceived as those contained in Islam.

Concerns for Humanity

In the North American setting, there is within African Americans the desire for freedom from racism and discrimination. There is the desire to be treated as a complete person--that is to be judged and evaluated on the basis on being human instead of the continuous and constant struggle to be treated as an equal. Currently, the news media is reporting that the issue of race and ethnicity continues to be the great divider of this country: an African-American man who was kidnapped and set on fire (burning 40% of his body) simply because he is African American; police brutality against African Americans in major cities which is common; the growth in the number of racial hate groups, including the Christian Identity movement, sponsored by the Klu Klux Klan and the White Aryan Resistance movements; and other signs of injustice continue to grow as economic conditions worsen.

> In addition to Identity, the names of groups in this movement include Klu Klux Klan, Posse Comitatus, and Skinheads, with hundreds of variations. They appeal to White people of all ages and concerns. No region of the country is without them. Their recruiting groups range from embattled farm communities to college campuses. Hate is their ideology, violence is their tactic, and militant bigotry is their unifying theme. Their particular targets are Jews, Blacks and homosexuals (Muldrow 1990:1).

Persons for whom experiences such as these are foreign or exceptions, cannot understand how such experiences formulate one's thinking about God.

However, it is clear from scripture that the biblical Jesus was one who could identify with this concern of African-American Muslims. After all, as the result of social and geographical dislocation, did not his ancestors serve as slaves in a foreign country, Egypt? Wasn't there an organized plot devised to discourage their spirits and to kill the male children (Exodus 1:8-17)? And again in the New Testament, were not his people again the receptors of another plot to kill the male children in Bethlehem (Matthew 2:16)? Were not his parents forced to escape and to live as refugees, exiles in Egypt for a time? The Bible proclaims that the social and political influences of Jesus' day joined forces with the religious leadership for Jesus' demise. God turned what was meant for evil into good, into a gospel of grace, for the salvation of all people. The praxis and anthropological models of contextualization could be used to erase the traditional interpretations of scripture, and allow African-American receptors to see the gospel anew (Bevins 1992).

Islam, in national and international communities, as represented in both written and spoken words, is sympathetic to the plight of African Americans. The move may be political and is a reflection of the goal to establish Islam firmly within the context of North America among an indigenous people. Or, perhaps it is because Muslims too have tended to be discriminated against and stereotyped, and have found themselves struggling against some of these very same issues as they seek to make their home here (*Minaret*, December 1992:35). This sensitivity is evident in Muslim oriented materials, activities and publications. Irregardless of the motives of the immigrant and naturalized Muslims who seek solidarity with African-American Muslims, where else in all of North American history, have African Americans, in the United States, received so much human affirmation?

Islamic Theological Beliefs

While some scholars disagree, Kenneth Cragg, Dudley Woodberry, and Dean Gilliland among other Islamic scholars have determined that the Qur'an and the Bible are referring to the One Creator God, though at times saying different things about God. The Prophet Muhammad issued a call away from the polytheistic worship of his day and toward the One God and Creator. In *The Myth of the Cross*, the Nigerian author Allhaj A. D. Ajijola writes:

> The greatest service Islam rendered to humanity was the exaltation and purification of the concept of God. Islam strove to deliver humanity from a multiplicity of gods on the one hand and from the incarnationalism on the other and to bring man back to the Unseen God (1975:170).

According to Islamicist Donald S. Tingle, the Prophet Muhammad's call to religious and theological renewal and revival, and to the worship of God was so severe that it did not leave room for the affirmation of the Christian doctrine of the deity of Jesus Christ as Savior and the Trinity (1985:7).

> People of the Book (Christians), do not transgress the bounds of your religion. Speak nothing but the truth about God. The Messiah, Jesus the son of Mary, was no more than God's apostle and His words which He cast to Mary; a spirit from Him. So believe in God and His apostles and do not say: 'Three.' Forbear, and it shall be better for you. God is but one God. God forbid that He should have a son! He is all that heavens and earth contain. God is the all-sufficient protector. The Messiah does not disdain to be a servant of God, nor do the angels who are nearest to Him (Qur'an 4:171-172).

Often Muslims will say that Islam is a simple religion to follow because it provides guidance for all (every aspect) of life. The Qur'an teaches that the purpose of human beings is to submit to God and it provides for daily life (spiritual, social, economic, political, and moral). It reminds people of their duty while on earth to themselves, to their family members and relatives, to the community at large, to others outside the community, and of course to God.

Theologically, Islam is perceived as the continuation of God's divine message which God revealed to all God's Prophets.

> Say: We believe in God and that which was revealed to us, and that which was revealed to Abraham and Ishmael and Isaac and Jacob, and the tribes; to Moses and Jesus and the other prophets by their Lord. We make no distinctions among any of them, and to God we have surrendered ourselves (Qur'an 2:137).

The Qur'an contains the message which was revealed to Prophet Muhammad, and in the final and complete revelation of God. The Qur'an, along with the *hadith* (the teachings and practices of the Prophet) and the various Schools of Law, form the religion of Islam, the teaching and guidance of God. Within these three levels of authority (the Qur'an, the *hadith*, and the various legal schools of interpretation) are found all guidance necessary to create a society and social institutions that reflect Islamic values and commitments.

Within the teachings of Islam, there appears to be six main tenets of Islam described by Joseph P. Gudel: Allah, Aneles, the Scriptures, the Prophets, the Hereafter, and the Divine decree (1985:18-19). I have selected four significant theological doctrines in which to explain the main tenets of Muslim beliefs as I have learned them from Muslims in the Los Angles area. They are: (1) the Oneness of God, (2) the responsibility of human beings, (3) the concept of worship, and (4) the concept of *daw'ah*, Muslim missionary outreach.

The Oneness of God

R. Marston Speight observes that by discovering the points of commonality and incisiveness of both Christianity and Islam, one becomes aware immediately that they represent the common belief that there is only one God, almighty and all merciful, who is the creator and sustainer of all of life. This discussion of the nature of God leads to the basic assumption that when human beings learn of God's power and mercy, or grace, they must respond in a threefold way, described by Speight as: a life of commitment to the divine will and authority; a life of gratitude for the gifts of God; and a life of responsible action in worship, charity and acts of righteousness. It follows from this that in response to God's action, the human's response to the understanding of God will be significant and will result in God's final judgment. This judgment is viewed by both Christians and Muslims as God's just response to the choices humans make concerning the will of God.

The Concept of Worship

Islam is a religion that emphasizes "intention" and "action." As one Muslim imam has said, "To worship God is to know Him and love Him as he wants us to, according to the Qur'an." This means to act upon His teachings in every aspect of life." The true believer is described as:

> Righteousness does not consist in whether you face towards the East or the West. The righteous man is he who believes in God and the Last Day, in the angels and the Book and the prophets; who, though he loves it dearly, gives away his wealth to kinsfolk, to orphans, to the helpless, to the traveller in need and to beggars, and for the redemption of captives; who attends to his prayers and renders the alms

levy; who is true to his promises and steadfast in trial and adversity and in times of war. Such as the true believes; such are the God-fearing (Quran 2:177).

Religious Practices

The five pillars of Islam define the most important acts of worship and provide the framework of a spiritual life that Muslims perceive pleases God. Each one of the pillars is performed with the awareness that it fulfills the divine and perfect will of God. The first pillar is the declaration of faith. Called the *shahadah,* it states "I bear witness that there is none worthy of worship except God, and that Mohammad is God's servant and messenger." It is the only pillar concerned with orthodoxy or "doctrinal correctness" (Denny 1985:105). The only declaration of belief necessary for one to become a Muslim is this confession that distinguishes the Muslim from every other worshipper in the world. This confession states unequivocally that there is only one God to be worshipped, and that the way and example of Muhammad is the ideal life.

The second pillar refers to the prayers *(salat)* that are prescribed five times a day as a religious duty required by God. The purpose of the prayers is to inspire belief in God and God's ways. Muslims say that by performing these prayers as prescribed, that the heart is reminded constantly of the things of God. As a Christian family member daily observes Muslim relatives excuse themselves in order to perform *salat* (prayer), the Christian is both awed and perplexed.

The third pillar is that of fasting *(sawm)* during the month of Ramadan. No food, drink or sexual intercourse is had from the rising of the sun to the setting of the sun. This is a time when Muslims commemorate Muhammad having received the revelation of the Qur'an. At this time Muslims are to practice patience, unselfishness, will power, discipline and to develop a spiritual awareness of social consciousness. The breaking of the fast at the end of Ramadan is called *Id al-Fitr*, and is accompanied by the giving of alms.

Zakat (almsgiving or charity) is the fourth pillar. It serves to remind the Muslim of his/her responsibility to the less fortunate. A payment equivalent to 2.5%

of one's net savings is what is required from the Qur'an. This money is given at the mosque toward furthering the Islamic cause--toward the building of mosques and schools, helping the needy, and so forth.

The pilgrimage to the *Kaa'ba* in Mecca (*hajj*) is the last pillar, one which is not compulsory, but is dependent on one's means or ability to make it. Every Muslim desires to make this pilgrimage before his or her death. The story of Malcolm X's pilgrimage to Mecca and his discovery of true Islam has led the majority of Muslims from the Nation of Islam into orthodox Islam.

Muslim Ritual Prayer: *Salat*

It is the second of these acts, ritual prayer, that we shall discuss in the next section. The act of prayer is as meaningful to the Muslim as it is to the Christian, for in prayer both the presence of God and the will of God are sought. The importance of prayer for the Muslim lies in the fact that it is centrally taught and held in reverence in the Qur'an. The prophet Muhammad prayed and taught his followers by example, both the position and attitude of proper prayer that is pleasing and acceptable by God.

The Nature and Practice of Prayer

The difference between Muslim and Christian prayer is obvious and distinct. For the Christian, the position, the structure and shape of prayers, like those found in the Bible, are various. No single model of either the form or the content of prayer is required by the Church. The case of Islamic prayer is different. While the focus of Christian prayer is sometimes directed toward God and other times to Jesus, the Muslim focus of prayer is directed always toward God. Because the Christian tradition is pluriform, various forms of prayers will be found in Christian practice.

This is not the case among Muslims. Muslims perform prayers in words and form that have had a continuous and direct historical relationship to their founder. The Qur'an directed that five daily prayers be said at the appropriate times. Qur'anic verses 17:178 and 20:130 indicate the established times. Sheikh Shu'aib, who has been working as the head of the Islamic Studies Department in Masjid F. Bilal, in

Los Angeles, has provided a table of the five daily prayers (1983:105), including the specific times in the North American context to correspond with the worldwide Islamic community.

If prayers are not said at the proper time, they are considered void and null. The morning, noon, afternoon, evening and night prayers are important and the Qur'an and the Hadith contain explicit instructions and guidance for *salat* in every conceivable circumstance. The Qur'an stresses that the prayers should be observed punctually and accurately, as practiced by Muhammad.

Recent studies affirm that contrary to popular belief, Americans in general are a religious people, with the majority professing belief in a Supreme being and expressing that belief through some form of prayer. Although religious beliefs tend to satisfy a variety of religious and social functions, through the vehicle of prayer, individual and communal, are expressed. These beliefs and the meanings they symbolize are then expressed in the symbolic forms and behaviors of those who embrace them, as evidenced in both their personal and public aspects of life.

While not all religions movements in the United States society are missional, those mentioned in the initial introductory dialogue are--the Yoruba religion, Santaria, Ethiopian Judaism, Islam and Christianity. Each of these religious systems professes, as foundational to their understanding of the believer's relationship to the object of worship, to be universal in practice, diasporal, and missional. Though Islam, Judaism, and Christianity are monotheistic, Christianity is often described as a religion of historical proclamation, while Islam is considered a theocracy. Islam perceives itself as the "middle" religion, standing between the Jewish idea which emphasizes God's justice, and the Christian idea which stresses God's love. It is through the act of ritual prayer that these distinctions and their theological implications become clear.

Muslim Theology in Prayer

Despite the particular religious systems, the act of prayer provides a theological key of understanding. Unlike Yoruba worship, Buddhism or Christianity, which engage the practitioner or believer in personal prayers involving intercession, petitions and individual devotions, Islamic prayer *(salat)* assumes a different understanding of prayer as the worship of God. According to Denny, "The *salat* is an intense, highly regulated, formal observance that features cycles of bodily postures climaxing in complete prostration in an orientation toward the *Ka'ba* in Mecca" (1985:106).

> At the heart of Muslim devotion is the *salat* , or "prayer service," consisting of several cycles of postures culminating in full bodily prostration from the beginning as a distinctive aspect of the new movement. The little Muslim group prayed together at night, in houses, but also out in public sometimes during the day, which occasionally brought ridicule and persecution. Praise and thanksgiving seem to have accompanied the prostrations (Denny 1985:74).

Ritual Washing

Wuduu is an obligatory act of purification before prayer. Cleanliness of self and of the environment to be used for prayer is a prerequisite in Islam, and is emphasized before approaching God. The Qur'an says: "O believers, when you get up for prayer, wash up your faces and your hands up to the elbows and wipe your heads and wash your feet up to the ankles. . . "(Quran 5:7). Clean water is used, beginning with the right hand, to wash the hands and arms up to the elbow, three times. The mouth is rinsed using water and the index finger, again three times. This is followed by a cleansing of the nose (sniffing and blowing out water), the face and both arms up to the elbows, each three times. The head is then rubbed with wet hands, followed by the ears. The act of *wuduu* is completed when the feet are washed, each three times, beginning with the right foot. Directly outside the mosque's worshipping area is located a designated place for washing oneself, as well as a place for leaving shoes.

Intention

One's intentions are prominent in this religion. Even the definition of faith in Islam involves "verbal assent, deeds and intention" (Cragg and Speight 1980:148). Therefore, as one initiates *wuduu*, even before the water touches the body, the believer states in his or her heart, *niyyah* or the intention to worship God. Because there is no report of Muhammad or his followers using specific wordings, one's intention is said in private. This is followed by saying, silently, "In the name of Allah, most gracious, most merciful."

At the close of this personal act of ablution, again the intentionality toward worshipping God is evident in the repeating of these words:

> I bear witness that there is no deity but Allah, He is one and has no associate. And I bear witness that Muhammad is His servant and Messenger. O Allah, join me with those who repent of their sins again and again, and join me with those who keep themselves neat and clean at all times (Tajuddin B. Shu'aib 1983:40-41).

The actual call to prayer is performed by an adult male. He stands on a raised platform or ground facing the *Kab'ah*, and calls out in a loud voice the following:

> Allah is the Greatest (two times)
> Allah is the Greatest (two times)
> I bear witness that there is nothing worthy of worship but Allah (two times)
> I bear witness that Muhammad is the Messenger of Allah (two times)
> Hasten to Prayer (two times)
> Hasten to real success (two times)
> There is nothing worthy of worship but Allah.

Additional words are required depending on the specific prayer offered. While the call to prayer is being made, the worshipper should sit silently and repeat the words after the *muadhdin*, and at the closure, the following supplication can be made:

> O Allah, Lord of this most perfect call,
> And of the prayer which is about to be established, grant to Muhammad the favor of nearness (to Thee) and excellence,
> And a place of distinction and exalt him to a position of glory which Thou has promised him (Shu'aib 1983:54).

The Call to Prayer (*adhan*)

Then the worshippers are to stand toward the Mecca for the actual prayer, regardless of whether the prayer being said is an individual or congregational one. The words used in the call to stand for prayer are words that confirm the major issues of the Islamic creed (the supremacy of Allah, the oneness of God, and the messenger

160

prophet Muhammad).   "Prayer is ready!" he (always male) shouts twice, and the hearers respond with, "May Allah keep it established forever!"

The Content and Form of Prayer

There are nine basic steps or elements to *salat*, and each must be made properly if the prayer is not to be considered void or invalid. In both the home and mosque environment, young children grow up observing their parents in prayer, and intentionally develop an attitude toward prayer that reflects both a naturalness as well as a sense of divine obligation.

Standing with hands raised to the ears, the worshipper says four times, "God is most great." This begins the consecrated state of prayer. As Denny notes, "From this time until the end, all attention and energy are focused on the correct performance of the rite" (1985:108). The recitation of the opening *sura* of the Qur'an is said while standing, with the hands placed between the chest and naval. This is the most often repeated passage of the Qur'an.

> In the name of Allah, Most Gracious, Most Merciful.
> Praise be to Allah, the Cherisher and Sustainer of the Worlds.
> Most Gracious, Most Merciful.
> Master of the Day of Judgment.
> You do we worship, and Your aid we seek.
> Show us the straight way.
> The way of those on whom You have bestowed Your Grace,
> Those whose (portion) is not wrath, and who go not astray (Qur'an 1:1-7)

Another verse from the Qur'an may be recited. The worshiper then bows with his/her hands reaching the knees and says "Glory be to God". Then, returning to the standing position, the worshipper praises God. "Our Lord, to You is due all praise."

Next, the worshipper prostrates to the floor, allowing the knees, toes and forehead to touch the floor, along with the palms of the hands placed flat on each side of the head. While repeating again that "God is most great," the worshipper assumes the sitting position (with legs and feet under the body, and palms resting above the knees). A second position of prostration is carried out, again ending with the words, God is great." "Finally," according to Denny, "the standing position is resumed, and this marks the end of a *rak'a*, the discrete, basic cycle of postures and utterances of which all *salats* are composed (985:109).

As the worshipper begins to conclude the prayer time a testimony is given to the unity of God, and to the prophet Muhammad. This is followed by a request for blessings for the Prophet and his family. Finally, the worshipper offers a short supplication, turning the face first to the right shoulder, and then to the right saying "as-salamu Alikum" meaning, "peace be upon you and the mercy and blessings of God."

This concludes the general prayer, which is to be performed by every Muslim daily. Accordingly, the number of *rak'as* or passages required are dependent on which of the daily prayers are being said. Friday is when congregational prayers are said, usually with an imam or any Muslim of moral life and sincere faith providing a sermon (*khutba*).

> Generally, the message includes an exhortation to the Muslims to obey God and actively follow and aplly the precepts of Islam. Although often the delivery is passionate and dramatic, after Muhammad's example, sometimes the *khutba* resembles a scholarly lecture. But is should not be too long, for as the Prophet is reported to have said, "The length of a man's prayers and the shortness of his sermon are a sign of his understanding, so make the prayer long and the sermon short, for there is magic in eloquence (Denny 1985: 111).

Women, infants, ill persons, the blind and the elderly are not required to attend.

Shared Muslim Leadership Goals

All Muslim leaders in the United States have definite religious, political and social goals. These goals may be articulated in various ways; however, they appear to be centered around five significant ends toward which effort is directed. These leadership goals, as well as the particular goals of W. D. Muhammad, will be discussed. In addition, an analysis of how these goals are processed through certain emic themes and are given shape in (Islamic) contextualized mission approaches will be included.

Leadership Goals

The first goal of leaders is to protect the Muslim way of life. This aim involves working toward changes that would make it easier for Muslims to practice their faith and pass it on to the next generation. For example, Muslims want permission granted in the school and workplaces that would allow Muslims to observe Islamic holidays. They also desire the availability of food that meets Islamic dietary laws. Concerning moral issues, they desire a drug free, less sexually permissive environment for youth.

Second, Muslim leaders promote Islamic education in the public schools as well as in their own Islamic schools. For years, Muslims have advocated for school textbooks and public library books that are free of anti-Islamic stereotypes. The removal of various misrepresentation of Muslims in the general media, children's cartoons, and adult films, in addition to textbooks and the promotion of Islamically correct literature is urged in many local communities by active Muslim groups. Miles Todd, a community organizer in South Los Angeles, is reported as saying, "When Islam is being attacked, it hurts and affects you no matter what color you are. . . . In my case, I am a Muslim first, an African American second" (*Los Angeles Times*, April 6, 1993 in "Islam Rising").

A third goal is centered around shaping the social environment within the United States by Muslims and for Muslims. This is done through Muslims becoming actively involved in the community, as well as by displaying Islamic pride as one takes stands on various community issues.

Influencing North American policies toward Islamic movements and populations overseas is another key goal of Muslim leaders in this country. Seeking to impact the affairs in Bosnia, Somalia, Egypt, Sudan, Kashmir and other countries where immigrant Muslims originate is important to some imams, who encourage Muslims to influence policies here. In addition, because of the unprecedented number of African-American soldiers who converted to Islam while serving in the Gulf War and in Somalia (profoundly impressed with the Islamic witness observed), and who married Muslim women while overseas, the international Islamic influence and political implications require more understanding among the African-American community.

A fifth goal that Muslim leaders seek to address is urging their followers to bring unity among Muslims of the various racial, ethnic and nationalities represented in the United States. One significant finding is that though a primary focus has been on understanding the leadership of W. D. Muhammad, he was unknown to some African-American Muslims. This was primarily the cause involving those African-American Muslims who were introduced to Sunni Islam through their college, or who relate to multi-ethnic mosques. Nevertheless, W. D. Muhammad must seek to encourage African-American Muslims to unite and to trust immigrant Muslims, and the leadership of immigrant Muslims must encourage their followers to trust and work with African-American Muslims (speeches of W. D. Muhammad, *Al-Islam: Unity and Leadership*, 1991).

Imam Muhammad's Additional Goal

An additional goal of W. D. Muhammad has been to "reconcile the enormous contradictions in the life of the African-American people" by presenting Islam as the "legitimate, responsible alternative" to the dilemma facing contemporary African America.

To free the African American from a locked-in patterns of failure, Imam Muhammad is offering an Islamic "exodus" of the mind out of America's epidemic moral decadence. This "step back" is a strengthening thrust forward to rediscover the well-spring of higher aspirations, creativity and moral discipline. There is historic precedence for this effort in pre-15th century Africa, the years before the arrival of the ominous European longships. The Qur'anic restructuring of the African mind produced a resurgence of scientific and technological advancement not seen since ancient Egypt and Zimbabwe. (The same torch of enlightenment had simultaneously crossed the Mediterranean and lit the European renaissance.) (W. D. Muhammad, *An African-American Genesis*, xii-xiii).

Several of his books, especially *An African-American Genesis, Religion on the Line* (1983), and *Al-Islam: Unity and Leadership* (1991) contain his analysis and remedy for problems plaguing the general African-American community.

These leadership goals are attainable, though to various degrees. For instance, one major concern of Muslims has been the need for chaplains in the prisons and armed forces. Posten reported that since 1977 the Muslim World League has already been engaged in "carrying the message of Islam to our Afro-Americans brothers who are unfortunately in prisons" (1990:303). On December 3 ,1993 a milestone occurred when the first Muslim Military Imam was appointed. Imam Abdur-Rasheed Muhammad, currently a prison chaplain, was inducted into the United States Army at the Pentagon (*Muslim Journal*, December 3, 1993).

Threats to the Achievement of These Goals

In an article entitled, "How Will Muslims Survive in America?" (*The Minaret*, September/October, 1992), three major threats to Islam and its future progress are discussed. These were part of a discussion presented by the Foundation of American Islamic Teaching and Heritage (FAITH), a newly founded California organization in September, 1993. The threats are identified as: (1) the mainstream American culture as reinforced in the media; (2) the general lack of Islamic education in society; and (3) the disunity among Muslims. Each will be discussed briefly.

Secularity and Mainstream American Society

Muslims, immigrant and African American, abhor the liberal attitudes and practices that are rampant in an open and free society, and as a result propose Islam to be the solution. The permissive, secular and capitalistic characteristics of modern mainstream society is identified as the problem affecting African Americans who are in need of a religion that will provide guidance and direction. W. D. Muhammad has phrased this favorite message in a variety of ways: "Excellence and Freedom: Our Common Motivation" and "A New Mind. . . On Race Pride and Opportunity. . .A Growing View of Direction for African Americans" are examples. Of the first threat, he comments:

Capitalism, separation of values and attitudes in a so-called secular society binds most Americans. In capitalism, individual wealth is the only motivation and the only measure of success. This contradicts the spirit of Islam and its values of social responsibility. Separation of church and state is also in opposition to Islamic teachings (1992:32-33).

Lack of Islamic Education

The lack of Islamic education is viewed as another threat to Islamic goals. The articles from *Minaret* analyze the situation in this manner:

The amount of Islamic education that Muslim youth receive in their country is nothing compared to their secular education. Trying to compensate in Sunday school programs is not adequate and even the few Islamic schools that do exist are not enough because they do not help the Muslims entering high school and college now. This means that most of the Islamic knowledge that Muslim youth acquire is through their parents. . . .Though this is to be expected, the pressures of living in a non-Muslim society require more formal learning of Islam to survive. Parents often unknowingly teach children cultural beliefs that are assumed to be a part of Islam. This makes it difficult for Muslims of different cultural backgrounds to associate with each other. . . . When Islamic identity is taken as part of a cultural identity, the unity of all Muslims is undermined, especially in a country where many cultures must co-exist peacefully. Lack of Islamic education also includes a lack of positive examples because we also learn from role models. In American society, it is difficult to sustain an Islamic identity without formal Islamic education (1992:33).

Muslims are trying to address this concern by operating an increased number of Islamic schools offering quality education.

Disunity among Muslims

Concerning the disunity among Muslims, the article further states:

This is one of the most crucial problems because it relates to many other problems such as the negative image of Muslims in this country. If we can't even live with out own differing opinions, how can we correct negative stereotypes about Muslims in society at large? . . . Strict ethnic segregation divides us in our mosques and social groups. The mosques are also degraded by power struggles that divide different families and factions. . . . National and ideological differences further divide Muslims in America. . . . Another source of disunity is the lack of respect for Islamic scholars. Instead of working out differences with scholars, an increasing number of power groups in various mosques are simply expelling them as if it was just a business decision (1992:33).

As missiologist Darius L. Swann has recognized, one cannot help raise the question, "Has North American racial segregation penetrated the Islamic communities" (1994)? This is the most crucial problem facing Muslims as well as Christians, and there are no easy solutions.

The Muslim Use of Contextual Models and Approaches

Several missional approaches are taken by Muslims in an effort to contextualize their religious beliefs and practices. Key approaches will be described as they are evident in the Los Angeles context. Among these are the transcendental, counter-culture, and translational approaches in addition to several key contextual strategies.

The Transcendental Contextual Approach

The transcendental model focuses not on a particular religious content to be articulated, but on the subject who is articulating. "The hope is that if one is personally authentic in one's faith and in one's being-in-the world, one will be able to express one's faith in an authentically contextual manner" writes Bevin (1991). This transcendence is done while acknowledging that Islam calls for the Muslim theologian to be more protective of the received tradition of the language and worldview of the Qur'an. Therefore, by accepting this divine revelation of Qur'an, one is free to focus on the self as the theologizing subject.

The Notion of Divine Revelation

The value of this model is that it engages the theologian in a commitment to doing theology, recognizing the importance of both the individual as a prime locus for constructing a truly contextual theology and expressing God's revelation within human experience. This not only leads to new formulations of the faith, but demonstrates the importance of orthopraxis and God's revelation among the experiences of the people of God. From a Christian perspective, Robert Schreiter in *Constructing Local Theologies* (1985) identifies five criteria for deciding the genuineness of a particular local theological expression, and they are evident in the practices of Muslims as well as Christians. The criteria are: an inner consistency, a definite worship and liturgical practice, an orthopraxis, an openness to criticism, and the ability to challenge other theologies are evident when this particular model is utilized. This is significant for two primary reasons: the fact that Islamic theology is embodied in ritual, and the fact that theology is conceived in terms of expressing one's present experience in terms of submission and obedience.

A unique presupposition of the transcendental model is the premise that while every person is a result of both historical and cultural factors, the human mind operates in identical ways in all cultures and all periods of history.

As real as historical and cultural differences are, a historical or cultural subject's way of knowing transcends those particular differences. No matter where one knows or when one knows, one begins the process in experience, organizes this experience by means of concepts, judges the truth or falsity of one's conceptual understanding in judgment, and integrates the knowledge arrived at in judgment by means of a decision. What the transcendental model claims is that if one gives full rein to this transcendental, transcultural process as one tries to express one's faith, one will necessarily come to an expression of faith that is truly one's identity as a historical and cultural subject (Bevins 1992:100).

The Faith organization mentioned previously, has attributed the growth of Islam to dedicated workers with "intelligence and foresight to see that Islam can endure the test of time in America for all ages" (*The Minaret*, 1992).

The Muslim Use of the Counter-Cultural Approach

As mentioned earlier, Bevins introduced another model in 1993 that was built on the work of George Hunsberger presented in *Missiology* (October 1991). At the heart of this mission model is the belief that religion must challenge culture. The prevailing culture is taken seriously, and with suspicion, and thus shapes the way Islam is articulated as a set of doctrines. Similar to the anthropological model, the counter-cultural model is able to make use of the wisdom learned from intra- and inter-religious dialogue in order to help develop a theology that is relevant to felt needs for change.

The Issue of Identity

However, unlike the anthropological model which is centered around one particular cultural group, the Islamic communities in Los Angeles are not homogeneous units, rather they are very diverse culturally. Muslims must be constantly reminded that cultural beliefs which are assumed to be a part of Islam, but which are not, must be abandoned. "When Islamic identity is taken as a part of a cultural identity, the unity of all Muslims is undermined, especially in a country where many culture must co-exist peacefully" is a warning frequently given (*The Minaret*, 1992:33). This warning speaks against the anthropological models and affirms the goals and nature of the transcendental approach, for emphasis on the cultural identity instead of on the Muslim identity makes if difficult for Muslims of different backgrounds to associate with each other.

The Islamic identity, however, is extremely important and is sustained through Islamic identity (in the family, education and community) that is primarily stressed over against identification with mainstream America. An example of this is evident in the fact that the Muslims realize that the contextualization process is not static, but continual. The FAITH organization has identified three contemporary challenges that Muslims must address as "causing erosion of Islam in the United States" (1992:32). They are: (1) to identify values of American culture (capitalism, values and attitudes toward secular society, the separation of religion from daily life, and the motivation and means of measuring success by individual wealth) and to show how they contradict the spirit of Islam, which focuses on the values of social responsibility and no separation of religion and state; (2) to make a concerted effort to reach and hold Islamic youth who are attracted to the popular life-styles of their non-Muslim friends through Sunday activities in addition to normal Islamic activities; and (3) to address the concern of the general lack of Islamic education within the American society. The same issues are reiterated in the *Parents' Manual: A Guide for Muslim Parents Living in North America* (1976), prepared by the

Women's Committee of the Muslims Students' Association of the United States and Canada.

The Muslim Use of the Translation Contextual Model

Because of the unique nature of the Qur'an and Muslims' attitude of infallibility toward both the content of the Qur'an and Qur'anic tradition, the translational mission model is reversed. Rather, everyone must learn Arabic. Translation model would mean that the Qur'an was translated into vernacular languages. One weak point of Islam is that Muslims seldom do this. Local imams and other Muslim leaders stress the importance of learning the Arabic language as a Muslim. As a result, at least the *shahadah* and parts of the Qur'an are memorized. *The Muslim Journal*, the official Muslim national weekly, contains basic Arabic lessons in addition to the various tapes and computer disks available, in order that both the spirit and the letter of Islam are communicated.

Transcultural Communication

However, there is a major need to go beyond the Arabic vocabulary to the deep structures of meanings that is central to the dynamic equivalent translation approach. This is evident in the fact that though great effort is made to learn Arabic in order to read the Qur'an, the reality is that Muslim leaders and teachers must go beyond the traditional formal translation approach, and as Kraft describes, "endeavor to be faithful to the original . . . message, and to the intended impact that message was to have upon the original readers (1979:271). The attempt to understand the Islamic faith in terms of a particular context is, as Bevins notes, "really a theological imperative"(1992:1). Such a strong emphasis on the Qur'an, as the translation model takes toward the religious text, holds well with the theological and religious orientation of Muslims.

However, unlike the use of the translation approach, this model is used to insist on the divine message of the Qu'ran as an unchanging and unchangeable message. In addition, the fact that the Muslims who utilize the translational method do not necessarily have to hold a fundamentalist view toward Islam. What is essential is that they maintain a traditional view toward Islamic law and tradition which is key to their faith understanding. According to Donald S. Tingle, the Prophet Muhammad's call to religious and theological renewal and revival, and to the worship of God was so severe that it did not leave room for the affirmation of the Christian doctrine of the deity of Jesus Christ as Savior and the Trinity doctrine (1985:7).

Often Muslims will say that Islam is a simple religion to follow because it provides guidance for all (every aspect) of life, primarily due to the emphasis placed on the translational mission approach. The Qur'an teaches that the purpose of human beings is to submit to God and it provides for daily life (spiritual, social, economic, political, and moral). It reminds people of their duty while on earth to themselves, to their family members and relatives, to the community at large, to others outside the Muslim community, and of course, to God.

Muslim Contextual Strategies

The prevailing scholarship related to Islamic institutions and practices in the United States of America reveal a community in process--one engaged in construction and reconstruction. Upon reflection, a thematic approach indicates why the topic of Muslim contextualization deserves special attention. The convergence of three different interests is evident through specific and yet interrelated forces at work. The first is related to the interrelationship of the Islamic religion as Muslims from various linguistic, ethnic, and cultural groups converge within urban America. The second speaks of the emerging neighborhood social and economic institutions and organizations based on a Qur'anic model. The third factor is related to the conscious and intentional development of a Qur'anic model of Muslim community in the North American context. I will briefly comment on each.

The first speaks of the interrelationship of the various linguistic, ethnic, and cultural Muslim groups under the rubric of Islam. As intercommunal and relational issues increase, so too does appreciation for the need to work in collaboration. Various behaviors and modes of thought that served immigrant and naturalized

Muslims well in the countries of their origin are now challenged by pluralism in a democratic society. They are forced to expand and change in order to meet the present contextual challenges. African-American Muslims who are unencumbered with such deeply rooted traditions and customs are better able to play a decisive role in the shaping and formulating of the new Islamic identity that is emerging. Of particular interest is the change in the ethnic and cultural allegiances of the new Muslim populations as their self understanding develops. While their pattern reveals strong ethnic ties initially, there are also strong indicators of the willingness to work together for the common good of all Muslims.

As African-American Muslims take time to address issues of social change through various and often changing strategies, they are discovering the freedom to establish relevant religious institutions based on a Qur'anic interpretation in a western context. The Qur'an provides a system of economics based not on private ownership, but rather on economic exchanges conducted according to Allah's ownership and law. This system integrates and affects not only public and private life, but also economics and politics in an effort to appropriately address issues related to credit, loans, and interest rates. The notion of Islamic economics, while currently being debated in academia as a meaningful scholarly area of specialization, does represent an attractive alternative concept to prevailing dominant models of capitalism on the level of local communities. This is especially appealing among disenfranchised persons. Spurred by interest in the idea of Islamic capital investment, new economic enterprises are evident in various neighborhoods where some Muslims live and/or work. Such neighborhood social and economic organizations and institutions, owned and operated by African-American Muslims, represent a long-standing traditional felt need value of the African-American community; that of economic empowerment.

And this final issue underscores the fact that contextual strategies must exist in dialogical relationship with the sacred written word. Muslims in the United States do speak of the development of the Islamic community based on an assumption that the future of Islam is best served with mutual recognition and cooperation between and among all Muslim believers. Through collaboration across mosque/ masjid/center boundaries, Muslims seek to contribute to strategies and plans that support Islamic religious and spiritual beliefs. Based on the unitarian principle of the absolute oneness of Allah, and the belief that all existence is one without any bifurcation or compartmentalization of public and private life, Muslims are enabled to distinguish between forces that both encourage and discourage Islamic faithfulness.

A concern for secularization, modernity, and de-Islamic forces in American culture, promote the Islamic desire to create meaning within Muslim communities. This perspective does not negate individual conscious and personal moral norms, for they are important, but what it does accomplish is the establishment of a community consciousness in an Islamic understanding of orthopraxy. For instance, among African-American Muslim women, this raises new issues such as polygamy as a viable option within Islam, and the question of health examinations for women performed by male physicians. Among other Muslims, this is evident in the range of topics that must be addressed, such as divorce, management of property, democracy, the American legal system and the nature of Christian and Muslim dialogues.

Appendix D contains a taxonomy developed to indicate the various involvements that Muslims associated with the mosques of Los Angeles County engage in. This taxonomical analysis has attributed to an enlarged perspective of the contextual nature of how Muslims engage in witnessing to their faith (Spradley 1979:137). As for the componential analysis, each item listed in the left hand column was contrasted and located in one of these various dimensions of contrast: personal commitment, Islamic intrinsic value, a religious reality, a *daw'ah* focus, or a value to ensure the future. This has provided for a detailed investigation into one or more of the above central scenes, while at the same time making it possible to construct a more holistic view of contract dimensions, and thereby discovering the important emic themes previously discussed.

In studying the Sunni Muslims, three central observations become apparent. The first is the fact that the majority of African-American Muslims, who represent 42% of all Muslims in the United States, are persons who have consciously rejected what they have perceived to be biblical Christianity. As former Christians, or persons related to Christian homes, these persons believe that their experience of Christianity and the biblical interpretation of Christianity are one and the same. This is evident in the many Christian and/or biblical images and references made, and to the Catholic religious tradition that is often repudiated.

Second, in rejecting Christianity and its violent historic past of racism and discrimination, the African Americans who turn to Islam are embracing an idealized version of that faith (Gilliland, 1994). Research indicating the number of Muslims who have become disillusioned with Islam, and have rejected it on this ground is not available to date.

Third, in the African-American Muslim's search for an authentic relationship with God through religious expression, the presence of Muslim immigrants who have common goals with the African-American Muslim community, has assisted in creating an environment where a strong Muslim identity can be developed. This became obvious when interviewing an active African-American Muslim who was not very familiar with Imam W. D. Muhammad. Significant themes such as religious identity, communal unity, spirituality, and self-affirmation as understood and conceptualized by African-American Muslims must be recognized by Christians in order to encourage relevant communication with Muslims.

CHAPTER 6

PERCEPTIONS OF ISLAM IN THE PROTESTANT
AFRICAN-AMERICAN CHURCHES

It is not possible to discuss the perceptions of Islam in the Protestant African-American churches without first understanding the pluralistic influences that help give shape to those perceptions. North American pluralism according to historian Thomas Sowell in *Ethnic America: A History* is not an ideal for which North Americans started and aspired, but rather it is an accommodation to which they were eventually driven by the destructive toll of mutual intolerance in a country too large and diverse for effective dominance by any one segment of the population (1981:10). The interplay of a multiplicity of external factors such as various cultures, ethnic groups, worldviews, religions and languages within a pluralistic society have impacted the life experiences of Protestant African-American churches in such a way that the internal concerns and issues facing the church have caused the external challenges of pluralism to assume a secondary importance. In this chapter, the churches' self-understanding, as well as key internal factors affecting the life and ministry of the churches will be discussed. Then the accumulative results of the explanatory questions from the survey will be presented along with a discussion identifying internal factors which have served to divert the churches' attention from the challenge of Islam. The response of the questionnaire serves as a reliable indication of the respondents' awareness of the Islamic presence in the African-American community of Los Angeles County, as well as their attitude toward addressing the Islamic challenge.

The Churches' Self Understanding

The Protestant African-American churches, the majority which are located in the traditionally Black denominations, are responding slowly to the religious pluralism within the Africa-American community for a variety of factors. Though we live in a multi-cultural and multi-religious society that has demanded openness in areas such as social justice and human rights concerns, Christian attitudes toward Muslims and persons of other faiths have not, until recently, required an attitude of openness and understanding. Until recently, the number of African Americans converting to non-Christian religious communities by birth or in response to mission outreach was considered inconsequential, and no need for investigation was considered necessary. Christian attitudes and actions toward non-Christians remained ambiguous and ambivalent, with a lack of relevant Christian witness.

Mission Call

The worship, witness and service of these churches reflect an understanding of mission and ministry that has historically been three-fold in nature: first, to be obedient to God's calling by addressing, as a people of God, the common challenges that African-American people face in fulfilling their basic, physical, social and psychological needs as a result of faith in God. These African American churches today must continue to bring the gospel message to bear witness to all current realities. The importance of effective communication of the gospel in light of complex religious traditions, a growing fixation with violence, drug abuse and other coping mechanisms, sexual degradation of children and adults, and the secularization of society in general, must become a priority.

Build Bridges Cross-Culturally

Secondly, it has been important to the indigenous African-American denominations to build bridges cross-culturally with Africans on the continent both for evangelization and political purposes. Quaker Paul Cufe, Baptist Lott Carey, Methodist Amanda Smith, Episcopalian Alexander Crummell, and Presbyterians William and Lucy Sheppherd represent only a few of the early African-American missionaries who participated in cross-cultural missions to Africa at the turn of the twentieth century.

> There have been several meetings in the United States dealing with the question of the relationship between African Americans in the United States and people of African descent everywhere in the world. . . . It was December of 1895 that Professor John W. Bowen, who was on the faculty of Gammon (Theological Seminary), led in the discussion of the relationship between African Christians in the United States and those in the homeland of Africa. It was a very important conference; probably the first one in which a full expression of the missionary concerns of Black Americans was brought forth (Wilmore 1989: 273).

In addition, relationships with Africans, as well as with persons from the Caribbean, Jamaicans, Haitians, Cubans and others from the formerly British West Indies; Afro-Brazilians, Afro-Beliizians, and Afro-Nicaraguans and others from Latin American countries, and people of African descent in and throughout Europe were also important beyond religious concerns. Since the late nineteenth century, a growing concern for all persons of the African Diaspora has evidenced itself in the concept of Pan Africanism, in better relations between Africans and African Americans, and in the attitudes of African- American missionaries involved in cross-cultural missions. The latter was evidenced in the recent conference of ecumenical African-American missionaries held in 1992 at the Interdenominational Theological Center, Atlanta, GA.

Concern for an Holistic Gospel

Thirdly, is the African-American churches' ongoing need to bring the Christian gospel to address the larger issues of human inequality in general. The African-American churches therefore must continue to seek to proclaim a holistic gospel that does not bifurcate evangelism and theology, peace and justice, and truth and ministry, liberation and salvation to women and men wherever they are. Just as the ministry of Jesus Christ was to the whole person, so too is the church's ministry. This is especially true as people seek meaning and relevance in daily living.

Internal Concerns Facing the Churches

Factors of pluralism and the implications of living in a pluralistic society have impacted the internal life of the church in more ways than most churches are willing to admit. Pluralism has affected the life of the churches in the African-American community in four crucial areas: ecumenism, issues related to classism and economic, gender inclusivity. How the two critical external factors of (1) increasingly multi-cultural (transitional) neighborhoods and (2) growing awareness of religious pluralism affect the internal life of the churches' witness and education, and nurture are in the early stages of research and investigation. It is in understanding how the church has struggled in response to these issues that sheds light on why the churches have a low awareness of the external factor of Islamic growth.

The tendency to hold on to the image of the "traditional" Black church, which adequately served the needs of a rural people, is not adequate to meet the needs of the contemporary urban African Americans. Traditional church practices and means of theologizing need to be re-examined in order to meet the needs of people who live in and are impacted by a pluralistic world. While the message of the church does not change, the need to be aware of how much tradition has shaped our way of experiencing, perceiving, imaging and speaking is great. Often Christians fail to realize that it is very difficult for persons who live and move outside the church to understand and comprehend responsible Christian discipleship. The biblical assumption undergirding pluralism is that although we do come from different starting points, if we take the reality of Jesus Christ seriously, in word and in deed, we will end up with the same conclusion, that we all are in reality made in the image of God, fallen, and have available the opportunity to be re-created as sisters and brothers in Christ.

Pluralism and Ecumenism

The pluralism within the African-American ecumenical Christian communities and the ability to put aside doctrinal differences and church politics in order to engage in common community ministries present a great challenge, particularly among the fiercely proud independent African-American denominations. Though some ecumenical efforts are effective, the difficulties of working together across denominational lines is evident in the acknowledged state of crisis facing the African-American community (*Progressions* 1992:7). It is the result of an accumulation of an unhealthy matrix of social, spiritual, physical and psychological realities that threatens the very fabric of a strong self-identity and communal life. In reality, the crisis is one of the spiritual leadership working in partnership to address critical issues that face congregations located on almost every corner in some urban centers.

The solutions call forth a response to the questions of unity and ecumenism. Many of the problems facing the African-American community are too complex to be addressed by any single congregation or denomination: they require the partnership of all parts of the body of Christ working together. As partners within the body of Christ, are these churches willing to put aside their "personal and political agendas" to bring healing, hope and wholeness to the people in their midst?

Although Lawrence N. Jones, the former dean of Howard University School of Divinity, observes that "the transcendent reality that unites most African-American Christians and congregations is a concern for the quality of life, for justice and fairness, and for a humane existence for their members and communities" (*Progressions* 1992:21), there is no denying that ecumenism does not come easily. In recent years it has become easier as interdenominational activities increase and efforts are united to combat some of the social concerns of the community.

Classism, Economics and Pluralism

Not enough attention has been given by the African-American churches to the critical issues of classism in America. As the economic pie is cut into smaller pieces in order to serve the growing needs of more racial and ethnic groups, the dissatisfaction and anger of those who feel disinherited and disenfranchised became more obvious. It is a reality that economics (largely) determine our ethics and influence our theology, and that class is determined by economics. The implications of this greatly affect the witness of congregations within their immediate communities.

Economic Issues

Therefore, another concern of the African-American churches is economic development and economic justice issues. While it is a basic premise that one's social location affects one's perception of how reality is perceived (*sitz im leben*), without a strong spiritual system of beliefs, it is easy for a church's highest motivation to become economics. At the same time, economic needs of people must be acknowledged and addressed within the context of the realm and presence of God's reign and God's concern for the whole of personhood.

While some churches are doing remarkably well in providing models of Christian economic development, the majority are not. "The New Agenda of the Black Church: Economic Development for Black America" is the lead article in *Black Enterprise* (December, 1993) in which author Lloyd Gite describes how various congregations have begun to launch economic redevelopment projects for their communities. Church members of various denominations throughout the country are learning what they can accomplish within local communities when their monies are pooled together in order to provide much needed jobs, businesses, shopping centers and senior citizen housing. Rev. Floyd Flake, whose congregation used a $10.7 million HUD grant and built a 300-unit senior citizen housing project in New York in 1978 (and since has established numerous service institutions including a school and a multi-service center housing a prenatal and postnatal clinic, in addition to buying and rehabilitating more than 15 boarded up buildings) is quoted as saying, "If our churches ever learn the power that they have, we can turn the urban communities of American around and have control of them" (1993:57). In Los Angeles, the article focuses on one such recent project:

> Shortly after the 1992 riots in Los Angeles, the mammoth 9,500-member First African Methodist Episcopal (FAME) Church of Los Angeles swung into action,

as the church created the FAME Renaissance Program to fund community services, business and economic development programs through private and public funding sources. FAME Corp. is a non-profit organization established by the church. . . . So far, the program has approved about 34 loans totaling more than $500,000.

However, its not just the mega churches that are attempting to address the economic needs of the African-American communities. Smaller congregations have also discovered ways to help the community, and should be encouraged to do so.

Without such involvement. . . . Black communities across this country would face extinction. 'The risk of not doing it is greater than the risk of doing it,' declares Adams of Hartford Memorial. 'If we take the risk, we can provide employment opportunities, and our children can begin to acquire the skills that will take them up the ladder of economic independence' (1993: 59).

The Issue of Classism

From another perspective, Lincoln and Mamiya speak about the increasing bifurcation of the African-American community into two main class divisions: a "coping" sector of middle income working class and middle class African-American communities, and a "crisis sector of poor African-American communities made up of the working poor and the dependent poor." The class divisions, for most practical purposes, is growing, and due to the changing demographics of middle class African Americans, the inner cities have become the home of the poor who are both physically and socially isolated.

In past generations, some of the large urban Black churches were among the few institutions that could reach beyond class boundaries and provide a semblance of unity in the Black communities. The challenge for the future is whether Black clergy and their churches will attempt to transcend class boundaries and reach out to the poor, as these class lines continue to solidify with demographics changes in Black communities. Young Black men in poor urban communities represent the largest sector of the unchurched, and young Black women also are a rapidly growing portion. The question is 'What can be done to extend the ministry of Black churches to the urban poor?' (Mamiya 1992:3).

As one who has worked with African-American communities, Mamiya had made the following suggestions as to how churches can begin to take some steps in reaching the poor. First is the call for all African-American churches, regardless of size, to begin missions to the poor by sending in missionaries to hard-core poverty areas. According to him:

the importance of these outreach missions is that they are the first step in organizing the poor. Historical and social scientific studies have shown that religion is an important way of bringing discipline and order into peoples lives. . . . Young men who attended church had a higher change of getting out of poverty conditions. Why? Because of their disciplined use of time . . . because religion brings with it not only a worldview but a means of introducing order and discipline (Mamiya 1992:3).

The second step suggested is the need for more community organizers and community organizations in poverty areas to help train lay members and clergy in the task of community organization. "The goal of community organization is to empower the poor, to give a voice to the oppressed, to mobilize the collective power of poor people to confront and challenge the collective power of bureaucracies and entrenched interests" (1992:4), observes Mamiya. This, according to him, becomes a way of attracting young African Americans to the church. "What is important is to go where the young people are and hang out, try to win their trust and confidence, and then provide resources and directions for their lives" (1992:4), he states.

The third step consists of the African-American churches developing a prison ministry. More than 90% of all African-American churches have no prison or jail ministry, in spite of the fact that the United States has the highest prison population in the world and that estimates suggest that half of the prison population is African American. Did not Jesus say to visit those in prison?

And the last suggestion made by Mamiya addresses the need for the ministry of the churches to be concerned about the self-esteem and self-identity of all African- American children, regardless of class. He says,

Low self-esteem and low rates of racial self-identification among Black children strike at the core of the doctrinal position of the Black Church and pose a challenge to it. Throughout their history in this country, Black Christians have sought to affirm the worth of each human personality, that each person is a child of God, even in the midst of the worst and most dehumanizing conditions. It becomes extremely difficult to fulfill the central command of Christianity--to

love your neighbor as yourself--if you have difficulty loving and affirming
yourself (1993:5).

The suggestions that Mamiya offer are already observed in many instances
throughout Los Angeles, to some degree. The use of African American images and
perspectives in church curriculum and Sunday School materials is growing. The
need to establish ethnic schools in order that members can learn about Black history
and the Black biblical presence in Scripture is being recognized. I intentionally used
the model that Mamiya offers in this article not only because he is aware of the
competition that the Muslims are engaging in for the souls and allegiance of African-
American men and women and youth (especially those living in poverty), and their
history of successful prison ministry; but because his ideas and challenges have been
emphasized in the responses given in the local survey introduced in the first chapter,
and presented in chapter four. He concludes his article by observing:

> The future of the Black Church in the twenty-first century will depend as much
> on how it responds to the poor in its midst as the externals of racism, the
> abstractions of ecumenism, or the competitive threat of a resurgent Islam. Past
> tradition has cast the Black Church as the proverbial "rock in a weary land"--the
> first and the last refuge of those who call it home, and all those who live in the
> shadow of its promises (1993:6).

The African-American Elite

Lois Benjamin in *The Black Elite: Facing the Color Line in the Twilight of
the Twentieth Century* (1992) balances this study by focusing not on the underclass,
but rather on the elite and professional, the "Talented One Hundred." Benjamin
reminds us that religion is important also to the professional African American.
Many maintain ties with the traditional Black church, for the "Black church is the
place that provides a safe harbor and spiritual refueling to anchor Blacks in the midst
of racial storms" (152). For many who live and work in predominantly White
communities, it is important that their children "have kinship with the Black church
and the Black community, because of the whole ceremony of the Black church, its
hymns, and its spirituals" (152). The "Talented One Hundred" also indicated that the

majority who grew up in the predominantly African-American denominations, often drifted away from the church as young adults (perhaps experimented with other religious faith such as Islam, Eastern philosophies and African ideologies, in addition to traditional religions), and later returned to the African-American churches with a new understanding and appreciation for that church. Even if for professional or political or religious reason one unites with a White congregation, usually a dual affiliation is also held with the traditional Black churches.

Pluralism and Gender Inclusively

Fourth is the gender concern, and this has created a two-pronged challenge for African-American churches, internally and externally. Internally, African-American churches are reluctantly considering anew God's ministry to, for and with women of all ages. Unlike the majority of the mainline and some Pentecostal Anglo churches, the African-American churches tend traditionally to take a conservative approach to the gender issue, particularly as it related to the ordained ministry of the Word and Sacraments. The following observation makes this painfully clear:

> In the sanctuary of a Black Baptist church in Chicago in 1971 at a meeting of the National Committee of Black Churchmen, the following incident took place. Two Black women approached the pulpit at different times during the meeting: one was a theology student, so that she could place a recording device; and the other was a Presbyterian church executive, who wished to address the committee. The pastor approached each woman and asked her to remove herself from the pulpit area, explaining that the women church officers had passed a ruling that no woman could stand behind the pulpit for any reason. They wanted to insure that no woman would be elevated over another in the church, and they insisted that the image of the clergy should remain exclusively male. This incident is one illustration of the fact that traditionally in the Black Church, the pulpit has been viewed as 'men's space' and the pew as 'women's place' (Lincoln and Mamiya 1990:274, quoting Jacquelyn Grant).

The description above is indicative of the problems and challenges that women in the ordained ministry continue to face today by both men and women; not much has changed. Women called by God to leadership in the church, especially in the preaching and teaching ministries, pose a challenge (and in some cases a threat) to many of the predominately African-American male church leadership and ministerial organizations. Issues such as biblical support for the ordination of women, as well as the appropriate use of spiritual gifts that women bring to ministry are still being questioned by some African-American churches outside of the mainstream integrative denominations.

This reluctance to recognize and allow women to share as full partners in ministry remains, despite the fact that women (the elderly, widows, wives, single women and others) continue to constitute the overwhelming majority of church support and membership, and despite the proven positive record of pioneer female clergy. As Jacquelyn Grant argues, "the Black women's tri-dimensional reality proves a fertile context for articulating a theological perspective wholistic in scope and liberating in nature" (1989:224). The necessary attention given to addressing the crucial issues facing African-American men in contemporary society is urgently needed, but should be carried out within a larger concern for the dignity of all humanity.

Externally, these churches also tend to be insensitive to the larger societal issues concerning women. Outside of the churches the impact of economics, political and justice issues, quality health care, the feminization of poverty, and the reality of mothers heading single-parent families, can scarcely be overlooked in any realistic appraisal by those concerned about the mission of the church. Is the church, like the example of Jesus, ministering in such a way as to present the full gospel as good news to women, or will it, like the culturally accepted attitudes of Jesus's day, be used to simply maintain the status quo?

The Factor of Multi-Culturalism

A fifth concern is for the cultural pluralism that is evident in traditionally urban African-American communities such as the city of Los Angeles. Despite the fact of the popular media's attempt to shift the blame of the Los Angeles rebellion (1992) on Korean and African American "hatred," this ignores the historical fact that there have been very few inter-cultural clashes in the city of Los Angeles involving

African Americans. In fact, peaceful co-existence was evidenced early in California's history when fifteen of the original forty-four individuals who founded today's Los Angeles were African Americans; the others were Mexicans.

The plurality within the African-American neighborhoods in Los Angeles County finds the presence of several Caribbean nationalities, various Hispanic ethnic groups, Samoa Americans and various Asian cultures. Latinos and African Americans have a long history of peaceful co-existence which can be traced to the original contacts of the races, as evidence in the presence of the Garifuna (also known as the Garinagu) community in Los Angeles; these are the descendants of escaped Africans who intermarried with the Arawak Indians about 300 years ago (Pearstone 1990:132). Because of the strong anti-Japanese movement which brought many to Los Angeles prior to 1910, Japanese and African Americans learned to live together. The same is true of the Chinese, who with African Americans lived for many years in a section of Los Angeles which was originally known as "Calle de los Negroes," and eventually became Chinatown in the 1880s.

However, ever since 1965, when laws restricting immigration were liberalized, intentional cross-cultural ministry has become a relatively new concern for African-American congregations, who now find themselves, for the first time, minorities in the midst of rapidly changing multi-cultural neighborhoods. The desire to reach out to persons of other cultures with the immediate church community has resulted in some faithful African-American congregations attempting to learn a new language, offering educational classes in English as a second language, Alcoholic Anonymous classes in Spanish, providing free hot meals, making meeting space available for Ethiopians, Koreans, and others; and offering other social services for undocumented workers and other newly arriving immigrants.

Concerned African-American churches participate in community programs that foster understanding and unity. As one who has pastored in South Central Los Angeles, I have witnessed how Latinos, American Samoans and African Americans can work and fellowship together in areas of common interest. As Korean

Americans and African Americans learn to respect and communicate with one another, to understand their cultural and racial differences, and to appreciate their human commonalities--each will be enriched, and will perhaps discover that our cultural journeys have been similar. Each, however, must be willing to approach the other without racial prejudices and to learn to appreciate the communal strengths of each other. Not only because Asians have had to historically relate to religious pluralism in their native countries, and also within their immediate families, but also because the two ethnic groups (African Americans and Asians) have had some similar experiences within the USA, there is a possibility that one part of the universal Church can inform another in the task before us.

> My consciousness was shaped by the civil rights movement led by African-Americans, who taught me to reject the false choice between being treated as a perpetual foreigner and relinquishing my own identity for someone else's Anglo-American one. For me, African-Americans permanently redefined the meaning of 'American.' I came to understand how others had also been swept aside by the dominant culture: my schooling offered nothing about Chicanos or Latinos, and most of what I was taught about African-Americans was distorted to justify their oppression and vindicate the forces of that oppression. . . . Likewise, Korean-Americans have been and continue to be used for someone else's agenda and benefit. . . . In a sense, they [the Korean-American shopkeepers] may have finally come to know what my parents knew more than half a century ago: that the American Dream is only an empty promise . . . I only hope that we can turn our outrage into energy, because I still want to believe the promise is true (Elaine H. Kim, *Newsweek*, May 18, 1992).

Experiences such as the one suggested above would indicate the importance of the ministry of reconciliation emphasized throughout the New Testament--Christ's reconciliation of humans to God, and the Christian's engagement in reconciliation as the body of Christ. Reconciliation is needed in many areas of life, but especially within a pluralistic society. The church, as an incarnational sign of the reign of God in the ever-changing African-American community, can witness to the universality of the gospel of Jesus the Christ (though on a local scale), in much the same way as the *hajj* gives witness to the unity of Muslims across racial, cultural, worldview and ethnic boundaries.

The Characteristic of Religious Pluralism

As African-American churches seek to be faithful in their mission and ministries, perhaps the greatest challenge of all is presented in the form of religious pluralism. There are at least six generic religious movements observed in the African-American community (the first two which have previously been mentioned): (1) African Americans in the indigenous and historically traditional African-American Protestant denominations (2) African Americans in predominately White Protestant and Catholic traditions; (3) African Americans in Judaism and the ancient Christian traditions (such as the Ethiopian Orthodox Christians, Ethiopian Hebrews, the Black Israelites, and the Falashas); (4) African Americans in the Islamic communities (Hanifi, Sunni, Ahmmadiyas, and the Nation of Islam); and (5) African Americans who practice the "New World" religious traditions and synthesis such as Yoruba, Santeria and Vondun. While a few of these religious movements have strong nationalistic appeal, (6) others not mentioned such as Bahaias, Christian Scientist, and the New Age movement are clearly pluralistic and inclusive in their religious outlook. What they all have in common is their goal and desire to address the spiritual needs of African Americans.

In addition, racially and ethnically pluralistic religious traditions such as Ba'haism, Jehovah Witnesses, the Unification Church, Buddhism, the New Age movements, and cults such as the Peoples Temple, MOVE, and the Davidican cults (with their emphasis on diversity and harmony) are also attractive to some African Americans. The African-American community traditionally, in general practice, has accepted religious pluralism without question as an integral part of their communal life.

However, the motivation, resources and dedicated commitment by which some strategic missional activities are being carried out by persons of non-Christian religious faiths, and their success in converting Christians, has raised consciousness and is causing some church leaders to take notice and to begin to address this issue of religious pluralism with a relatively new interest and concern. In the preceding chapters, we have seen the challenges of both popular Islam (the Nation of Islam) and formal Islam (American Muslim Society). As Christians reflect theologically, we cannot ignore the presence of other religious traditions that function as some of the diverse ways that God speaks to us from the broader culture which lies beyond our own limited experience and the historically specific Euro-centric tradition of Christianity (Whitehead and Whitehead 1980:20). Religious pluralism, as Roger Greenway states in *Discipling the City* (1992), affects every aspect of urban life--politics, public education, the financial world, and the military. Africa-American Christians cannot afford to ignore this reality.

The five factors presented are greatly impacting and influencing the pluralist challenge facing African-American churches today: (1) race and ethnic differences, (2) ecumenical relations, (3) gender inclusively, (4) the issues of classism, and (5) religious pluralism. Until the churches can adequately address these internal factors, there will be few resources available to address the issues presented by the challenge of Islam.

Response to the Questionnaire

The challenge of pluralism, as presented in the responses to the questionnaire entitled "Religious Pluralism in the African-American Community," has identified significant key issues that African-American congregations must struggle to address if they are to witness faithfully within religious diversity. The majority of these issues have been addressed indirectly throughout the presentation of this study. There are, however, certain major areas of concern raised by four specific questions. Each question along with some representative responses from the questionnaire, are presented with comments.

The Church, a Barrier to African-American Progress?

Question 16: When a Muslim says that the Christian Church represents more of a barrier to African-American progress than Islam does, what do you think that Muslim (usually a former Christian) means?

Overwhelmingly, an examination of the responses attributed the remark to the history of the churches' identification with racism, and Euro-centric (or White) Christianity.

Muslims mean that Whites have used the Bible the same way they used the chain and whip--to keep the Black man in check, by putting guidelines in it, and having the world follow it, but they do whatever they need to get and gain power;

Because of the past history of Euro-centric Christianity, they fail to see themselves in Scripture;

Christianity taught Black people to be weak and submissive to those who tended to harm them;

Euro-centric slant and traditional internal exclusion of Africentric themes;

were frequent and representative responses. Others referred to the *deceit and oppression practiced by the early Christian church . . . and the spiritual attraction of Islam.*

Secondly, a smaller number of respondents, in answering this question, indicated the Islamic influences:

Islam is not segregated along racial lines as Christian groups in this country are;

Muslim religion teaches emphasis on self worth, personal dignity, courage, supporting and lifting up the African-American community; and

Muslims picture the Christian church as being divided among themselves, while they stress unity and togetherness.

And lastly, African-American churches were represented as contributing to the image of the church representing a barrier to African-American progress:

Because the Muslims observe the contradictions between the walk and talk of White Christians (and some African Americans, too, as a matter of fact);

Muslims believe that Christians only worship on Sundays and don't help the community.

Explaining "The Deceit and Oppression Practiced by the
Early American Church"

It is clear from this survey that one of the most important tasks facing the African-American church is the need to help both Christians and non-Christian African Americans to understand and communicate what one respondent referred to as the *deceit and oppression practiced by the early Christian church (racism)*, i.e., the church's identification with White racism. Until the church is able to explain how and why the church and racism interlocked, and identify this process as syncretism and **not** biblical Christianity, very little can be done to correct the damage inflicted on the self-dignity and self-image of people of color, especially people of African descent, in the name of Christianity.

In order to avoid the notion of syncretism, the church (or, for that matter Islam) must seek not only to guide selectively, reinterpretation and ramification, but must also respond to the deeply felt needs of the people sought to be reached; for if contextualization is to be done effectively, as Luzbetak, observes:

> It is not a question of either/or but both/and. All that we have thus far said about felt needs and about the importance of social analysis comes into play. An elitist or culturally irrelevant religion, rather than one deeply aware of the felt needs of the people, will merely encourage untheological forms of popular piety (Luzbetak 1990:373).

Awareness of the Islamic Challenges Needed

Question 11: According to the information presented in the pie chart, 42% of all orthodox Muslims in the U.S. are African Americans. As high as 90% of the new converts to Islam were African Americans. Prior to receiving this questionnaire, does the high percentage choosing to worship in orthodox Islam come as a surprise to you?

The largest percentage of respondents indicated that the growth of Islam, as suggested, did not surprise them. They contributed their previous awareness, or knowledge, to a variety of factors. Many had encounters with Muslims in other cities across the nation, and described them as both visible and vocal. The Muslims' sense of ethics, self-confidence and ritual prayer, as well as the fact of Islam's numerical strength in Africa were also identified. Only a small number of respondents admitted having actually studied or done research on the Muslim movements.

In quite a few instances, however, the respondents expressed definite surprise. One respondent observed: *The strong belief in the Gospel that brought us through from slavery . . . it's hard to believe we have strayed so far.* The fact that most of the converts were probably raised as Christians was raised and lamented by a few.

In response to the second part of question 11, "why or why not were you surprised at the growth of Islam among African Americans," two sets of responses were forthcoming. One set centered on Islam, and the other on Christianity. Concerning Islam, some representative comments were:

The Muslims emphasize areas lacking in the African-American community, such as responsibility, self-control, courage, strong manhood, etc.;

Given the economic, political, and spiritual oppression in some of the churches, what would you expect?;

Islam deals with solutions today and now, whereas Christianity deals with the after life; and,

African Americans, especially men, are seeking a religion they can relate to and that allows them to feel good about themselves in a positive and spiritual way.

In addition, the fact that Muslims carry themselves in a respectful way, are taught to be proud of their heritage, and are taught self defense against a corrupt and racist system, were also expressed.

The responses that reflected on Christianity were not as numerous, but at the same time were insightful.

Christianity does not and has not advocated equality of the races, nor does it promote entrepreneurship; and

Muslims are dissatisfied with those professing to be Christians.

Respondents indicate that a contextualization of Christian mission and ministry by the African-American churches in light of religious pluralism is needed, particularly in light of the growing presence and commitment of Muslims. However, this must be accomplished by an understanding of Muslim missionary methods and means.

Faith in the Church's "Ability" to Meet the Challenge

Question 18: What will it take to increase the church's "ability" to meet this challenge?

On this question of the church's ability to meet the challenge of Islam, the respondents were almost equal in their responses concerning confidence in the church's ability to meet the challenge posed by the Islamic movements. Only a slight margin (40 to 36) expressed confidence in the church's ability. Four main themes were expressed: the need for awareness of the challenge, relevant leadership, consideration of the resources of the church, and a two-pronged missional training approach.

Increasing the awareness of African-American churches and Christians was singled out as the best way of beginning ministry sensitive to religious pluralism.

Concerning the leadership of the churches, several respondents stated that church leaders need to lead in preparing the congregation to witness and evangelize in the African American community. *Church leaders need to stop guiding people with so-called fundamental religion which most often is another form of racism and White indoctrination* was one response offered. Instead, *give people a sense of pride about Christianity. Leaders must not only teach and preach essential Christianity, but practice it also.* Respondents feel that leadership must educate people by setting priorities in the church, showing them the "how," and seeing them through. Youth, however, expressed another desire: that the church would communicate with youth better: *Show them that Christianity is better, not just have someone tell them.*

Resources available to assist the churches in this effort included prayer, the Holy Spirit, a trainable membership, some believers who are both "bold and strong," teaching members how to "get serious" about their faith, and building relationships specifically with non-churched families in the community.

A two-pronged missional training approach was identified. One emphasis is focused on deepening the understanding of the biblical faith, what it means and how one goes about living a life dedicated to Christ. Also suggestions were made to the need to know how to practice Christianity in the home, community, workplace and school. This set of responses indicated what Dr. William Pannell has stated, and points to a profound insight that African-American church leaders need to wrestle with: the difference between the "Black Religious Experience" over against the "Distinctly Conversion Experience" (a lecture in the course, "Evangelism in the African-American Church, Winter, 1993). What the difference is and how the difference impacts one's daily living is importance for the sake of the individual Christian, as well as for the ministry of effective evangelism. The second emphasis reported was the need of the church to develop a genuine interest and study and concern for non-Christians; and, to learn how to communicate effectively with them without "attacking" them.

Faith in the Church's "Willingness" to Meet the Challenge

Question 18: What will it take to increase the church's "willingness" to meet this challenge?

The largest percentage of respondents indicated a deep concern over the church's "willingness" to meet the challenge of Islam. Twenty-two churches reported a favorable attitude, while 38 said either "not so good" or "poor." Twenty respondents honestly checked "I don't know." Obviously, there is more confidence in the church's ability to meet the challenge posed by Islam than there is in the church's willingness to address the challenge. Indications are that the desire for unity and community is stronger than the desire to see another divisive factor (now religion) imposed upon/within the African-American community.

While one respondent suggested that it will take a tragedy or some politically powerful Muslim group gaining political control in the United States before the church becomes willing to address Islam, the largest percentage of respondents said in numerous ways what one expressed clearly; that is, the greatest need is *to move the major emphasis of most churches from racism (and church politics), and to focus on the other qualities of Christianity such as justice, self-help, building community, and courage for living, rather than just on forgiveness and love.* In a number of instances it was indicated that true commitment to the African-American community, as well as greater awareness of the subtleness of the Islamic impact on our community, family, and church could help to increase the church's willingness.

The training of missionaries for local work (just as we have missionaries overseas), as well as church members; the acceptance of female ministers; holding pastors accountable for helping Christians to more clearly understand the challenges; and the desire to *stop talking, and start living the faith fully in our daily living* were among the most representative responses.

Christian and Muslim Contextualization Approaches

As it has been clearly demonstrated, the concept of contextualization is central to the inculturation and globalization of not only Christianity, but other religious faiths. Besides Christianity, there are several other religions that seek significantly to proselytize and make converts among the African-American community. These would include the Jehovah Witnesses (clearly indicated on the survey), Buddhism, Yoruba religion, the Ethiopian Jewish religion and Islam. However, the two prominent forms of Islamic influences, popular and official, that have been considered here, in terms of various mission approaches, strategies and motivations, can be categorized by their dominate features of ethnocentrism, accommodation, or contextualization. As indicated previously, these terms-- contextualization (emphasis on context) and inculturation (focus on culture)--have been used freely by Christians. However, without the Christian theology and doctrine poured into them, they can be generically conceived and utilized by any missional religious communion. Therefore, in order to understand the dynamics and potential of Islamic missionary activities, and in an effort to formulate an appropriate Christian response, the generic concepts of mission models and approaches must be considered. One has only to visit the Masjid Bilal located in central Los Angeles to observe the commitment of both African Americans, Middle Easterners and others to establish a strong center for learning and propagating Islam and its beliefs.

Christian Considerations of Contextualization

Since 1972, there has been tremendous discussions on the concept of contextualization, its motivation and its approaches. Louis Luzbetak (1991) has identified three different types of contextualization which could assist in the development of a theoretical framework: a translational type, a dialectical type, and a liberation type. Christians need to be aware of what approaches are used by both Muslims and Christians in their attempts to contextualize. The dynamic equivalence approach, based on Bible translation theory developed by linguists and anthropologists (Nida, Taber and Reyburn earlier, and currently Kraft, Shaw and Luzbetak) is helpful in understanding how God-talk is communicated from the written word and speaks to a particular context. Its value lies in its concern for the essential messages of the text to be translated in meaning and impact in ways that identify as closely as possible equivalent to the meaning and impact that was held by the original hearers (Kraft, 1979).

The translational model, along with the triple dialectic approach, is valuable for the same reason. This is an approach initiated by theologian Karl Barth who has influenced current missiologists such as Robert Schreiter, Dean Gilliland, and David Tracy to develop mission models that consider the relationship of both the Gospel and the Church tradition, and the values, needs and traditions of the local culture. Luzbetak writes:

> The dialectic to which we refer is the tension and constant, deeply respectful back-and-forth challenge and exchange that should be going on between the three poles directly involved in contextualization. The three poles are the Gospel, the universal traditions of the Church, and the local culture. It is especially through such challenges and invitation to counter challenges from these three perspectives that genuine unity in diversity can be achieved and true contextualization realized (Luzbetak referring to Schreiter, 1991:81).

Building upon the dialectical method of Karl Barth, new models of mission have begun to emerge. Schreiter's, the triple dialectic approach; David Tracy (1979) with the concept of "revisionist model," which offers both a criteria and method for doing theology; and Dean Gilliland's (1989) identification of contextual theology as incarnational mission model (with a focus on the evangelistic, nurturing and witness/service dimensions), all speak to the attempt to formulate a relevant response.

Similar to the ethnocentric theoretical models of Christianity which tended to characterize missions in the nineteenth and early twentieth centuries (Luzbetak 1991: 64-66), the adaptation model has as its goal to fit the historical systematic theology (Western) and Christian traditions (Euro-centric) into particular cultural situations. This approach assumes that the epistemology, axiology, and ontology of a particular people or historical theological understanding has relevance for all peoples and all times. Many African-American congregations found in primarily European-American denominations (i.e., Presbyterian, Reformed Church of America, Episcopalian, and others) can be described as emerging from adaptational models.

The synthetic model is another commonly utilized. It is based on four elements (the gospel, Christian tradition, culture, and social change) that interact in such a way as to involve persons in the process of theologizing. Social change and how it affects mission (positively as well as negatively) and the challenges it poses, is an area that requires further study. Cultures, peoples and mission opportunities are not static, and thus require a dialectical process that moves toward truth. The problem, however, is to ensure that it is carried out with a clearly biblical theology.

The semiotic model is best presented by Robert Schreiter in *Constructing Local Theologies* (1985). The methodology involved in this model has to do with discerning the symbols or signs of the culture, and utilizing these as significant indicators as to how to contextualize theology. Unlike most models, the semiotic model takes into consideration the presence of previous theologies that have already influenced the lives of people. When we consider the Nation of Islam, for example, the focus is usually on periphial Islamic influences. However, there is a failure to recognize the biblical influence inherent within the Nation of Islam's socio-theology. A keener recognition of this could assist the churches in better understanding of some of the issues of change taking place in that movement. As a model fit for the Western trained society there may be some value for further consideration if local persons are central to "simply, clarify and give ownership of the Bible and the whole gospel to the community of faith in a given place" (Gilliland 1989:317).

The Traditional African-American Christian Model

The praxis model is based on the assumptions of mission as contextualization and that people can only realize the truth of God (revelation) when they participate actively in theologizing. According to David Bosch, the late head of the Missiology department at the University of South Africa:

> The rediscovery of the contextual nature of all theology has had particular importance for what has become known as 'liberation theology' in all its forms. At least since the time of Constantine, theology was conducted 'from above' as an elitist enterprise (except in the case of minority Christian communities, traditionally referred to as 'sects'); its main source (apart from Scripture and tradition) was philosophy, and its main interlocutor was the educated nonbeliever. Contextual theology, on the other hand, is theology 'from below': its main source (apart from Scripture and tradition) is the social sciences, and its main interlocutors are the poor and the culturally marginalized (1991:61).

Bosch accredits J. J. Segundo with the discovery that not only is all theology contextual but that this is the only way in which theology can become meaningful by stating, "Segundo expressed the new 'epistemological break' as taking the form of a 'hermeneutical circle' in which praxis has the primary and reflection becomes a second (not a secondary) act of theology."

The validity of the praxis model, particularly as it relates to African Americans, is both the recognition that culture shapes the way Christianity is articulated, and the validity of the human as the place of divine revelation and a source for theologizing that is equal to scripture and tradition (Bevins 1992:48). Mary Motte (speaking of "The Poor: Starting Point for Mission"), C. Rene Padilla (referring to the "integrity of mission"), and Michael Amaladoss (reflecting on evangelization as liberation) in *Mission in the Nineteen Ninety's* (1990) provide provocative reflections on the praxis model.

Vincent J. Donovan in *Christianity Rediscovered* (1982) is an example of how the African context missiological issues are encountered utilizing this approach to missions. James H. Cone and other African-American theologians uphold the praxis models primarily because of what they identify as the oppressive nature of older approaches of traditional theology which ignores the African-American experience, and makes the African-American churches invisible and inarticulate. In addition, traditional Christian theology has, as Cone identifies, failed to speak of hope and truth to the marginalized because it continues to be dominated by the powerful (1986, 1989, 1993).

Muslim Contextualization and Mission Approaches

African-American Christians need to be helped to recognize and understand the nature and the extent of Muslim missionary and outreach activities within African-American communities. These activities express a religious and spiritual reality that is causing people to view Islam, for the first time in such large numbers, as a viable alternative to Christianity. One key hypothesis is that knowledge of God as the basis for interpreting human nature and the act of God as the basis for a praxis of interpretation is evident in the life of Muslims. Discovering the points of commonality and inclusiveness of both Christianity and Islam have been most helpful. Islam and Christianity represent, according to Woodberry, Speight, Denny and Cragg, the common belief that there is only one God, almighty and merciful, who is the creator and sustainer of all of life. It is my assumption that the theological commonality between the two faiths are one of parallel witness rather than opposing witnesses.

It is assumed, therefore, that belief in God leads to the basic assumption that when human beings learn of God's power, mercy (or grace), they must respond in a three-fold way, described by Speight as: a life of commitment to the divine will and authority; a life of gratitude for the gifts of God, and a life of responsible action in worship, charity and acts of righteousness (1989:126-134). It follows from this that in response to God's actions, the human's response to the understanding of God will be significant and will result in God's final judgment. This judgment is viewed by both Christians and Muslims as God's just response to the choices humans make concerning the will of God. Contextualization concerns itself with how that life of commitment is translated and takes shape in a particular situation, shaped by the social and religious environment. The various mission approaches, strategies and motivations can be categorized by their dominate features of ethnocentrism and accommodation (i.e., the Nation of Islam) and accommodation and contextualization (American Muslim Society).

Though Cragg, Posten, and Denny all describe Islamic missionary activities and various mission approaches, admittedly, Hesselgrave and Rommen confirm that Islamic contextualizers are confronted with a unique set of problems based on the belief in the unique understanding of the Qu'ran's special revelation and infallible authority.

> Consistency here demands that the book be delivered, interpreted, preached, taught, and memorized--but not translated. The traditional position of Islam is that the Koran translated into another language is not really the Koran. In a sense, all inquirers into the faith must themselves become contextualizers. They must learn the Arabic language and culture. As Islam has come to rely less on power and more on persuasion to propagate the faith, practicality has demanded translations (1989:136).

The rise of Islam also reflects changing theological, political and social conditions within the African-American community. Islam is viewed as a religious option deemed viable both personally and communally by a growing segment of the African-American community. How Muslims continue to organize and become institutionalized with this society in order to solve personal and social problems from a religious and/or spiritual perspective is significant as this is a movement which represents a new thrust of adaptation and contextualization within the United States context.

An Illustration

The Foundation of American Islamic Teaching and Heritage (FAITH), a California-based organization which holds a series of public debates on the future of Islam and Muslims in the United States in the next century, provides an excellent source for examining Islamic contextualization and its motivation. Although the term itself is not referred to, the spirit and characterization of contextualization is surely operable in an article entitled "How Will Muslims Survive in America?" (*The Minaret*, 1992).

> It is also here [North America] that great Islamic thinkers, scholars and members of the enlightened elite have come forth to share their knowledge of inspiration with us all. We don't have to look to any other country for guidance and support because our support is right here. All of these people and their work will not disappear just like that, but rather it will survive because of one important point. To keep Islam alive, there must have been a struggle and we must have certainly met that challenge. Islam is alive in America because practicing Islam is what has been missing in the past (1992:32).

This important article provides an important foundation from which to identify and examine some of the key missional approaches and contextualization models at work within contemporary Islam among African Americans.

The Nation of Islam and its model of mission cannot be overlooked because of what it represents--a powerful and influential folk Islam, that has frequently become the step ladder leading to the American Muslim Society. The various mission models and approaches evidenced in these two Muslim movements will inform the development of an authentic and relevant model of Christianity contextualized for the mission of evangelization and re-evangelization of African Americans in the midst of the contemporary challenge of the Islamic faith.

CHAPTER 7

SUMMARY AND CONCLUSIONS

The missiological implications call to attention the fact that while the worldview perspectives and personal experiences and concerns, within the North American context are basically the same, African-American Muslims and African-American Christians differ with regard to the theological framework from which they view life. The goal of this project is to provide a means and a model by which a criteria for the development of an authentic and relevant model of Christianity can be identified and implemented for the mission of evangelization and re-evangelization within the religiously plural African-American community.

This study has been concerned with the Protestant African-American churches' inability to discern where their current position is within the contemporary religious milieu, and to engage in mission appropriately. The research used anthropological, historical, and missiological tools and techniques. Each research tool has its own limitations and strengths, but by utilizing various approaches, the credibility of the research results has been enhanced. As a historical study, the aim of the investigation was to give concrete descriptions of the key persons, events and movements which have influenced the growth and expansion of an Islamic presence within the United States from 1619 through 1994. It is through this background that the missiological concepts of worldview and contextualization principles were applied to the particular domain of the American Muslim Society, orthodox Islam, as practiced within a specific locale. This provides an opportunity to reflect on the definitive beliefs and practices that are meaningful to Muslims. Based on this knowledge, both a criteria for mission and a model for mission are presented.

The Islamic Appeal: Four-Fold

The study reveals that the search for an authentic relationship with God through religious expression, coupled with a violent historic past of racism and discrimination and an influx of Muslim immigrants who have found community and common goals with the African-American Muslim community, is the most crucial factor explaining why African Americans are attracted to Islam today. Factors both external and internal to the church are contributing to the rise in the number of former Christians and non-Christians who are seeking spiritual solutions in Islam.

Four primary interrelated factors concerning the Islamic appeal as perceived through Muslim religious beliefs and practices are: truth, reasoning, the perception of the Islamic community as united, and the cultural appeal for historical knowledge. In order to create an effective ministry, these four must be comprehended by Christians as they seek to witness to Muslims and potential Muslims within the African-American community.

Religious Truth

The first factor is that the African-American Muslims have found that the American Muslim Society has conformed to their concept of religion. Islam represents an authentic relationship with God, based on the assumption that the truth is literally communicated in the Qur'an. If the spiritual journey of Malcolm X, who was successively a Christian, a member of the Nation of Islam and a convert to Sunni Islam, is an indication of the common spiritual journey taken by many, we would have to acknowledge the possibility of the emergence of at least a third generation of Muslim believers who might embrace and advocate the Qur'an and Islamic teachings. The religiously educated are able to maintain the conviction that they have found truth in the Qur'an. Because the family unit is from the Islamic theological perspective, the basic unit of the faith community, the Muslim that encounters the Christian is well articulated about his or her faith as "truth." The new convert's contribution to the growth of Islam is the result of both an intentional acceptance of a totally new way of religious thinking and doing, and of the holistic worldview of Islam, which does not make distinctions between the religious and non-religious aspects of life. Therefore, the need for churches is to assist Christians in understanding how religions and religious truth are evaluated in the daily market place.

In addition, this has become a complex and often confusing environment in which the word "truth" is either associated with every religious system, or to complicate matters further, there is a growing concern that there is simply no "truth" at all.

> But the fact of the matter is, in the world today, that is not where the conflict lies. The conflict does not lie in competing versions of truth. The conflict lies in whether there is any truth over which to compete. The loneliness, despair, depression and hopelessness that are epidemic to the modern world are not caused by an inability to choose which religion to follow. Many are coming to suspect that they can more accurately be traced to the notion that there is no truth at all. The first step to undoing the excesses of scientism and totalitarianisms of all kinds is to reestablish that medicine is available--the place you can purchase it is called the spiritual dimension of humanity, and the medicine itself goes by the generic name of hope (Muck 1991:10).

Any attempt to comprehend the dynamics involved in creating an appropriate Christian apologetic and ethnotheological response requires both a theological and anthropological understanding on behalf of Christians. In the case of African-American Muslims, the content of religious knowledge and the undergirding and prevailing worldview and philosophical assumptions must be understood as well. These things being so, the final chapter of this study will consider an approach that may work with Muslims or potential Muslim converts, based on the Christian concept of truth.

Reasoning

More and more theologians, African-American Christians as well as Muslims, are recognizing that contextualization is an imperative, not an option. Larry Posten presents the case from the Islamic perspective in his dissertation on the subject of the Muslims' struggle to contextualize (1990:312-318). If Posten's study on Muslim *daw'ah* had included African-American Muslims, the greater extent to which Muslims are appealing to the theme of reasoning in adapting to the message of Islam in their cultural environment would have been recognized. More is being done in the area of Muslim contextualization than Posten would lead one to believe. Just as the universal church of Christ must contextualize the biblical gospel in order for it to be heard in each local situation, so must Muslims contextualize their concern about propagating their faith. While every Christian communion in its own locale and each generation must struggle with the processes and means related to this concern, the same missiological concerns must be addressed by Islamic leadership.

By appeal to reasoning, Muslims consider their community as intrinsically superior to Christianity. To make such a claim assumes that people have in themselves the moral power needed to live in submission to God. According to Islam, the history of Christianity itself is an obvious demonstration that it lacks moral power. The violent historic past of racism and discrimination, which has been undergirded by the use of Christian theological beliefs and practices, is consistently mistaken for biblical Christianity. Approaches to biblical Christianity that require reasoning and intelligent thinking are the ones which will have effect in meeting the modern Islamic critique of Christianity.

Concerns of Epistemology, Ontology and Axiology

Africentricity has played a major role by contributing to the phenomenology of knowledge, both in terms of content and structure. A corrective toward addressing the dilemma of African Americans who have rejected Christianity and embraced Islam on the basis of "true brotherhood," can be found in discovering the importance of these three interrelated areas of study--epistemology, ontology and axiology-- which speak of ultimate knowledge, purpose and value. While the issue of the relationship of Christianity and culture is instrumental in shaping the worldview of African Americans, it is one which is rarely discussed among the dominant Christian American culture. However, the Civil Rights era seems to have ushered in a grass root effort among African Americans to gain knowledge and understanding of the assumptions and presuppositions framing Eurocentric and Afrocentric understandings of life and the world. This has been done primarily through careful scrutinization of black religious studies in three areas: regarding the nature and grounds of knowledge (epistemology), the nature of being and the kinds of human existence (ontology), and the study of values and value judgment (axiology).

Examples of the life and words of early African-American Christians such as Frederick Douglass, who "wrote a candid letter to his fellow communicants of the Zion chapel, saying that he had to 'cut loose from the church' because he had found the American church, writ large, to be a 'bulwark of American slavery' . . . was now committed to a new faith [anti-slavery], one for which he would speak the word" (McFeely 1991:85), must be understood and addressed. Carter G. Woodson acknowledged the necessity of two kinds of education for African Americans: self education, in addition to modern education. The epistemological, ontological and axiological assumptions of life, raised in the face of religion, were never far from their interpretations of life.

> The so-called modern education, with all its defects, however, does others so much more good than it does the Negro, because it has been worked out in conformity to the needs of those who have enslaved and oppressed weaker peoples. For example, the philosophy and ethics resulting from our educational system have justified slavery, peonage, segregation, and lynching. The oppressor has the right to exploit, to handicap, and to kill the oppressed. Negroes daily educated in the tenets of such a religion of the strong have accepted the status of the weak as divinely ordained, and during the last three generations of their nominal freedom they have done practically nothing to change it. . . . The same educational process which inspires and stimulates the oppressor with the thought that he is everything and has accomplished everything worthwhile, depresses and crushes at the same time the spark of genius in the Negro by making him feel that his race does not amount to much and never will measure up to the standards of other peoples (Woodson 1933:xiii).

Because these crucial concerns are as important today as they were five decades ago, and because of the need to address them within the context of biblical theology, this discussion is critical. The concepts of ethnic cohesion (Tippet 1987:287) and the multicultural model (White and Parham 1990:5) are important as they provide a more realistic foundation upon which to build a theological framework. The cultural factors which influenced the unique development of Americanized Christianity, and led to the growth of religious pluralism within the African-American context, reflect a historic and systematic examination of the experiences and struggles of African Americans which cannot be denied as Christians today seek to develop their theological mission in the midst of this environment.

The gospel must be presented anew--as believable, reasonable and relevant. Several Afrocentric scholars and pastors have began to study the African heritage of the Bible, and the receptivity has been encouraging. Valuable for content as well as methodologies proposed are: *Must God Remain Greek? Afro Cultures and God-Talk* (Robert Hood); *Troubling Biblical Waters: Race, Class and Hope* (Cain Hope Felder); *Martin and Malcolm and America: A Dream or A Nightmare* (James H. Cone); *Just A Sister Away: A Womanist Vision of Women's Relationships in the Bible* (Renita J. Weems); *The Coming Race Wars? A Cry For Reconciliation* (William Pannell); and, *Biblical Strategies for a Community in Crisis* (Colleen Birchett). These are a few of the exciting Christ-centered studies of theological reflection which make use of the method of Afrocentricity in order to contextualize the Christian message. They provide hope and point toward new and dynamic ways of presenting the truths of God Word's and God's will.

The Islamic Community Perceived As One

While the Muslims of southern California (or nationwide, for that matter) present themselves as a unity, the Christian community, because of its many denominations and divisions cannot. Therefore, a third appeal is the perception of the Islamic community as a united religious body with a common belief and practice. The growing presence of international Muslim immigrants who have found community and common goals with the African-American Muslims, has helped to aid the cause of African-American Muslims greatly. Support and encouragement that exist on several levels (local, national and international), and the resources available for furthering the Islamic cause in the United States are great. However, the perceived model of unity, as witnessed in the *hajj*, made possible across racial and ethnic lines in the name of religion is attractive to many.

The Cultural Appeal for Historical and Social Identity

The fourth factor of appeal is related to the issue of Identity. Knowledge concerning the presence and contributions of Africans, and Islam, throughout the history of civilization that usually accompanies the Islamic presentation is alluring. The Bible, like the Qur'an, is understandable as people realize the importance of issues of identity, both historical and social. And yet, while the aim of Scripture is relationship, at this particular juncture in history, the quest for knowledge has a tendency to overpower the quest for relationship. Therefore, the quest for identity, which often accompanies Qur'anic presentation is appealing to many.

Racism, Culture and Social Identity

While the correlation between the factors of religion and ethnicity have often been neglected or underrepresented in sound academia, the current proliferation of global ethnic and/or racial wars is bound to change this. Ethnic cleansing in Bosnia-Herz, apartheid in South Africa, and Neo-Nazism in Germany and the current rise of Anti-Semitism in the United States are our most obvious examples from the contemporary setting. It cannot be assumed that theology remains neutral to such principalities and powers. The factors of ethnicity and racial identity cannot be ignored in any setting where authentic theologizing is taking place. Because of the peculiar nature (a bifurcation of life that separated the spiritual from the physical) of the dominant Christianity that was proclaimed in theological beliefs and practices to enslave and later domesticate Africans and African Americans in the 15th through the mid-nineteenth centuries, there were various religious and theological responses. As exemplified in the following quotation, the factors of race and religion continued to govern negatively the worldview of many Christians in the North American context. The attitude of G. T. Gillispie, a reformed theologian of the Presbyterian denomination, stated in 1954, is still persistent and is evident in the beliefs and practices of some persons identified as Christian leaders today within the dominant culture.

> ... the Bible contains no clear mandate for or against segregation as between the White and negro races . . . it does furnish considerable data from which valid inferences may be drawn in support of the general principles of segregation, an important feature of the Divine purpose and Providence throughout the ages (Virgil Cruz and Jean Cooley 1992:9).

The rise in the Christian Identity movement which consists of "churches" and sects that hold doctrines of racial purity and anti-Semitism, and advocate violent overthrow of the government, all in the name of Jesus Christ (Muldrow 1990:1); and other racial hate groups going under the banner of Christianity, including the White Aryan Resistance movements; and in the thwarted attempt to committed violence aimed at the First African Methodist Church in Los Angeles and its worshippers, are recent examples. Christian voices such as those of William Pannell (1993) and C. Rene Padilla (1985) must be heeded.

> The idea is that people 'like' to be with those of their own race and class and that we must therefore plan segregated churches, which will undoubtedly grow faster. We are told that race prejudice 'can be understood and should be made an aid to Christianization.' No amount of exegetical maneuvering can ever bring this approach in line with the explicit teaching of the New Testament regarding the unity of men in the body of Christ [The author proceeds to quote Col. 3:11 and Gal. 3:28. . . . By what authority can it preach man's reconciliation with God through the death of Christ while at the same time denying man's reconciliation with man through the same death, when both are equally important aspects of the gospel (Eph. 21:14-18)? As Dr. Samuel Moffett put it at the Berlin Congress, 'When racial discrimination enters the churches, it is something more than a crime against humanity; it is an act of defiance against God himself' (Padilla 1985:31).

One significant result of the dysfunctional relationship between ethnicity and Christian theology in the United States has been the conversion of African Americans (Christians and non-Christians) to Sunni Islam which is proclaimed by Muslims and perceived by others to be a religion of "quality of races before God."

Racism, a reality of racial diversity, is an answer to a system that routinely discriminates against so-called minority peoples. The church's participatory role in this reality has resulted in what Mark Heim (1985), and Lesslie Newbigin (1989) refer to as the "bad conscience of Western humanity."

> We are painfully aware that the confident proclamation of final truths in the past has included the claim of racial superiority and the right of Western Whites to rule others 'for their own good.' And among these conventional truths which seemed so obvious to earlier generations was also the conviction that Christianity was the one true faith. Racism, economic exploitation, and sexual discrimination all flourished to some extent in the shadow of these convictions (Helms 1985:18).

The Problem of Evil and Sin

Another area where the African-American worldview differs from that of the European American's (and therefore needs contextual considerations) is evident in the whole issue of enormous sin and evil. In fact, in *Reason and Religious Belief: An Introduction to the Philosophy of Religion* (1991), the authors identify the problem of evil as the greatest case against God's existence. The social location (where evil and suffering is evident physically, social or psychologically) of the so-called liberation theologians and churches within a particular setting, thus have within their worldview a frame of reference for theologizing which outsiders find foreign and unacceptable. Stating that there are numerous examples of thoughtful people who have rejected religious belief because of the world's evil, the example of theologian Eugene Borowitz is cited, who in the face of the Holocaust concluded that "God is dead." The author remarks:

> Whether encountered in the indescribable horror of the Holocaust, unrelenting hunger in underdeveloped countries, violent crime in large cities, political corruption, or the desperate suffering of terminal cancer patients, the presence of evil in our world cannot be ignored. Evil in one form or another touches all of us. Some think that theists have no intellectual right to believe in God unless they can somehow square that belief with the existence of evil (1991:93).

This is certainly the case concerning the European slave trade and Christianity. However, though this is the experience of some, I would suggest that it is not the "denial of God" that is the result of unexplained suffering and evil within the African-American community, but the "turning away from God" to other gods that is the temptation. As Cain H. Felder has stated, there is an astonishing diversity of religious beliefs and practices found within the history of people of African descent throughout the Diaspora around the world (1989:155). This temptation is implied in both the Old Testament and the New (e.g., Psalm 138:1, Acts 21:38, 1 John 4, Rev. 13), and conforms to the missiological principle that states that during the times of transition, turbulence or evil, people seek spiritual solutions. In part, this is what caused the prophet Jeremiah to cry out: Is there no medicine in Gilead (Jeremiah 8:22)? Missionary minded religious people of every conceivable religious group are aware of the spiritual void persons today are experiencing, and the religious searching that occurs.

The Nature of the Challenge

The Islamic community, as is the African-American community, is in transition, both influenced by national and international factors. This transition provides many opportunities as well as challenges for the Church. Writing about the concept of worldviews, Brian J. Walsh and J. Richard Middleton (1984), define worldview, not as a system of thought, such as theology or philosophies, but rather as a perceptual framework, a "vision of life" (20), and a "vision for life" (32). According to them, world views have spiritually formative and cultural power in the lives of their carriers--they provide a model of the world, guide and direct life, determine values; and rest on faith commitment. Therefore, it is crucial that the challenges of pluralism be met relevantly and authentically by concerned Christians.

Walsh and Middleton make an important observation that helps to elucidate why some Christians are converting to Islam: "One day we come to realize that our worldview is not the worldview of the Scriptures; we see that it is not consistent with our confession that Jesus is Lord. Then we need either to deny our confession and look elsewhere, or to begin to overhaul our basic way of looking at life and living it" (39). Many of the African-American Muslims today represent those who saw the inconsistencies related to a so-called Christian world view, and rather than to begin to engage in a whole process of re-learning, they chose simply to reject Christianity and look to Islam. However, the verdict is still out, and time will tell how successful these persons, Muslim converts, have been in making the worldview adjustments required to be a Muslim according to the Qur'an.

However, it would be a mistake to assume that because Muslims reject Christianity, they have rejected Jesus Christ. Although the Qur'an mentioned Jesus, many Muslims have never been exposed to the biblical Jesus who by his own words proclaimed:

> The Spirit of the Lord is upon me, because he has chosen me to bring good news to the poor. He has sent me to proclaim liberty to the captives and recovery of sight to the blind, to set free the oppressed and announce that the time has come when the Lord will save his people (Luke 4:18-19).

Having now made these observations, what follows are missiological implications for faithful and effective mission and witness within the African-American religiously diverse communities. The nature of the challenge before us is multifaceted. It must be concerned with renewal in the church, effective Christian communication, training for Christian witness, a holistic concern for persons, and an incarnational ministry.

Revival of the Church

Herein lies the primary missiological challenge: the willingness to become renewed through revival. Is the Christian church in the North American context willing to allow God to transform her understanding of herself in order to discover her calling and mission amidst religious pluralism, and more specifically in the face of Islam? Is the Church, like the apostle Peter, willing to be converted in order that the Good News may go forth? How many Christians and churches, precisely because the Christian worldview is rooted in faith in Jesus Christ, are able and willing to grow to the point of critiquing their "Christian" worldview in such as way as to see that it is not consistent with our confession that Jesus is Lord? From the Native

American, African-American, most Latino Americans and many Asian American perspectives, the 300-plus years of encounter with Americanized Christianity (which has supported culturally destructive systems and influences), does not give realistic, practical evidence of a worldview that has been shaped by the Scriptures under the guidance of the Holy Spirit. How much longer can Americanized Christianity (as opposed to biblical Christianity) flourish in this present society? Revival is needed throughout the churches in America. Perhaps due to the pulls and inter-connectedness of other domains of life (political, economic, and others), the moral and spiritual core of Christianity is not as evident as it should be. However, the challenges of pluralism call forth Christians who are willing to allow God to impact their worldview, and bring biblical Christian understandings and values to bear on all the various domains of life. The command given to humanity to rule over the earth (and not people), the worship of God, and the clashes of the powers and principalities (good and evil), are helpful biblical themes for challenging and transforming the worldview of the Christian.

The churches, in addition, must equip Christians to be prepared not only to share their faith, but also to tell and show why Christianity is important. The model is Jesus Christ, in his teachings and ministry, and in his attitude as he related to persons of other faiths. Those who are most effective will be those who go in love and righteousness, and learn to see life through the eyes of the Muslim and respect Islam, and who are able to talk about things that are of importance to Muslims, while at the same time bearing witness to Christianity, a universal religion. Kenneth Cragg has suggested that we should begin as Christians to study the Bible as though a Muslim was looking over our shoulder. We must be willing to study the Qur'an in the way the Muslims study it in order that the Holy Spirit, using the text of another religious body, can lead us to Christian understandings. Also, the Christian should seek to develop a spirit of cooperation with Muslims rather than antagonism, especially in areas where Christ calls us to be in ministry.

The Multicultural Worldview Theory

It is unfortunate but true that the mission models used by the colonial European Christians all too commonly consisted of conquering a population and then securing the conquest by baptism as a sign of submission (Luzbetak 1991:93-94). Less than a hundred years ago, Christian accommodational missional approaches were characterized by paternalism and racism. Methods of extending the church by suppressing ethnic and cultural factors, and by means of mission societies with ethnocentric dominant features predominated among Christian approaches to not only persons of African descent throughout the world, but to most non-Europeans. As a result, these types of activities done in the name of Christianity have produced a particular response among both Christian and non-Christian African Americans which is evidenced in any worldview analysis. This has paved the groundwork for at least a hearing of the Islamic perspective among African Americans.

For instance, in terms of the African-American worldview theme which emphasizes the importance of community, it would appear that certainly in the area of religious beliefs, the Muslim perspective is more compatible to that of the African Americans (emphasis on the group), than it is to that of the European Americans which is dominated by a strong sense of individualism. Consider Shelia Larson:

> . . . who actually named her religion (she calls it her 'faith') after herself. This suggests the logical possibility of over 220 million American religions, one for each of us. Shelia Larson is a young nurse who has received a good deal of therapy and who descries her faith as 'Sheilaism' (Bellah 1985: 221).

This emphasis on individualism and individual salvation and morality does not agree with the community centered value found in the African-American worldview in which the individual within the context of community is considered most important.

The worldview of the Muslim needs to also be seen as equally intelligent as that of the Christian because when viewed from a broader, inclusive perspective it does represent another adequate view of reality. Insights gained from this study which focuses on Muslims' perspectives on the religious beliefs system should create within the African-American Christian community a desire to renew and revive Christian commitment to the universal mission to which God has called these uniquely endowed African-American churches. The missiological response should enable and empower these churches to respond with biblical faithfulness in both belief (an appropriate apologetic) and in practice (appropriate contextualized models).

Effective Communication

The Church needs to evaluate the ways and means in which she communicates the gospel message. As Christians, we believe that the good news of Christianity is supracultural. Theologians speak of a "gospel core" which is "Christ incarnate." A basic metaphor that reveals this thinking is that of the kernel and the husk: the kernel of the gospel is surrounded in a disposable, non-essential cultural husk (Bevins 1992:182). One of the implications of this research is that Christians must seek to communicate the kernel and not the husk, and to do so in such a manner as to challenge Muslims to see Jesus Christ in a new and different light as Savior. This metaphor is more appropriate to the African-American experience at this time. For example, to place as much emphasis on Jesus as the spiritual child of God, and less on the physical, is a beginning. This is not to imply that Jesus was not truly human and divine; however, in a materialistic and physically expressive society such as exists in the United States, it is important to emphasize the spiritual nature of the human being. Also, there is a need within a religiously plural context to return to the biblical concept of God as Spirit.

Because of the unique world view perspectives of African Americans, it is important that Muslims have an opportunity to hear the gospel "anew" and with clarity, from a non-Eurocentric, non-Anglo perspective, which does not represent colonialism, imperialism or racism. For me, the implications of involving both African and Arabic speaking Christians in this ministry are exciting. It calls forth for the participation of Christians from other parts of the world who are willing to share and live out their faith within the setting of the African-American community. This also speaks to the need to consider engaging all the church in effective communication, and not simply the preacher.

Training for Christian Witness

Church leaders and persons involved directly in witness and ministry among religious pluralism need to be trained in understanding Islam, and other religious faith active in the community. Because Islam and its influences are relatively unknown by most, Christians need to know who the indigenous Muslims are, what they believe, and why they are. A corrected historical knowledge of African peoples in the expansion of both Christianity and Islam would provide a perspective which could serve more adequately as a launching pad for mission.

African-American Muslims are often aware of this broader history and utilize it (often mixed with half-truths) as a missiological strategy. Yet the average Christian, Euro-American or African American, is usually ignorant of these matters and does not know how to respond. Unfortunately, Christians today still tend to dismiss the universal appeal of Islam and do little to help the church to interact with this and other religions. As a result, we fail to grasp how Islamic influences have been contextualized in the African-American community. Bill Musk's *The Unseen Face of Islam: Sharing the Gospel with Ordinary Muslims* is a helpful book for training purposes because it presents with clarity, the religious function, forms and meanings of both official and popular forms of Islam (1992).

The Pentecostal Response

Based on the responses obtained from the questionnaire and the theological beliefs of the Pentecostals, it becomes apparent that those who are most able to maintain a balanced perspective on evangelism and social responsibility and are most likely to respond to Muslims, are persons who are committed to the Gospel of God in Jesus Christ. Dr. Lawrence N. Jones, the former dean of the Howard University School of Divinity, recently made the following observation.

The past quarter-century has witnessed revolutionary social change, teaching us that today's realities may be tomorrow's curiosities. These changes have altered the world in which African-American Protestant churches exist. Their position of authority has been challenged and, to some degree, diminished by the Muslim community and other non-Protestant organizations of believers (1992:21).

By considering the leadership of the Muslim communities in America, we have begun to perceive, as Jones astutely observed, how the position of authority of the African-American Protestant churches has been diminished by the bold, clearly articulate Muslim leadership. It appears that Pentecostal lay and ordained leaders have the ability and the willingness, in addition to a clear sense of motivation, to present a bold and clear articulation of the gospel in words; whether they are willing to do so in deeds as well (on a large scale basis) is yet to been seen. How the important life themes of spirituality, community, personal and religious identity, and self affirmation are presented in Christian witness as viable religious issues relate to the current religious pluralism still remains a challenging task to the majority of both Pentecostal and Protestant churches.

It is important to recall some of the characteristics related to the role and nature of Muslim leadership in the United States. These key characteristics of Muslim leaders, historically and present, include the facts that:

1. Muslim leaders are not chosen or approved by the dominant culture. This is at odds with mainstream African-American Christian leadership, as exemplified in the person of Dr. Martin Luther King, Jr. who primarily sought the friendship of White Christians.

2. Recognition that the crucial problem for African Americans today is the issue of identity. For the Nation of Islam, from its inception the identity issue was equated to "race." However, for the Muslims of the American Muslim Society, identity is equated with religion as a unifying factor.

3. The failure of African Americans to fully realize the new opportunities for personal development are capitalized upon in the Islamic presentation.

4. Recognition that the long, deep struggle of African Americans has been to retrieve their full humanity. Muslims reject the idea of individual effort, for an allegiance through an affirming communal theology and ideology.

5. A strong belief that Islam is suitable for Africans and those of African descent (and Christianity is for those of European descent) is evident. This concept has been espoused and supported in Christian missions, particularly during the Victorian era.

6. Spiritual roots of Christianity are found in the presentation of Islam.

7. The Muslim leader is aware of his important role as a cultural interpreter.

The historical development and struggles of the African-American Pentecostal churches appear to make them the best prepared candidates for holding awareness and attitudes conducive to addressing the Islamic challenge. According to *Progressions*:

> The field research underscored the growth and dynamism of Pentecostalism, which emphasizes speaking in tongues, faith healings, prophesying and other gifts of the Holy Spirit. The Church of God, once dismissed as a lower-class sect, has emerged as a substantial mainstream organization.
>
> Equally important is the expansion of the Neo-Pentecostal movement within the old-line denominations, especially the African Methodist Episcopal Church. *The Black Church* speculates that half of Black churchgoers might be part of these movements in the next century (1992:7).

Though in a different context, Roswith Gerloff has also documented the vitality of the Black Pentecostal churches as a dynamic worshipping, equipping and missionary agency in Britain (1992).

Pentecostalism among African Americans appears to be the most willing to provide a needed remedy: churches willing to identify and engage in mission motivated by biblical mandate and relevant to the issues affecting poverty and justice within the religiously plural urban area. The biblical motivation and desire as evident in this present call for faithful is evident.

All of our theological reflection concerning mission and evangelism needs to be informed on one hand by the Scriptures and the Holy Spirit, and on the other hand by Christian experience in witness among Muslims, and by the questions which Muslims address to the church. The Bible needs to inform the manner in which we express mission in Muslim context. . . .These twin realities (theological reflection and experience) informed our vision and plan for being faithful and fruitful witnesses among Muslims (Woodberry 1989:13).

Authentic approaches to Muslim witness, mission and evangelism require that the leadership of African-American churches are called to a new task that requires a new understanding of the key elements of mission, urbanization, poverty and justice, and leadership training. While the other elements will be included in the recommendations chapter, the more urgent need here is to discuss the need for a new leadership paradigm for Christian leaders in the face of religious pluralism. A new contour or framework of a new paradigm of mission must emerge in response to the contemporary challenge of Islam aimed at building Christian spirituality.

A New Leadership Paradigm for the Church

Developing a biblical theological response to the contemporary challenge of Islam related to the criteria above, requires that African-American churches make inquiry into a new paradigm of mission that has as its core the emphasis on three major elements: mission as contextualization, mission as common witness, and mission as eschatology, "as action in hope" (Bosch 1991:60). This requires that African-American church leaders on the various levels of the church, local as well as national, commit themselves to a dynamic process of theological reflection (being as well as doing) as they seek to listen and respond to God in the face of religious pluralism.

In the *Journal of the Religious Education Association and the Association of Professors and Researchers in Religious Education* (Spring 1992:282), Steve Fortosis has presented a helpful taxonomy indicating the development and growth toward which leaders engaged in Muslim witness and mission should strive to achieve (see figure 4). This is not to suggest that there is a stage of "perfection" that Christians reach. Rather, it points to stage three, as a level of competency that is always changing, evolving, and in process.

Stage One: Formative Integration
(Evolving Characteristics)

Fluid convictions
Theological Dogmatism
Juxtaposed motives/attitudes
Feeling-orientation
Conditional love
Black/White morals
Less biblical knowledge/discernment
Egocentric reasoning

Stage Two: Responsible Consistency
(Evolving Characteristics)

Solid convictions
Less theological dogmatism
Purer motives/attitudes
Faith/orientation
Less conditional love
Black/White/gray morals
Greater biblical knowledge/discernment
Others--centered reasoning

Stage Three: Self-Transcendent Wholeness

Deep consistent intimacy with God
Secure theology fosters flexibility
No duplicity between public and private self
Unwavering faith even in unexplainable tragedy
Compassionate/redemptive with others failings/weaknesses
Universalized moral framework; confronter of public/private injustices
Thorough biblical knowledge/wisdom
Self-transcendence for the sake of others

Figure 4

Stages of Christian Formation
Fortosis (1991)

An understanding of Christian leadership in this manner will make it possible to reflect on and understand the three faulty, but common assumptions about conversion identified by Harvie Conn in 1978 at the North American Conference on Muslim Evangelism: our understanding of conversion as a one-step decision; as an individual decision; and as purely spiritual. The overall goal of the leader is to be challenged and to challenge others to give credence to a life of Christian growth, rather than to a single set of doctrinal "propositional truths."

The missiological implications of this research call to attention the fact that while the worldview perspectives, personal experiences and concerns of African Americans as a community emerge from a common historic social experience within the North American context, the quest for religious and spiritual answers is basically the same. African-American Muslims and African-American Christians differ with regards to the sociological and theological frameworks espoused by their leadership. Christians moved only by the love of God, and love for humanity, are desperately needed to engage in mission to African-American Muslims and potential Muslims.

These are the agents of mission who can make a real difference. It is Kenneth Cragg who said that our passion as Christians should be to make Christ known not only because he is knowable, but because knowledge of Christ is life. This is really the "truth" that Muslims are seeking. Therefore, we must be concerned not only with what Christ is to us, but how Christ seems to them, the Muslims. African-American Muslims who have participated in this research have shown me that Christians must take seriously this calling and the full implications of this mission in its historical, traditional and social context. For the nature of the challenge is spiritual.

Conclusion

In conclusion, the great need of the African-American Protestant churches is for committed Christian leaders (clergy and laity) to guide congregations in becoming mission centers, living out an incarnational model of ministry. Such a church is able with authenticity and relevance to present, in word and deed, the liberating, compassionate, healing, prophetic and saving power of God meeting humans needs. Too often, Christian congregations located in the African-American communities do not identify with or relate to the felt needs of the people in that particular community. The greater amount of stewardship--time, talent, money and energy--is spent at the sustenance level. Even among the seven traditional main African-American denominations, too often issues related to church polity and denominational agendas, as well as unresolved issues related to classism and womanist issues, prevent the church from being as sensitive as it could be to the pains, hurts and confusion of the many outside the doors of the church. In the face of such a multifaceted challenge as presented to the churches by the growth of Islam, within the African-American community, there is a temptation to simply withdraw and ignore the challenge. However, a change in priorities as indicated in this research, based on historical and existential knowledge of Islamic development and goals, in addition to the desire to engage in relevant mission within the current religious pluralism, could result in a renewed and revived church.

As a missiologist, it is also my opinion that the ability to properly address the challenge that Islam poses to the Church is a task far too great for the African-American churches to face alone. It calls for the assisted insights and experiences of the "holy catholic Church." African-American churches need to be encouraged by and in dialogue with the universal Church concerning its experiences with Islam. African-American Christians also need to be in dialogue with the American Muslim Society as well as with the NOI. From a global perspective, African-American Christians need to know that the competition for Africa is not only fierce but often brutally violent between Christianity and Islam as they compete for the religious commitment of the Africans. Protestant African-American Christians need to hear the voices of African Christians who are encouraging African Christians that they

> should not allow the possibility of conflict with Islam or other religions to determine their agenda for mission theology and practice. Rather they must seize the reality of religious competition as a challenge for them to articulate ways of bold and humble proclamation of the gospel of Jesus Christ.

Tite Tienou goes on to say how this must be done.

> Denigration, conquest and triumphalism have too frequently been ingredients of Christian missionizing in Africa. . . .One need not denigrate the followers of other religions in order to magnify Christ and his gospel. . . .Consequently, the way forward is to produce a theology of Christian mission which convincingly demonstrates that the gospel can be proclaimed boldly and without compromise, denigration or conquest. This is one of the most urgent themes for reflection by African mission theologians in the years to come (1993:242).

The study of Christian and Muslim encounters, positive and negative, in other historical periods as well as geographical locations may also prove insightful.

From another perspective of doing theology in Africa, there is significant and timely warning that can be applied to the African-American experience, related to the issues of cultural identity. In *My Faith As an African* (1990), Jean-Marc Ela writes:

> Instead of talking complacently about inculturation, which in the end, never stops singing the praises of 'negritude' and authenticity, we should prepare ourselves to confront the basic questions of the Africa evolving today. . . .Any appraisal of the problems of faith organized narrowly around the recovery of the past will never allow us to stand beside Africans as they ask their questions of today (1990:171).

Currently great emphasis is placed on Africentricity and discovering the historical African identity of the African American, and this is necessary in order to understand how God has revealed Godself throughout the history of African Americans. However, the reality may be that the younger African-American generation may have less of a longing for connectedness with the past and more of a need for resources to deal with today and tomorrow (Effa 1989:37). With the guidance of the Holy Spirit, African-American churches must move in the direction of hope in the future through authentic and relevant contextualized missions.

Missiological Implications

Leadership evidenced in the African-American community in the form of imam and residential scholars of the mosques, Islamic educators in both Islamic parochial schools and advocates in public schools, and the presence of business persons active throughout the community are symbolic of the various missional leadership models used to communicate deeply held Islamic beliefs and practices. As a result, four factors must be addressed by the missional church.

Islam Perceived As a Viable Religious Option

The first factor is that the African-American Muslims as found in the American Muslim Society (Sunni orthodox) represent an authentic relationship with God through religious expression. The typical Christian, however, may or may not be able to articulate the faith in the face of Islam, and usually becomes defensive with little understanding of Islam.

Because of the growing presence of Islam as a world religion actively involved in *da'wah* (missionary) activities within the United States and in the African-American community in particular, the worldview of the Muslim needs to also be seen as equally intelligent because when viewed from a broader, inclusive perspective it does represent another adequate view of reality. North American Muslims, both immigrant and indigenous communities are in transition, and they too are struggling to make sense out of their faith in light of modernity. Kenneth Cragg reminds us of the theological void felt by them as he reflects on Shabbir Akhtar's "A Faith for All Seasons" (1990) in this rather lengthy but significant quotation:

> I think that for many contemporary minds, Muslim and others, the 'riddle' and the 'silence' go much deeper into sharper measures of disquiet and perplexity. This is partly so by the evidence of Islam itself, the unloveliness of fanaticism, the dishonesty of obscurantism, the political cynicism, and the violation of human rights. Is there no Shirk or 'denigration of God,' we must ask, in the violence done by our perversity to the design and intention of God? Is our human scene well diagnosed as 'getting along reasonably well despite a few disappointments'? Or are we not required to take our theology into a more radical perception of what it must take for God to be God in light of a radical honesty about the way humans are humans? . . . While adamant in his resistance to Christian sentimentality, as he sees it, Shabbir Akhtar is also frank in his recognition of 'the shallowness of Muslim responses to the challenge of modernity.' He acknowledges the need for urgent self-criticism and cites Surah 2.286: 'Lord, do not burden us beyond what we have strength to bear,' applying the words to 'the silence of God being increasingly oppressive . . . on the heart of every believer' (1993:162).

Lamin Sanneh suggests the same phenomena in the context of Africa (1976, 1984). Consideration of the fact that evangelical theology is heavily influenced by a Western individualistic worldview, and Islamic theology is heavily group oriented, for the African American who is also group-oriented, and places value on community orientation, family and authority (similar to the African worldview), the paradigm shift is not as great for African Americans, and yet as a viable religious faith option, there are theological voids. Insights gained from this study should allow Christians to focus on Muslim leadership, discern the voids, and seek to address the challenge of Islam which God has called and uniquely endowed African-American churches.

Islam: A Response to Christian Syncretism

The creative, dynamic process of contextual theologizing and dependency on the Holy Spirit that gave rise to a Christian theological understanding among African Americans, that sustained people throughout the period of enslavement, that gave birth to African-American denominations and churches in the late 18th and early 19th centuries; and that exemplified itself in the indigenous worship and outreach within the community must be reclaimed and proclaimed. The Muslim appeal continues to reflect the negative results of the encounter of African Americans with the historic traditional Eurocentric American Christianity. Muslims seem unaware of James Cone's *Black Theology* and, William Jones's *Is God a White Racist?*, and Albert Cleage's founding of the Shrine of the Black Madonna, and to the growing number of Africentric churches.

The Failure of the African-American Churches

Thirdly, the African-American churches must also claim their responsibility in failing to communicate and to pass on to present generations, in relevant and authentic ways, foundational Christian beliefs and values. While Christians are aware that the future of the African-American churches are at stake, few of them are actually venturing outside of the doors of the churches to be in ministry in the community. Instead, the majority of the missional activities are regulated within the church building, which in many instances, is not perceived as a place of welcome and friendship by those within the community.

Muslims continue to identify not only with the African-American community, but "within" it. This has contributed to their continued effectiveness and attractiveness, particularly among a people who tend to be disenfranchised and are in need of human dignity, support and empowerment. Unlike some churches which relocate or sell their church buildings when the neighborhood changes, the mosque remains and seeks to further address the social, religious, and political needs of the community. While the local mosque has served as the center of worship, systematic observation has shown that the mosque is also the center for many outreach activities and ministries by Muslims. A myriad of community concerns have been addressed by them as well as by the larger African-American community. These include community services such as voter registration, college preparation classes, African-American and Islamic study programs, prison services, and drug abuse and gang counseling and intervention.

Muslims are, as indicated in the taxonomy presented earlier, involved in a variety of kinds of activities throughout the African-American community. One of the more popular forms of outreach, in addition to drop-in centers, is in the form of a cafe or restaurant. Throughout the nation, including Los Angeles County, are many such cafes, bakeries, and restaurants which cater to Islamic dietary requirements, but also help to create a sense of community within community. I have often frequented the Muslim mosque and the cafe located in Altadena, and have discovered it to be a place of community, and a place where issues and concerns of the community and for the community, especially self-help economic and politics, are communicated.

Common Goals: African-American and Immigrant Muslims

Fourthly, the growing alliance of international Muslims (immigrants) and the African-American Muslims (indigenous to the North American context) has helped to aid the cause of establishing firmly an Islamic community in North America. The Dar al-Islam community, located in New Mexico, as well as Islamic centers across the country, serve as examples in which the Islamic values of kinship, acceptance, leadership and unity are the apparently perceived goals. Consider the first North American Muslim "Pow Wow" was held June, 1993 in Dar al-Islam. Under the Qur'anic banner of "We have made you tribes and nations so that you might know one another," the goal of this grass root organization was to bring together Muslims of all backgrounds from all over the United States and Canada.

> There was a sense that there is a certain urgency to beginning work on the next phase of Islamic work in America. The last decade was the mosque building phase, and the focus was on local communities and physical structures. We have now entered an *ummah* (community) building phase, and the focus is on relationships and linking those communities and the individuals within communities. We must begin to build bridges, find common ground and connect the various elements of the community (*The Minaret*, July/August, 1993:38).

The active participation of Muslims in the second Parliament of World Religions (August, September 1993) held in commemoration the first Parliament of World Religions held in 1893, as well as the event of the 30th annual convention of the Islamic Society of North America ("Muslims for a Better America"), are indications of a willingness and desire of some Muslims to work with other religious and moral people.

Together these contemporary factors comprise the most crucial features related to why African Americans are attracted to Islam today. It is crucial that the Protestant African-American churches begin to address a task so enormous by obtaining a clear understanding of the contemporary Islamic leadership, particularly its motivations and goals. Motivated by a desire to be in dialogue with Muslims, it is a necessary element of faithful contemporary Christian witness required within a religious plurality that will hopefully thrust the church forward:

> . . . to creative new attitudes and practices of mission that enable Christians to work as if all depended on us and, yet trust God's grace for those we cannot reach, confessing that God will deal justly and mercifully with them in ways beyond our ability to perceive (Covell 1991:170).

The Context of Proclamation

As it is stated with clarity, the Protestant African-American churches must give greater concern to the presentation of the Gospel. James Cone writes:

> Because of Malcolm's unrestrained critique of Christianity and uncritical devotion to Elijah Muhammad's Nation of Islam, White Christians ignored him and Black Christians paid too little attention to his critique of their faith. By their turning a deaf ear to Malcolm, the public meaning of Christianity remained almost exclusively identified with the cultural values of White Americans and Europeans. More than anyone else in American or White people's moral and religious values. . . .
> I do not think that anyone can be a real Christian in America today, or perhaps anywhere else, without incorporating Malcolm's race critique into his or her practice of thinking about the religion of Jesus. . . . Black Christians prefer to refer to Martin King when talking about themselves or about their ecumenical relations with Whites. King is less offensive to their Christian sensibilities (1993:296).

As Muslims and potential Muslim converts learn about Islam, it is often compared and contrasted to Christianity: a high form of Islam placed against a low form of Christianity. The Christianity that is most often referred to is one that most Protestants would not recognize. Priest, holy water, and spookiness were words used to describe Christianity. The explanation of the failure of Christianity is often given within the framework of Christians having been led astray by those who did not understand Jesus Christ, namely his disciples. What Jesus said was later tampered with. That is why, according to the Muslims, we do not have the Bible in its original languages today. The belief that Allah is not a human is enumerated many times, along with the fact that you do not associate anything or person with Allah. The Muslim God, unlike the God of Christianity, does not need to rest.

The Nation of Islam leaders, on the other hand, will use the study of Egyptian hieroglyphics to show how Christians reinterpreted the Egyptian belief in the "SUN" to give it their own meaning, i.e., the "SON." Jesus is revered, but it is obvious that Christians are concerned misinformed heretics. Their basic argument is that Christians have spent 2000 years trying to analyze God, rather than to live a godly life. Rather than simply submitting to and obeying God, Christianity has sought to know and understand the mind of God, which they cannot.

The Church needs to evaluate these perspectives, and the ways and means in which she communicates the gospel message. As Christians, if we believe that the good news of Christianity is supracultural, it is important that the focus is on communicating the message and meaning of Christ according to the Bible, and not as defined by popular culture. Much of what is known by non-Christians concerning biblical teachings has been obtained through unknowledgeable sources.

While the task of presenting the gospel "anew" in a society such as exists within the United States appears tremendous, God has and is equipping concerned Christians to meet the challenge. The concern is whether Christians are willing to become equipped in order to engage in the necessary missiological reflections that will lead to the churches becoming "Christ incarnate" in word and deed in the communities in which they are present.

CHAPTER 8

RECOMMENDATION: A CULTURALLY SPECIFIC
MODEL OF MISSION IN A RELIGIOUSLY PLURAL SOCIETY

One of the key goals of this study is to identify a missiological model of ministry and witness that could result in an authentic and relevant mission and ministry within a religiously plural African-American community. The development of a biblical contextual response to the contemporary challenge of Islam requires that African- American churches pursue a new paradigm of mission that has as its core, a major emphasis on elements: mission as contextualization, mission as common witness, and mission as eschatology, "as action in hope" (Bosch 1991:60). The result would be the creation by Christians of a biblical model and method of ministry that is holistic in its concern for faithful mission and witness among Muslims. An effort such as this requires that African-American churches commit themselves to engage in a dynamic process of theological reflection (a doing of theology) as they seek to listen and respond to God in the face of religious pluralism. The efforts of both modalities, missionary focused congregations, and sodalities, ecumenical mission minded bodies, working in partnership are necessary to create the environment for a relevant and authentic mission. The Project Joseph Outreach Ministry to Muslims, headquartered in Pasadena, California was the only sodality operable.

The point of departure for such a theological inquiry must begin with a clear understanding of the nature and purpose of the church. Charles Van Engen (1991) has provided a paradigm for re-thinking and living out the purpose of the church by re-discovering the biblical essence and purpose of the local church. By analyzing scriptural descriptions of the church, *koinonia, kerygma, diakonia and martyria,* (fellowship, proclamation, service, and witness), Van Engen demonstrates that the missionary Church emerges when its members increase their participation in the Church's "being-in-the-world" through active participation in each of these activities (1991:89).

This participation should be carried out in a spirit of humbleness (seen in the example of Jesus himself), of teach-ability (the Holy Spirit as the teacher), and of obedience (to God alone, as Lord of the conscious). The Christians must be intentional about what it means to be in the world representing the One who is "the way, the truth, and the light." They are called to be, as Jesus said, "gentle as a dove and wise as serpents." *Uncommon Decency: Christian Civility in an Uncivil World* (Richard J. Mouw, 1992), *Telling the Story: Evangelism in Black Churches* (James O. Stallings, 1991), *We Have Been Believers: An African American Systematic Theology* (James H. Evans, Jr., 1992), and *Unapologetic Theology: A Christian Voice in a Pluralistic Conversation* (William C. Placher, 1989), each speak to the manner in which people should be trained for Christian mission.

A Holistic Concern for the Total Person

The starting point for an appropriate apologetic that is concerned for both words and deeds must become interested in a theology of wholeness for the total person, and not just for religious or spiritual aspects of life. In response to the question: "How would Jesus Christ approach a Muslim?", the biblical answer is clear: "As a human being with many needs." Interestingly, an analysis of themes present in African theologies of mission reveal areas of commonality with an African-American theology of Christian mission in this concern for wholeness. Desmond M. Tutu, in speaking about the role of the people of God in God's kingdom, and relating it to Leviticus 19:2f (. . . "be holy because I your God am holy"), says:

> . . . so that human beings, who were made in the divine image of God (Gen. 1:26-32), were expected to reflect God's character, conducting themselves in a manner that was intended to mirror the divine conduct and concerns....In proclaiming the kingdom of God, we should seek to work for a recognition of truth that we are

created for interdependence, for togetherness, for fellowship, for family. We are meant for a delicate network of cooperation and interdependence (Gen. 2:18f). That is the fundamental law of our nature, and when that law is flouted, all kinds of things go desperately wrong (1991:33).

Tite Tienou has also been helpful in his identification of themes of mission theology, which, though designed for African Christians, are also applicable to the African-American situation. He has identified four: (1) the need to craft a theology that adequately consolidates and secures the gains of Christian mission; (2) the need for African Christians to be liberated from the complexes associated with African identity so that they can participate fully in the mission of the crucified and risen Lord; (3) in an age of religious crisis and confusion, the need for theologians to articulate reasons for continued focus on expanding the Christian faith; and (4) the need to establish theological bases for dealing with the staggering socio-economic and political crisis of the continent (1991:239-240). Though all four trends are not equally applicable to the North American context related to African-Americans Christians, there is enough commonality to produce beneficial dialogue. African Americans also need to develop an effective mission theology, free themselves from operating from deficits instead of strengths, articulate reasons to commend the faith to others, and develop theological perspective which address acute societal concerns and questions.

The Need for an Incarnational Ministry

Incarnational ministry is related to the task of the church to be in the community representing the liberating, compassionate, healing, prophetic and saving power of God meeting humans needs. Too often, Christian congregations located in the African-American communities do not identify with or relate to the felt needs of the people in that particular community. Even among the seven traditional main African-American denominations, too often church polity and denominational agendas, and unresolved issues of classism and gender prevent the churches from being as sensitive as it could be to the pains, hurts and spiritual confusion of many outside the doors of the church.

As a result, local people tend to view Christianity as irrelevant, lacking integrity, or "not contributing to the progress of African Americans." An incarnational ministry must take seriously the African-American worldview, including its epistemology, its ontology, and its culture, and develop a corrected analysis of the conditions that oppress people, such as injustices and poverty. Historically, the African-American understanding of the Christian faith, which gave birth to the spirituals, gospel music and Black theology, as gifts to the Church in the North American context, has been a source of solidarity for people, providing hope and prophetic vision in the midst of a shared suffering. This incarnational ministry must continue today with a new sense of urgency, and a new sense of community devoted to the mission of God.

A Biblical Approach to Religious Pluralism

In a social environment where other religious believers of various ages, ethnicities, economic classes, and worldview are also striving to give witness to the "uniqueness" of their beliefs, there needs to be determined an appropriate theological framework for identifying, analyzing and developing a biblical response to religious pluralism. There must be a theoretical foundation upon which a biblically faithful and relevant theological framework can be developed. The African-American Christian who seeks, out of a sense of gratitude to God, to be faithful to the Great Commission, will regard with all seriousness these words:

> Go, then, to all peoples everywhere and make them my disciples: baptize them in the name of the Father, the Son, and the Holy Spirit, and teach them to obey everything I have commanded you. And I will be with you always, to the end of the age (Matthew 28: 19-20).

He or she will seek to live a life that gives evidence of that faith in both words and deeds.

Encouraging religious advocates of the various religious faiths to share their faith with others; protecting members from perceived false religious teachings; and reaching out to members of other religious groups with a message of true salvation as we perceive it. . .all religious faiths have these in common. What then, is an appropriate Christian theological response to such a multi-religious environment? What type of theological framework is needed to inform and motivate African-American Christians to face the challenge of religious pluralism? One is needed which engages the Christian in a dynamic process of continuous "being" and "doing," of "reflection" and "action," which moves from discovery to an affirmation of those things discovered, and which engages the total person in a constant process of theological beingness, as exemplified in this scripture.

> The women went to Peter and his friends and gave them a brief account of all they had been told. After this, Jesus himself sent out through his disciples from the east to the west the sacred and everliving message of eternal salvation (Mark 16:9-10).

Following the example of the God (who so loved the world that he sent his only Son into the world not to be its judge, but its savior [John 3:16,17], for the purpose of eternal fellowship with God), and the method of God (John 1), the incarnation, it becomes obvious that the church must begin as God did, with the receptors in mind. Therefore, the emphasis on communicating the biblical word of God, must be on the receptors, who are in this instance, African-American Muslims and potential converts to Islam. The purpose is that they might hear, with clarity, the message of God, believe in God as revealed in Jesus Christ, accept the gift of salvation offered, and become involved in the community of God on earth.

Theological Assumptions

Identifying an appropriate biblical theology which is able to adequately address first, the universal needs of humanity, and secondly, the particular needs of a unique sub-set of humanity which have risen out of the physical, social and psychological experiences of four hundred years of enslavement and racism is essential. The kidnapping and enslavement of Africans by both Muslims and Christians on the continent, and the experiences of the Middle Passage and the African Diaspora which resulted in the mass deaths of African civilians by Europeans, often in the name of Christianity, during and following the period of enslavement, as well as the systematic cultural practices of violence and racism which have continued up to today needs to be addressed with theological comprehensiveness (Molefi K. Asante and Mark T. Mattson, 1992).

This is not merely a perception of reality, but is a social reality of fact of life within the North American context. This context continues to affect how African-American people perceive themselves, and of course, their Creator. Both Benjamin Tonna (1985) and Roger S. Greenway (1992) offer helpful insights into this dilemma, from the perspective of urban ministry. Theologian James Cone, since the 1960s, has been one consistent voice among many who has systematically reflected on the relationship between theology and culture. Dr. J. Alfred Smith, pastor of the Allen Temple Baptist Church, Oakland, California, and theologian, has framed the challenge before the African-American church in one reflective question: How do you make sense out of life for a people who know more about failure than success?

Several biblical themes could be identified to describe God's work and rule in the world in relationship to the challenge of religious pluralism, liberation and covenants, for example. Yet, Jesus spoke often about the reign of God, and in his person announced its reality. George Eldon Ladd's *The Gospel of the Kingdom* and *Signs of the Kingdom in the Secular City*, edited by Helen Ujvarosy, provide keen insight into applying this theme to contemporary mission. In this present environment where other religious believers are also striving to give witness to the "uniqueness" of their beliefs, and where cultural, ethnic and racial factors are primary, a dominant overarching theological framework, such as the reign of God, will allow the churches to focus on purpose and meaning for humankind, according to God. Teachings and examples for identifying, analyzing and developing a biblical response to religious pluralism should emerge.

The importance of claiming the "Reign of God" as an appropriate biblical framework for providing the theological background from which to develop a sound response to religious pluralism in the African American is important for several key reasons. First, it makes its usefulness in focusing on the concept of God, who for most monotheistic believers, is known as Creator, Sustainer, Ruler and Judge, and the nature of God. Secondly, this approach will allow for a more realistic and consistent assessment of divine reality with the locus being in the Word of God, as opposed to human centered theologies. And thirdly, this focus on the divine reign instead of the human reign will continuously point us to the creation of a biblical framework that interprets history as not being out of control, but rather as meaningful and purposeful. George Hunter, in stating the need for the church to offer people hope in the reign of God, quotes from Ken Chafin to illustrate this point.

> [Unfortunately, much of the Church has] taken the doctrine of the Second Coming, which is a very valid New Testament doctrine, and turned it into an esoteric doctrine, and turned it over to the crazies and the confused Zionists. We have failed to realize that the doctrine, originally perceived, was the doctrine of Hope. The doctrine rightly communicates the confidence that the Creator God who came in Christ is still in charge of the universe; it's not out of control, and He will bring it to conclusion and fulfill His purposes and promises. I think that if you can undress the doctrine of the Second Coming from all the gaudy clothes it has picked up, it has a far more significant appeal to secular people than anyone realizes (Hunter 1992:63).

With this in mind, it is my belief that the theme of the reign of God, will in addition, address the concerns that initiated and continue to sustain the move of Christians from Christianity to other religious communions in search for an authentic relationship with God.

The biblical perspective on religious diversity gives evidence that religious pluralism is a normal state of existence for the people of God. Throughout biblical history the people of God had been called and challenged to know who they are and whose they are. The loyalty and courage of Abram and Sarai called from the religions of Ur, Joseph in Egypt, and Ruth converting to the God of Naomi, and of

238

Priscillia and Aquilla living among the gods of the Romans, indicate that in spite of religious pluralism, there have always been a people, devoted and committed through faith, to the one God. In spite of idolatry and apostasy surrounding them, there have been women and men conscious of their calling (vocation, purpose of life) to be a people called to live under the rule of God's reign.

The implications are two. For those Christians who are nominal in their faith commitment, or who are doubting the relevancy of Christianity, the church must find ways to lovingly, but firmly remind them that:

> Since you have accepted Jesus as Lord, live in union with him. Keep your roots deep in him, and become stronger in your faith, as you were taught. And be filled with thanksgiving. See to it then that no one enslaves you by means of the worthless deceit of human wisdom, which comes from the teachings handed down by men, and from the ruling spirits of the universe, and not from Christ. For the full content of divine nature lives in Christ, in his humanity, and you have been given full life in union with him. He is supreme over every spiritual ruler and authority (Colossians 2:6-10).

It is important that Muslims who worship the One God should be encouraged in their spiritual journey as well. At the same time, however, it should be made clear to both Christians and non-Christians that the same God is not fully known to the Muslims because of their rejection of God's revelation in Jesus the Christ. The Qur'an is not direct revelation, but rather is reflected from the Bible. Therefore, the prophet Muhammad and his message are inadequate for salvation because he is merely human, and his message is of human, and not divine origin. Without knowledge of Christ, it is not possible to comprehend God fully as it is written:

> This is the new being which God, its Creator, is constantly renewing in his own image, in order to bring you to a full knowledge of himself. As a result, there is no longer any distinction between Gentiles and Jews, circumcised and uncircumcised, barbarians, savages, slaves, and free men, but Christ is all, Christ is in all (Colossians 3:10b-11).

Now, given the fact that Christians have a specific gospel message to witness to, and acknowledging that there is a particular biblical framework for viewing religious pluralism, this is an adequate place to begin the development of a biblical theology toward Muslims.

The Old Testament

A survey of the Old Testament reveals the history of a particular people ("a light to the nations--so that all the world may be saved," Isaiah 49:6), spanning many generations and their encounter with pluralism in the fullest sense of the word: multi-cultural and multi-ethnic, with peoples of differing nationalities, languages and worldviews, and not least of all, multi-religious. During the era of Abraham (the so-called Middle Bronze Age), as the origin of the Hebrew people's spiritual awareness was being formulated, there was a pantheon, bureaucratic hierarchy of gods and goddesses.

Each one was responsible for a particular aspect of nature or society. The Sumerian supreme beings included Anu, the high father god and Ishtar, goddess of fertility. While the Moabites worshipped Chemosh, the Amorites worshipped Marduke as lord of Babylon. The Egyptians believed in many gods with Osiris, Isis, and Horus being the major gods worshipped. And yet in the midst of this religious plurality, there developed the concept of monotheism that affirmed that besides God (known to the Israelites as Yahweh) other gods were supposed to exist, but Israel without any exception was forbidden to worship them.

In the Decalogue (Ex. 20:3; cf. Deut. 5:7) the commandment says: "You shall have no other gods before me." This may imply the existence of other gods, but under the covenant, Israel was permitted to worship only Yahweh, and in this the Old Testament religion never yielded (Gehman 1970:633).

Mosaic theology reveals Yahweh's nature, not only in the covenant and decalogue, but also in the names by which God is referred. However, scripture clearly indicates that given who God is and how God had revealed God in their lives, the people of Israel turned away from God, and began to serve other gods.

They stopped worshiping the Lord, the god of their ancestors, the God who had brought them out of Egypt, and they began to worship other gods, the gods of the peoples around them (Judges 2:12).

The Assyrians, the fall of Israel (800-700 B.C.), the decline of Judah, and the Jews in exile (587-538 B.C.) were experiences that placed the people called by God for a special mission, in direct contact with people of other religious faiths and beliefs. It was the prophetic voice of Amos and Hosea and Micah, and the others who constantly reminded Israel to be faithful to the One God.

An article by Stephen Breck Reid has been most helpful in identifying three biblical attitudes toward religious pluralism that are significant for this study--(1) the importance of the issue of identity in a religiously plural world; (2) the religiously plural nature of cultures as inevitable; and (3) the fact that Scripture provides at least two guidelines for "the delicate work of maintaining the identity of a believing community in a religiously plural culture" (1991:27). When one reflects on the historicity of the Jews (in the Old Testament) and the Gentiles (in the New Testament), and the struggles of the post-Apostolic church (particularly in circumstances where culture and Christianity are not closely identified), these factors become obvious.

The first guideline Reid calls attention to is the fact that an understanding of how the biblical texts developed in a religiously plural culture can help us understand the interaction between the church and the contemporary religious pluralism of today. In the examination of four historical periods of the Israelite religious development, it becomes clear that not only does religious pluralism correspond with cultural pluralism, but also that the religiously plural culture itself served as a resource for theological reflection.

> Instead of a monolith in the early formation period of Yahwism we see a dynamic conversation between religious communities. We see this is the depiction of God as well as a period of acknowledgment that other peoples in the regions had other gods; we find monolatry, not monotheism in the early period. . . .Thus far we have established that the understanding of YHWH demonstrates influences from three traditions: El, Baal and the God of the Ancestors. The canonical process proves adaptable to a religiously plural culture (Reid 1991:31).

Reid's second guideline states that in a religiously plural culture, every religion is forced to articulate its essential.

> Israel early on developed two fixed points that anchored its interaction with the religiously plural culture. First, 'the intimate relationship with the deity' remains a pillar of identity for the believing community. Second, in a religiously plural culture the people of YHWH must 'eschew any preoccupation with objectification of God.' The religion of Ancient Israel remained at core an iconic, without icon. YHWH remains beyond representation (Reid 1991:31).

One only needs to recall the various historical periods in Israel's history to identify the factors of religious pluralism, the temptations it presents to God's people through God's messengers. For instance, during the period of the decline of Judah and neo-Babylon (700-587 B.C.), when prophets Zephaniah, Nahum, Habakkuk and Jeremiah lived, theirs was the message of sin (against God and others) and the call to repentance. And during the time of the Jews in exile (587-538 B.C., and when Lamentations and Ezekiel were written), and during the time of the rise of Persia (Deutero- Isaiah), the themes of "a Redeeming God," "Nations called to God," and "the Servant of Yahweh" were proclaimed.

The New Testament

The Book of Acts is by nature and description, a dynamic multiethnic (look at the day of Pentecost!), multicultural (Jewish, Roman, Samaritan) book that gives evidence of a multireligious (monotheism and polytheism, religious tolerance as well as intolerance) background in a pluralistic setting. Even the pluralistic form of Christian practice was evident in Acts, in that some Christians received the Holy Spirit at baptism (2:38; 19:5-6) or before baptism (10:44), and as in the case of the Samaritans (8:17), some time subsequent to baptism. In chapter 8 is the story of Christianity first reaching the non-Jewish regions and peoples.

Significant among those who became Christian is an Ethiopian (Nubian) minister of Candace, queen of the Ethiopians, who had come to Jerusalem to worship. He was a God-fearing person. As he was returning home, he had one-on-one contact with a Christian who took the time to befriend and communicate with him.

Saul, at that time in history, disliked those who advocated God in Christ, and ravaged the church (Gal. 1:13). Paul's persecution of the Christians and Stephen's death represent a particular crisis situation, and the persecution that resulted led to the Gentile mission in Antioch, a multi-religious urban context.

> Some of the believers who were scattered by the persecution which took place when Stephen was killed went as far as Phoenicia, Cyprus and Antioch, telling the message to Jews only. But other believers, men from Cyprus and Cyrene, went to Antioch and proclaimed the message to the Gentiles also, telling them the Good News about the Lord Jesus. The Lord's power was with them, and a great number of people believed and turned to the Lord (Acts 11:19-21).

In much the same way that the story of Daniel and his friends was exegeted for its understandings related to the implications of religious pluralism, so also could these readings. For instance, what are the implications of the two-pronged mission strategy utilized in verses 19 and 20? Why did some of the disciples go to the Jews only (M-1), and others went to both Jews and Greeks (M-2, M-3), representing their approach not only to persons of another culture, but also to advocates of another religious belief system?

It must be pointed out that Afrocentric writers (James Cone, Cain Felder, Robert E. Hood and Molefi Kete Asante, to name a few) would affirm this anthropological approach, believing that any presentation of the Gospel geared toward African Americans must include references to the persons of African cultural and ethnic background. Persons mentioned in the New Testament such as Simon of Cyrene (and his two sons Alexander and Rufus); Simeon who was called Niger and Lucius of Cyrene; the Ethiopian Eunuch; and Candace, a queen of Ethiopia around the time of Christ who is credited with bringing Christianity to her country, and others cannot be dismissed, but should be used to counteract anti-African sentiments that have been identified theologically with either God or Scripture. This has been a successful model that is utilized in many African-American churches in theological, historical and experiential activities.

Early Christian Approach

Religious pluralism, and how the early church approached it, is evident in the passage of Acts 17, especially verse 23. Paul, as one who has experienced the grace of God in Christ Jesus, became upset then he saw the idols of the city of Athens. Whether the Gentiles mentioned were persons considering conversion to Judaism, or whether the Jews mentioned had begun to interpret the resurrection as another god, we are not certain. What is sure is that Paul in Athens became engaged in the dialogical approach with advocates of various religious and philosophical systems (Jews, Gentiles, Epicureans, Stoics and others).

Paul took the altar dedicated "To an Unknown God," and used that to present the gospel of Jesus Christ. "That which you worship, then even though you do not know it, is what I now proclaim to you," reads verse 23. Paul started where his listeners were and proceeded to tell them about the God of creation and history (verses 24-27), the God of the present ("Yet, God is actually not far from any one of us. . . we too are his children," verses 27-28), and the God of the future, of judgment (verses 29-31). Though the Greeks had thousands of gods, known and unknown, Paul did not hesitate, in a godly way, to tell them of the God who remains faithful always. The response he received is one in which the faithful church should also anticipate: some will desire to know more, and others will not; and some like the woman Damaris and the man Dionysius will join the Christian community, and believe (verses 32-34).

A Theoretical Framework for Addressing Religious Pluralism

In seeking to determine a contemporary theological response to Islam, several distinct concerns must be addressed. A contemporary approach to understanding Islam and religious pluralism in general is one that initiates the process by careful, earnest, and thoughtful consideration of two similar yet distinct questions: (1) How should a Christian approach another religion (that is, what it advocates)? and (2) How should a Christian approach a believer of another religion? The first question is one that raises epistemological and ontological concerns. The second one is a moral question. Both are considered in *Reason and Religious Belief: An Introduction to the Philosophy of Religion.*

> Answers to these questions require that we consider the truth-claims of the various religions. The questioner seeks to understand sympathetically the religious claims of other persons, to interpret what they mean and what significance they have for believers' lives, and to evaluate critically the alleged truth of those claims. On the other hand, to ask how we should approach other persons is a moral question. Advocates of other religions should be treated, at the very least, as the ethics of our religion demand persons should be treated.... It is often forgotten that evaluating a person's truth-claims and relating to persons are separate issues (Peterson 1991:221).

While we can respond to the question of how to approach a believer of another religious faith by appealing to the examples, precepts and experiences of God's people throughout the Bible (and especially in the life and teachings of Jesus Christ), the second question posed is more difficult to answer, for there are among Christians, several basic approaches. The third question raised is how to assess or evaluate a religious system for truthfulness. The final question is related to the criteria of authenticity and appropriateness related to contextualization. Each must be given adequate attention. What should emerge is a new paradigm of mission.

Basic Approaches and Assumptions Concerning Reality

There are several ways to approach the study of religious pluralism. Steve Bouma-Prediger, a Christian philosopher and adjunct at Fuller Seminary has suggested Ian Barbour's typology of religious views as an attempt to understand the assumptions and presuppositions that lay behind views held of other religious communions (see figure 5). The value of this typology is that it provides a means for evaluating both the positive and negative aspects of views held toward religious pluralism. I recommend that the biblically appropriate view for Christians to assume is contained within a mixed perspective which represents in this typology a description of both the claim of absoluteness concerning the revelation of God in Jesus Christ, as well as elements that affirm pluralistic dialogue. Perhaps John

Frederick Denison Maurcie, in his 1846 Boble Lecture entitled *The Religions of the World*, has summed up an appropriate and seeking perspective when he writes:

> Each religion, he suggested stresses a vital aspect of divine truth while only Christianity holds all aspects together in absolute harmony. Christianity in contact with other religions, can therefore supply the wholeness they need to become effectual. Christianity, though like all systems, suffers decay and stands itself in needs of the revitalization that contacts with other religions can supply (Bennett 1991:117).

A Criteria for Assessing Religions

Are all religions equally true? And by what criteria do we assess religions? Keith Yandell has suggested that criteria is needed to evaluate religious systems for truthfulness. This moves beyond claims as to simply whether one religion is true and the others are not, but provides a ground for the rationale of the various religious beliefs that are encountered by Christians (Figure 5).

Barbour's Typology of Views

1. Absolutism or exclusivism

   a. There is only one true religion and all others are simply false.
   b. Since only one religion is true, there is one exclusive path to salvation.
   c. Problems: absolutized finite expressions of the infinite, sanctions, intolerance

2. Approximations of truths or supersessionism

   a. Other religions have elements of the truth that are most completely presented in one particular religion.
   b. Since one religion is the fulfillment of all others, other religions offer real though limited paths to salvation.
   c. Problems: condescending attitude and closed to learning from other traditions.

3. Identity of Essence or Global Religion

    a. All religions are in essence the same though expressed in different cultural forms.

    b. Since all religions are basically identical, there are many valid paths to salvation.

    c. Problems: disagreement over common essence, fails to take seriously genuine difference, and conflicts with lived religious experience.

4. Cultural Relativism

    a. Every religion is a unique expression of a different culture--incapable of being compared, evaluated, or reduced to some essence--and true in its own context.

    b. Since each religion has its own distinct character, there are many different valid paths to salvation.

    c. Problems: religions are not in fact self-contained and incapable of being compared, self-reference of problems.

5. Pluralistic dialogue

    a. Other religions are affirmed even though one religion is taken as more adequate such that loyalty to one tradition is combined with respect for others.

    b. Since no judgment is passed on other religions, there may/may not be other paths to salvation; in any case mutual enrichment through dialogue is important and necessary.

    c. Problems: fails to take seriously the claims to universality of some religions; can lead to relativism.

Figure 5

According to the authors of *Reason and Religious Belief* (1991), Yandell suggests the following criteria for assessing religious truth claims.

    1. The propositions essential to that religion must be consistent with each other.

    2. Knowing that the religious system is true must be compatible with its being true. If the truth of the system entails that we cannot know it is true--for

example, if, like Madhyamika Buddhism, it claims that all views are false--that is reason to suspect its truth.

3. The truth of a religious system must be compatible with what must exist for it to be true. For example, the claim that Ultimate Reality has no distinctions is incompatible with the claim that religious statements that affirm this are true and not false.

4. If the only reason for offering the religious system is that it promises to provide a solution to a problem, and if fails to do so, there is no reason to accept the system. For example, if a religious system was introduced to resolve the problem of pain and suffering, and it clearly did not accomplish this, there would be no reason to advocate that religious system.

5. Essential truths of the system should not contradict well-established data, for example, in the sciences or psychology.

6. Ad-hoc hypotheses to avoid evidence contrary to the religious system count against that religious system.

7. A system should be able to account for and explain broad reaches of human experience.

8. (Added criteria.) It should satisfy some basic moral and aesthetic intuitions, and provoke and inspire persons to live more morally responsive and responsible lives (Michael Peterson et. al., 1991:231).

While knowledge of these theoretical understandings of theological discourse are very helpful within Christian dialogue in a religiously plural world, it should be noted that has been primarily through the evidential (inductive, factual improbability) and existential (actual experience) realities that Muslims have formulated their beliefs and attitudes toward both Islam and Christianity. For instance, the importance of the present human experience in theologizing in both the Christian and Muslim religious journeys are obvious by African Americans can be seen in the example of the Nation of Islam which is not concerned with rejection by orthodox Muslims in the United States. Founder of the Nation of Islam, Elijah Muhammad, according to Lincoln, admitted that some of the teachings and practices of the Nation were clearly at variance with orthodox Islam because of the particular experience of African Americans in the United States.

So while the pursuit for religious knowledge is sought in order to better participate in the dialogue of religious plurality, the importance of this research indicates the significance of the present human experience in both traditional Black theology as proclaimed in the churches, and in the Islamic movements as well. The individual as a theological source for persons who have rejected Christianity in favor of Islam is often presented in conjunction with arguments of reasoning and "truth," to indicate the irrationality of Christianity as some Muslims perceive it.

A Criteria for Assessing Contextualization

There is yet another important set of criteria that must be considered. More and more theologians are conceding to contextualization as an imperative, and not as an option. The universal church of Christ must contextualize the biblical gospel so that it is heard in each local (particular) situation. Every Christian communion in its own locale and each generation must struggle with the processes and means related to this concern.

Who will make the judgment as to whether a particular contextualized approach is truly Christian or not is, as Peter Schineller observes, a difficult question because "there will be disagreements, and in many cases, winners and losers. It will take time and effort to move to viable solutions" (1992:52). After presenting a timely discussion on syncretism, and providing case examples from within Christian history, Schineller suggests a criteria for evaluation of a particular contextual development that consists of the employment of a hermeneutical circle which consists of three poles: the Christian message, the cultural situation and the pastoral agent or agents. This criteria includes: (1) faithfulness to the Christian message; (2) insertion into the cultural situation; (3) engagement by pastoral agents (leadership); (4) patience; (5) a sense of God at work in the world; (6) a sense of the people of

God; and (7) listening to the Christian message in all its richness and to the various human cultures in all their diversity.

A Word About Syncretism

It has been said that one person's contextualization is another's syncretism. It is appropriate at this juncture to say a word about syncretism. "Syncretism: Good? Bad? Inevitable?" is the title of an article by Peter Schineller (1992) in which he observes that though syncretism is a "positive, necessary and helpful word to describe the development of a tradition in new cultures," the word itself has been so misused and misunderstood, that he suggests the development of criteria for distinguishing adequate versus inadequate inculturation would address the question that syncretism raises (1992:52). Thus, he develops the criteria presented above. The value of this criteria is clearly evident when one considers at least two of the nine historical cases presented by Schineller of syncretism that African Americans today must continually respond to in the face of Islamic challenge: the fact of 1,400 years of slavery rationalized by biblical Christians, and the fact that Christians adapted the celebration of the birth of Christ from a pagan winter feast of the sun. These two examples of syncretism continuously engage the Christian in a defense of the Christian gospel that the average Christian is not able to explain or articulate.

In order to avoid this notion of syncretism, the church (or, for that matter Islam) must seek not only to guide selectively, reinterpretation and ramification, but must also respond to the deeply felt needs of the people sought to be reached; for if contextualization is to be done effectively, as Luzbetak, observes:

> It is not a question of either/or but both/and. All that we have thus far said about felt needs and about the importance of social analysis comes into play. An elitist or culturally irrelevant religion, rather than one deeply aware of the felt needs of the people, will merely encourage untheological forms of popular piety (Luzbetak 1990:373)

Critical Realism, the approach taken in this study, affirms that there are indeed two realities, a human perception of reality and an absolute view of reality revealed by God (i.e., "R"). It is the responsibility of the Christian to take both seriously. There is an absolute reality that represents God's revelation, such as we have in Scripture. However, when it is interpreted by humans, we read and interpret it according to our "r," (our small, limited understanding of reality), which has been shaped by our experiences, our traditions and the particular context. Objective reality is seen by God only, for it represents omnipresence, omnipotence, and all knowingness. It is God's reality that judges our contextual efforts.

A Theological Model and Method

Among the many models and methods of theological reflection for Christian ministry suggested, James Whitehead and Evelyn Whitehead (1980) have identified one model which I find adaptable for Christian ministry within a religiously plural setting. It is a theological model that consists of identifying three distinct but interconnected emphasis-- personal experience, culture and religious tradition. Each is actively involved in an ongoing process of theological reflection that consists of three stages, that include "attending, and assertion, leading to an appropriate action that is the decision for a concrete Christian witness and ministry" (1980:22). This method is best described in the figure presented by Whitehead and Whitehead (1980:22).

The Model

A biblical theology of religious pluralism affirms the universal spiritual need of all people. Muslims and Christians must carry our their missional responsibilities with integrity. Such a model confirms both the implicit and explicit grounds for missional actions on behalf of each religious group.

Personal Experience

"Personal experience" refers to the collective religious experiences of a particular religious body and its adherents. Personal experiences of Christians will challenge them to reflect on their own experience (convictions, feelings, ideas, biases) about the Christian faith in general, and about the Christian witness to Muslims specifically. The individual Christian should not be surprised, however, that in the process of witnessing to Muslims if one is also converted, like Peter, in his

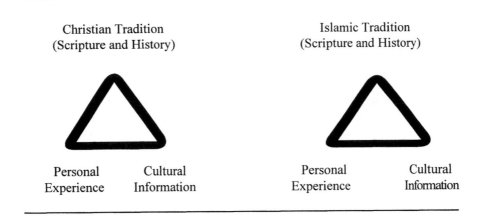

Christian Tradition
(Scripture and History)

Islamic Tradition
(Scripture and History)

Personal
Experience

Cultural
Information

Personal
Experience

Cultural
Information

Figure 6

Model for Understanding Religious Diversity

mission to the Gentiles. As Harold Dollar reminds us, the conversion of the Jewish

missionaries was somewhat more painful, sociologically, than was the conversion of

the Gentiles (1993:14). Ralph Winter brings the issue even closer to home.

> Will the 1990s allow us to realize that some of the most devout Muslims are
> closer to the Kingdom than (1) shaky Muslims who are apparently coming our
> way only due to their rejection of their own faith, or (2) purely 'cultural
> Christians' who don't really believe and obey anything? Isn't the Islamic cultural
> tradition--prayers, mosque, and entire way of life--far more redeemable than the
> ancient hellenic way of life with which Paul was willing to work? (1991:48).

A deeper understanding of what it means to be Christian, that is, of Christ, may be

the result of such a challenge. Because the second concept, that of "religious

tradition" (which includes scriptures and history) is self-defining, the third concept,

that of "cultural information" is in need of some clarification.

Cultural Information

Cultural information, according to Whitehead,

> refers to that information (confirming, ambiguous and demonic) which arises
> from the culture. It includes understandings--of the human person, of

community, of success and failure--which have influenced and continue to influence Christian efforts of self understanding (1980:19).

Or, in the case of Islam, we could say, to influence Muslim efforts of self-understanding, as well. For the Whiteheads, culture is perceived as dynamic, and social change is incorporated in their understanding of the culture concept. Stephen Charles Mott (1982) , from the evangelical tradition, and James Cone (1968, 1993) and William Pannel (1992, 1993), representing the African-American theological tradition, are among the theologians who identify biblical ethics and social change as inseparable, both influencing the culture. While cultural information from the dominant culture conveys the notion that Muslims in general are not to be trusted, the cultural information within the African-American community affirms that African-American Muslims can be and are usually trusted.

The Method

The methodology that is suggested here can best be described in the following diagram. Its purpose is to depict a dynamic and continuous process of theological reflection while engaging in mission and witness. This is taken from *Method in Ministry: Theological Reflection and Christian Ministry* (1980:22).

This model and method is adapted to fit the needs of discernment within the religiously plural environment, and is biblically and theologically appropriate. In the first stage, both knowing oneself and effective listening are essential. In the second stage, assertion is described as, "a style of behavior which acknowledges the value of my own needs and convictions in a manner that respects the needs and convictions of others" (Whitehead and Whitehead 1980:23). The third stage, the stage of decision and action, involves problem analysis as well as community implementation based on theological reflection on the Bible.

The ideal of Christian ministry is the formulation of a reflective community which is alive to the presence of God. . . . In a church that is truly Catholic, that is plural, different communities will come to differing conclusions in many concrete pastoral situations. . . . More often, however, these differences [that may emerge] will be appropriate and expectable variations that reflect the rich diversity within the Christian experience of God's Word and God's will (Whitehead and Whitehead 1980:26).

I. ATTENDING

Seek out the information on a particular issue of concern related to religious pluralism that is available in personal experience, religious tradition, and cultural sources.

II. ASSERTION

Engage the information from these three sources in a process of mutual clarification and challenge in order to expand and deepen religions insight.

III. DECISION

Move from insight through decision to concrete Christian witness and ministry.

Figure 7
Three-stage Method of Theological Reflection in Ministry

Mission and Theology

A faithful Christian witness to Muslims should begin with the concept of the oneness of God. R. Marston Speight observes that by discovering the points of commonality and incisiveness of both Christianity and Islam, one becomes aware immediately that they represent the common belief that there is only one God, almighty and all merciful, who is the creator and sustainer of all of life. This theology must not be separated from the mission, but rather should direct and guide it.

Areas of Commonality

This discussion of the nature of God leads to the basic assumption that when human beings learn of God's power and mercy, or grace, they must respond in a three-fold way, described by Speight as: (1) a life of commitment to the divine will and authority; (2) a life of gratitude for the gifts of God; and (3) a life of responsible action in worship, charity and acts of righteousness. It follows from this that in response to God's action, the human's response to the understanding of God will be significant and will result in God's final judgment. This judgment is viewed by both Christians and Muslims as God's just response to the choices humans make concerning the will of God.

Attending to Communal Felt Needs

Perceivably, several social and community oriented opportunities provide natural opportunities for Christians and Muslims to come together and dialogue, both informally and formally. If one focused on the model, and identified areas that represent "personal experience" and "cultural information" common to both the Muslim and Christian, what will be revealed are some significant areas where African Americans shared experiences as a particular ethnic group, (and individual members of it) can find a basis for cooperation, and mutual witness. For instance, considering the immediate and crucial events that have affected the Los Angeles African-American community for the past two years would reveal three key concerns--the need to address issues surrounding police brutality, racial and ethnic justice, and economic development. The issues surrounding racial and ethnic justices are evident in an article entitled, "The Myth of Racial Progress," and indicate that "clearly the racial divide is a grievous problem for America--and for the church (whose reputation is tarnished by a history of racial splits within its institutions)" (*Christianity Today*, Oct. 4, 1993:4).

Concerning the African American's need for economic development, it has been a well known fact held by critical thinking African Americans that ever since the Emancipation Proclamation, African Americans have emphasized three factors in solving the race problem in America. They are: economic development, self-help, and racial solidarity (Meier, 1988). Utilizing this historical information, along with biblical scripture in its fullness, African-American churches can become motivated to do much to respond appropriately to the social concerns of racism, economic development, self-development, and racial solidarity, acting out of Christian values and truths. The African-American churches have done much to address the issues of racial justice in this country (the churches' impact on the Civil Rights Movement is just one example), but what about the desire for economic development and self-development? Considering the large amounts of monies that are placed in the offering plates of African-American churches nationwide, the churches could do much in responding appropriately to social concerns as racism, economic development, self-development, and racial solidarity, informed by and resulting from Christian values and truths.

What the Muslims are doing in these areas and the activities they engage in as a result of bringing religious commitment to the realm of economics, indicate a much better understanding of the African-American worldview and community needs, in relationship to religious beliefs, than does the Christian understanding. While in 1982 it was reported that forty-six million Americans lived below the poverty level, as we enter the twenty-first century, it is unequivalently clear that Christians must wrestle with what the Christian faith requires of us in regard to our economic values and commitment (Finn and Pemberton 1985:1).

And what of the police brutality, and the societal structures that perpetuate oppression and injustices? Our approach must start with people, but must include structures. Structures are there for social usage, and as Christians, we are to influence the society for Christianity by influencing the people who influence the structures. "The goal must be to structure not pain and divisiveness, but new health and togetherness for all people," state Finn and Pemberton 1985:3-4).

What can Christians learn from Muslims in an effort to be faithful to both Jesus as Lord and Savior, and the African-American community for which God so loved that Jesus was willing to die for? They demonstrate the importance of being concerned for the people who are to receive the spiritual message, the receptors. The Muslim use of contextualization methods and approaches within the United States are a reflection of the goals, aspirations and objectives articulated by Muslim leaders. The goals they have identified reflect concern for the future of Islam in the North

American context. The various approaches taken toward contextualizing Islam, indicate the seriousness of the desire to create, maintain, and support a strong Islamic community.

A Faithful Witness

The search for a biblically faithful witness in the face of religious pluralism requires that, in spite of the theological differences, Christians must be prepared and willing to enter into dialogue and witness to Muslims. There will be areas of theological commonalities, such as the description of the nature of God as Creator and Sustainer, as well as areas of basic difference, such as the Muslims' emphasis on the gulf which separates God from all God's creation. This is a contrast to the Christian belief that the gulf has been bridged in the person (life, death and resurrection of Jesus Christ). It is helpful to recognize that though the Muslims claim to maintain a holistic view of reality, there is a definitive separation between God and human. This is primarily the result of the influence of the Muslim philosopher Ibn Sina of Avicenna:

> . . . who was the first to systematically develop the argument that all reality is divided into two categories, that which is necessary (God) and that which is contingent (creation). For the Muslim, this transcendence of God must never be forgotten (Tingle 1985:9).

However, for the Christian, God is both transcendent and yet present with us as "Immanuel." Where there are areas of difference, the Church must decide if the particular Christian belief is of human origin, and if so, then the Muslims are correct. However, if the message of the gospel is that God was reconciling the world to God, then the origin is of God. This model seeks to indicate how a dynamic Christian mission of theology must be experienced amidst religious pluralism if it is to be authentic (Figure 8).

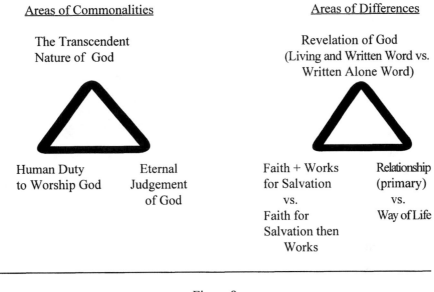

<table>
<tr><td>Areas of Commonalities</td><td>Areas of Differences</td></tr>
</table>

Areas of Commonalities	Areas of Differences
The Transcendent Nature of God	Revelation of God (Living and Written Word vs. Written Alone Word)

Human Duty to Worship God   Eternal Judgement of God

Faith + Works for Salvation vs. Faith for Salvation then Works   Relationship (primary) vs. Way of Life

Figure 8

Theological Reflections

The Revelation of God

Consider another example, that concerning the concept of God's revelation. If this was the concern arising from the Muslim and Christian encounter, understanding the meaning and nature of God's revelation would be crucial for Christians. The different types of revelations experienced (as doctrine, history, inner experience, dialectical presence and as a new awareness) would help to explain how and why Muslims and Christians differ in their understanding of God's revelation. The differences between the revelation of God as Living Word (Jesus Christ) and as Written Word (Bible or Qur'an) must be clarified, along with the nature of inspiration understood by Christians and Muslims. With such an understanding, Christians should become more faithful in both their own Christian growth, as well as in their witness. Or, consider a study of the biblical God utilizing the ninety-nine names and attributes of Allah as described by Muhammad Iqbal Siddiqi (1991). These and related learning experiences should be provided to encourage both Christian understanding of theological differences as well as commonalities.

Because this study presents a local theology, other elements residing within the African-American community should not be ignored, for they too are recipients of God's revelation and grace. The plurality of the African-American communities includes other ethnic Christians such as Asian-American Christians. Because Asian Christians have had historically to relate to religious pluralism in their home country and often within their immediate families, and because the two ethnic groups, African Americans and Asians, have had similar experiences of discrimination within this country, a possibility exists that one part of the universal Church can inform another in the task before us. Multicultural ministries would express the Christian reconciliation that is so desperately needed in our pluralistic society. A sign of the reign of God in the African-American community such as this, though on a local scale, can witness to the universality of the gospel of Jesus the Christ, in much the same way as the *hajj* gives witness to the unity of Muslims across national and ethnic lines.

Worship As Viewed Through Ritual Prayer

Another example of the need for such a method of theological reflection for missiology is taken from a comprehensive observation on the nature of Muslims' ritual prayer. Obviously the activity of ritual prayer is meaningful to the Muslim who practices it. The religious beliefs and practices of Muslims, as indicated in their daily prayer life, reflect several significant theological issues of concern for Christians. Theological reflections on this one practice, ritual prayer, reveals eight key characteristics of the ritual prayer of Muslims, namely: (1) as a means to empower; (2) to communicate something of the spirit of community; (3) to relate religious meaning; (4) to facilitate conscious awareness; (5) to indicate religious motivation; (6) to show how Islam has spiritually affected the believer; (7) to motivate; and (8) to serve as an activity around which every other aspect of life is ordered. Each one of these characteristics, when considered individually, may be considered irrelevant or marginal, but collectively they reflect a religious activity, an analytical unit, that conveys theological principles that are acted upon in the life of a Muslim believer, five times a day. Out of a total of at least eight characteristics evident in Muslims' ritual prayer, I will discuss four.

To Empower

The influx of African Americans to Islam is accompanied by a sense of enthusiasm and excitement that translates to a new religious commitment. Within the larger secular society, where Christian influence has been evident for generations and "cultural Christians" (Winters 1991:47) are the norm , Islam as a minority religion appears most committed to those things identified as "religious or spiritual." The individual Muslim perceives him/herself as the minority, but a "true worshipper," and one's daily participation in the prayers serve to strengthen that perception. The experience of empowerment is the result of disciplining oneself (which demonstrates the willingness and ability to learn the appropriate "holy" words, first in English and then in Arabic, and then mastering the bodily positions).

Furthermore, empowerment is obtained when one reflects spiritually that he or she is submitting to a historical practice that began with the prophet Mohammad. It is an activity clearly used to uplift one's daily life and to remind the individual of God throughout the day, and if one submits accordingly, he or she feels a sense of personal fulfillment. Unlike other religions where a one time confessional stance is taken, this confessional activity done daily involves the total person (cognitive, affective and evaluative), and allows people to feel that they are participating in it, geared to improve their present condition, both on earth and afterwards. This act demonstrates belief carried through to action. An act such as this, is a demonstration of what they believe, not merely words, but also through their actions.

To Communicate

Ritual prayer communicates something of the spirit of the community of Islam, a means of unifying adherents. One of its purposes is to influence people, and as a ritual produced by people, it is used by Muslims to teach that the religious community of Islam worldwide is united. Muslims all over the world are to pray facing Mecca at the same time during the daily prayers, repeating the same words. As a universal community, the ritual prayers are used to transform people's lives so that they have a greater ability to function within the *ummah*. As dictated by the Qur'an, the doctrinal and social practices developed by the prophet serve as a means of uniting people not only theologically but also ideologically.

To Relate Religious Meaning

The set of ideas developed in the Qur'an, and the form of prayer, given in example by the prophet Mohammad, can be viewed as two complementary processes. The first consists of a set of ideas about God, a holy language ("Arabic") ordained by God, God's nature and God's rule, and the other represents the form or posture of prayer. Concerning God, the words are a constant reminder of the unity and oneness of God, a call away from the dangers of idolatry. The prayer posture represents predictable and steady humbling of oneself before God. Moreover, the words themselves come from the Qur'an and are, therefore, reassuringly infallible and trustworthy.

To Facilitate Consciousness Awareness

In the belief and practices of Islamic religion we find a wide variety of reminders of the importance of "intention." Ritual prayers main purpose is to bring the believer in the presence of God and to remind that person of God's omnipotence and power. Some years ago I came across this description by a Muslim that until recently remained unclear.

> I think what prepared me for being a Muslim was being raised in the Baptist church. I was learning the idea of the power and the sovereignty of the law when I sang the doxology even though it included the Trinity concept, which we don't care for (Mallon 1989:49).

The meaning that has become clearer is that beneath the explicit words, lacks a reality that brings one into consciousness of the relationship between the divine and the created. This intentionality in our relationship to God is where Christians can learn something from Muslims.

Justification by Grace vs. Justification by Law

Having examined this one practice--ritual prayer--as an exercise for theological reflection, the final stage presented in the method is that of responsible decision making. This involves engaging the information obtained through personal and religious tradition encounters in a process of mutual clarification and, for the Christian, a recognition of biblical concern. In this case, considering the nature and meaning of Muslim ritual prayer, what does the Bible assert, and how does the Christian respond from a theological perspective? The book of Romans suggests an appropriate response to the theological issue suggested in ritual prayer: that of the issue of justification by the law of God. Muslim affirmation or justification through law is juxtaposed to the Christian's foundational belief in justification by God's grace. It must be noted that in the Qur'an, people are saved by grace, but faith plus works leads to salvation. God forgives whom God will. The implications of each (faith plus works for salvation, and faith for salvation then works) need to be understood from a biblical perspective as well as from a Qur'anic perspective.

Emphasis placed on clarity in communicating the biblical message is essential. As Muslims are invited to consider the message of the gospel, it should be presented with clarity and with relevance. "New Life for All Movements in African and Latin American" has formulated a presentation of the gospel message, that is, for several reasons outlined by Hunter, very appropriate for communication in today's multireligious culture (1992:87).

1. God created all people for Life.

2. People, in their sin, have forfeited Life.

3. God came in Christ to offer people New Life.

4. People can receive this New Life by Turning from their sins to Christ in trust and obedience to the Community of New Life.

5. People knowing New Life are called to be faithful in all relationships.

What God requires of human beings is dependent on how God is perceived. The Old Testament reflects a period in which among the various types of sacrifices offered to God, was included human sacrifice (Judges 11:1-40). But as the Bible makes evident, as people began to grow in human awareness and understanding, the general revelation of God developed more towards God's special revelation, and humans grew in their understanding of what God truly required of God's creatures. The prophet Micah is but one of many who wrestled with this life-shaking question and received the answer to what the Lord requires:

> What shall I bring to the Lord, the God of heaven, when I come to worship him? Shall I bring the best calves to burn as offerings to him? Will the Lord be pleased if I bring him thousands of sheep or endless streams of olive oil? Shall I offer him my first-born child to pay for my sins? No, the Lord has told us what is good. What he requires of us is this: to do what is just, to show constant love, and to live in humble fellowship with our God (Micah 6:6-8).

In the life and teachings of Jesus the Christ, the only perfect and living example, we see in the flesh exactly what is pleasing and acceptable to God: a life lived in perfect trust and obedience, and in care for the poor and the oppressed.

The Islamic system of belief, like that of Judaism is one which emphasizes legalism, or commitment to a set of religious laws. Muslims believe that God demands obedience in order to hope for salvation. This differs from the Christian belief which declares:

> There is no condemnation now for those who live in union with Christ Jesus. For the law of the Spirit, which brings us life in union with Christ Jesus, has set me free from the law of sin and death. What the Law could not do, because human nature was weak, God did. He condemned sin in human nature by sending his own Son, who came with a nature like man's sinful nature, to do away with sin. God did this so that the righteous demands of the Law might be fully satisfied in us who live according to the Spirit, and not according to human nature (Romans 8:1-4).

This issue of justification by faith and all that is theologically related to this biblical truth (God's grace, atonement and incarnation, for example) is at the heart of the Christian faith and is not negotiable. As Christians, we died with Christ, and he entered into our spiritual death. That act left us free to be raised in the newness of life with Christ Jesus. The Judaic law did not work; instead, it showed us our sinfulness. Without the shedding of blood there is no forgiveness; Jesus became the means of substitutionary forgiveness through the sacrificial system. When God saw and accepted the sacrifice of Jesus, God said it was competed (finished); by belief in God's work in Jesus Christ, that we are saved by faith.

What does this mean for the Muslim? People are often burdened with shame or guilt because they are unable to keep religious demands and laws. What happens, for instance, if a Muslim misses one of the ritual prayers totally, or is late? Or if she prays at a time deemed inappropriate for a woman? George Arthur Buttrick describes how these issues were of concern to the religious Jew:

> Legal and moral elements struggled for supremacy, and in times when spiritual vision grew dim it was natural that legalism should increase its hold. Men believed that God demanded complete obedience to a system of law which tended to grow more and more complex. The burdens which religious observance laid upon men consequently became almost intolerable, and religious belief failed to provide the incentives without which so great a weight could hardly be sustained. But this was a result which inevitably followed from the corrupting effect which legalism had upon men's understanding of the nature of God (Buttrick 1954: 375).

Expanding on the apostle Paul's message to the Roman church, Buttrick further explains that while justification by grace and justification by law are aimed at gaining a new standing with God, justification by works assumes that humans can earn acceptance by our own efforts, and by virtue of merit possess the right to stand unabashed before him.

> Faith, on the other hand, is a loving trust in and willing submission to God. If we respond to him as our Father, righteous in will and loving in purpose, we commit ourselves in humility to a relationship which he makes possible, but which we could never establish by ourselves (Buttrick 1954:376).

Guided by the spirit of God, decisions as to how to proceed in ministry and witness in a religiously pluralistic society will arise out of the continuation of this two pronged model (representing the process of interaction of Muslims and Christians), and by means of the process of attending, asserting and decision making within community, as a result of theological reflection of being and doing as the people of God.

The Muslims and Jesus

As we attempt to contextualize incarnationally among Muslims, Christians must keep foremost in mind that from the Muslim perspective, Jesus is only discussed in Christian and Muslim dialogues. The reason for this is that though Jesus is revered as a prophet of God, he is superseded by the prophet Mohammad as the final revelation. Jesus's deity as the Son of God, his oneness with God, his atonement for the sins of the world and his death on the cross are denied by general Qur'anic theology.

What is affirmed in Muslim theology is that Jesus was sinless; that someone was substituted for Jesus on the cross; that the crucifixion never happened; and, that Jesus Christ was taken bodily into heaven without having died.

> . . . They declared: 'We have put to death the Messiah, Jesus the son of Mary, the apostle of God.' They did not kill him nor did they crucify him, but it (Qur'an 4:157).

"In this surah, the Arabic is not clear. The 'it' refers either to the crucifixion or to Jesus who was fabricated," states Woodberry (March, 1994). W. D. Muhammad declares what most Muslims believe: that Jesus was a sign pointing to the Prophet Mohammad.

> The Qur'an does say that Jesus was the Word from his Lord. And this is in agreement with what the Bible says of Jesus. We understand that a word means a sign; that Jesus himself was a sign.....Jesus was a sign of what God intended for man--the good life that God intended for man, and how that good life has to struggle and even be abused and rejected. It has to rise and fall. But eventually God establishes His own good time. Jesus is also a sign of that which would come in the end of the world. And we do believe that Prophet Muhammad

fulfilled that major sign that Jesus pointed to for the future of the world (1988:25).

Though Muslims love Jesus, they believe that Christianity has been misunderstood, and therefore misinterpreted. Jesus loves Muslims. Just as he loves the Samaritan (Luke 10:25), the Roman (Luke 7:2), and the Pharisee (John 3:1) and the world so much that he gave his life in order that women and men may have eternal life. Because God is a God who knows his creation, in all its particularity as well as its universality, Jesus would begin his approach to the Muslims at the point starting where he or she is. The concern is for communicating the gospel to persons who are in a different place. Muslims have the greatest respect for Jesus as Prophet, so this becomes a point for beginning a Christian witness. Though Muslims reject Christianity, this does not mean that they have rejected Christ. More than likely, they have never encountered the Jesus of the Bible.

Missional Criteria: A Basis for Decision Making

In summary, if the African-American churches are to address the religiously plural environment with a sense of faithfulness and relevancy, priorities need to be changed. The Protestant African-American churches must be willing to be revived in order to address the issues related to nominalism, which often leads to a falling way from the Christian faith. The general social and moral decline of our culture must urgently be addressed by the churches (Pannell 1993:128-134). Christian leadership needs to educate Christians concerning the challenge of Islam through the development of an appropriate and relevant contextualized theology and mission such as is presented in this study. The focus of such a mission should be a two-pronged focus: (1) toward the Nation of Islam (popular Islam) as it often becomes a stepping stone for a religious journey leading toward the American Muslim Society; (2) towards the American Muslim Society (official Islam) as it has been in its contextualization within the African-American community. In light of the contextual and missional approaches discussed in this study, the communication of the biblical Christian faith in word and deed, requires the application of the following six criteria. These criteria are based upon a primary theoretical model of African-American churches as, to borrow a phrase from Pannell, "centers of evangelism" (Pannell, 1993).

(1) A new formation of an expression of theology should be directed toward the basic theological beliefs as expressed in the universal Christian church. The churches must continually engage in a theological self-critical examination to see if the responsibility of hearing, obeying and "being" the Word of God (as a sign of God's reign) is being carried out as faithfully as it could be. Based in orthopraxis, the churches are encouraged to theologize with a view towards bringing the gospel to bear specifically upon the African-American culture and worldview. A clearer distinction should be made between contemporary morals, which reflect society's beliefs and values (which are usually anti-Christian and anti-African American), and biblical Christian beliefs and values, which reflect just, trustworthy and eternal beliefs and values.

(2) The incarnational model is essential within an environment where proclamation of the Word of God must be accompanied by signs and demonstrations of the nature and power of the Christian faith. The churches' main concern must be to live out the biblical knowledge and revelation of God, to impact Christian faith that must be lived in a context of profound social, political and racial divisiveness. Also the means and methods used to witness among Muslims must be those embodied in the One who was incarnated.

(3) There is a need for integration of new social patterns with incarnational theology. The structure and the theology cannot be separated, but must reflect a holistic understanding of life ordained and sanctioned by God. New ways of doing theology also need to be encouraged. The Christian life should not be viewed as living according to a single set of doctrinal and propositional truths, but rather be exchanged for a view that gives credence to a life of Christian growth. A theology of African-American worship that perceives worship as empowerment for the 'gathered and the scattered church' will be rooted in New Testament references

to the divine ability to continue the work of Christ (Melva Costen 1993:118). New and intentional structures for Christian community, education, and fellowship should encourage the freedom of the Word of God (living and written) to permeate every aspect of life of the total person and not be limited to spiritual or religious concerns. The intellectual needs as well as the psychological and social needs of African Americans must be meaningfully addressed as Christians seek to evaluate the authenticity of their spiritual journey.

(4)   Relevant and authentic Christian faith must emerge from the perception that Christianity is basically relegated to the private spheres of life, and must become public. The perception that Christianity is concerned only about the soul and spiritual matters must be confronted. Christian values and ethics must be brought to bear upon secularity. Christian role models must be active in every phrase of life, exemplifying an attitude that is expressed in a popular church motto "unapologetically Christian and unashamably African American." A new pattern for living and relating that makes sense to this current generation is necessary to meet the needs of the future church as it seeks to conform to what we know about living in God's kingdom.

(5)   Lay involvement must be seen as the means to empowering biblically based evangelism and mission. The entire congregation, not the few individuals who are seminary trained, must be trained, developed, nurtured and led to discover what it means to do theology in a religiously plural society, with an emphasis on Muslims and Islam. Laity must be empowered to assume a proper and responsible lifestyle that acknowledges and affirms with gladness, the Christian understanding of stewardship and witness. Theology is done best by those who are most fully involved in the life of the society. The priesthood of all believers demands that each Christian becomes active in a local missionary congregation that engages in ministry as a body of Christ, and is not simply a collection of individual members.

(6)   The use of a creation centered theology, which affirms culture, human experience, and the world as a place where God reveals Godself is the starting point

for theologizing amidst religious pluralism. By means of an Afrocentric presentation of Christianity, persons' attention will be recaptured and drawn anew to the biblical message. The creation of a Christ-centered African American requires that the ecclesiology of the church must engage in and clearly articulate a pastoral, compassionate ministry which is relevant, authentic, and honest. Dynamically equivalent biblical meanings and experiences must be communicated effectively in order to develop meaningful opportunities for theologizing, worship, liturgies, ritual and meaningful discipleship that speaks to the needs of the church of the future.

Additional Themes of Concern

Based on the foundational belief that God is concerned with the total person, Christians must also become concerned for the total person. This suggests that Protestant African-American churches must remove their primary concern away from themselves, and be concerned for people within the community who are to receive the Gospel message. By seeking to address their areas of greatest pain and suffering from our spiritual reservoir, Christians demonstrate the presence and power of God, while at the same time inviting others to embrace the same presence and power.

Economics Needs

One attraction to the Nation of Islam is that Muslims are known for supporting an Islamic economic foundation within the African-American community and for addressing the economic needs of its people. Owning and operating farms, property and businesses are all attempts to get Muslims to think and act economically from a religious foundation. One Muslim informed me that Jesus's statement to give unto Caesar that which is Caesar's and unto God that which is God's, is a demonstration that all of life is not under the authority of God. An Islamic approach to economic development does exist according to the Qur'an, and the current state of the economic crisis in this country, particularly in the majority of the African-American communities, is causing some people to see and inquire into what the Muslims are offering. Only in recent years have the African-American churches begun to perceive the great need to develop a Christian economic attitude. The result has been in programs initiated by the churches' commitment to stewardship and social power.

Racial Concerns

While there appears to be within the North American setting a hesitancy to address issues related to race and ethnicity, there is within African Americans the desire for freedom from racism and discrimination and the desire to be treated totally human--that is to be judged and evaluated on the basis of being human instead of the continuous and constant struggle to be treated as an equal. The entire church must address these issues if it is to impact the African-American community significantly.

Urban Models of Authentic Approaches

Finally, in examining the current contextualization models that form the background development for African-American Christian theology, the implications for Christian contextualization are enhanced through the continued use of the anthropological methodology. The anthropological model offers great insight as a model that affirms that God's revelation is found within the complexity of culture and can be very useful when it is remembered that this is a means, and not the end. Its strength is that it testifies to the fact that it regards human reality with dignity, seriousness and intentionality. It starts where people are, rather than imposing concerns from other contexts. As stated in *Inculturating North American Theology*, there is a

> . . . concern with the affective and intuitive dimensions of religious experience that portray the human person as a self-defining process accountable not only to others for the consequences of personal choice, but also to God for the kind of person each individual chooses to become (Gelpi 1988).

What follows are three significant models that are proving to be very promising in reaching non-Christians. It should be stated that W. D. Mohammad is strongly against the second approach which emphasizes biblical theology, and especially Afrocentricity, with its belief in a divine human (Jesus the Christ). This is one of his primary concerns of Islamic apologetics.

An Exile Strategy of Education

Joseph Crockett (1991) has suggested what is known as the "exile strategy of education" for African Americans. The theme of the exile is used to interpret the longing for harmony in life, allowing the whole scripture to be viewed in terms of "assembly and dispersion, relatedness and estrangement, enjoyment and brokenness" (1991:16). The process of the exile strategy is fourfold, and the steps include:

(1)   Acknowledging the Condition: Presents information from the African-American experience. The intent is to make persons aware of the harmony or disharmony, wholeness or brokenness that exist.

(2)   Fashioning the Heart: Provides opportunity for persons to initiate the conduct that leads toward harmony with God and all of creation. This segment is grounded in the belief that persons my come to know God, become encouraged to live on behalf of God, and be equipped to fill their lives with meaning by the practices of faithful living.

(3)   Previewing and Expanding the Horizon: Places before the learner the scripture so that is may be in dialogue with the African-American experience or tradition. The expectation is that the scripture will support and/or challenge the learner's moral and ethical conduct and actions.

(4)   Reflecting: Allows learners to think about their conduct in relation to all of life. This segment adds the processes of the intellect to the task of making meaning (1991:18).

Afrocentric Worship and Mission

A second contextual approach involves the development of totally Afrocentric worship and ministries. The Rev. Albert Cleage, founder of the Shrine of the Black Madonna, has led an Africentric Christian church movement that appears to have made the "transition from a dependence on the white determined status quo to a true dependence on the loyalty of the Black community and a commitment to serve them," according to the editors of *The Black Church in America* (1971:11). This movement has encouraged others of both the Protestant and Catholic traditions, including such churches as former Catholic Father Stallings' Imani Temple (Washington, D.C.). Another distinctive style of Africentricity is found at the Trinity United Church of Christ (Chicago), under the leadership of Jeremiah Wright and his ministerial staff.

Biblical Recontextualization

A third approach is by means of emphasis on the African presence in the Bible through a process called "biblical recontextualization." In "The Bible, Re-Contextualization, and the Black Religious Experience," Cain H. Felder has described the process as

> The process of 're-construction' helps us gain access to this brave new world. It is a world which, frankly, was rather favorable predisposed to Black people. As evidence, consider only Acts 2:1, where Luke mentions among the prophets and teachers of Antioch Simeon, who was called Niger (i.e., 'the Black man') in an apparent Latinism. It was a world that was indebted to the Egyptian doctrine of salvation, taking seriously the glorious afterlife (I Cor.15:12-58, Phil. 3:12-16) (Felder 1989:165).

This process suggested by Felder, a New Testament scholar, would not result in a romanticizing of the African-American worldview, but rather would result in a re-discovery of some essential features of the Black religious experience in Africa including, but not limited to African Traditional Religions, and in so doing, enter a new dialogue of liberation and spirituality as found in the Bible (Felder 1989:165). Both of these methodologies provide opportunities for the African-American learner, especially ones whose contextual agenda is centered toward what it is like to be a "sojourner in this foreign land"--to discover what is biblically important (attitudes and behavior) within a religiously plural environment.

In an unpublished paper by Fred Jenkins at the Zwemer Institute is presented a biblical model for approaching Muslims. It was written at a time early in the transitional stage from Black Muslims to American Muslims when Muslim African

Americans identified themselves as Bilalians, named after the first muezzin and friend of the prophet Mohammad who was an Ethiopian. Jenkins suggests that for ministry to present-day Bilalians, the most promising passage appears to be the Ethiopian eunuch in Acts, chapter eight. The main points he emphasizes are five: (1) a willingness to go where a Bilalian may be found; (2) a sensitivity to the Holy Spirit and patience, followed by a willingness to listen to ascertain felt needs; (3) an offer of assistance as a Scripture scholar; (4) wait for an invitation to explain their meaning; and (5) a desire to meet the Bilalian where he is, then to teach him the truth about Jesus.

Muslims in the United States

**An estimated 5 million Muslims--or about 2% of the
total U. S. population--live in the United States.
A look at their ethnic background:**

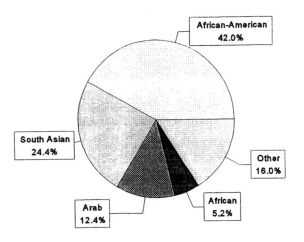

Source: World Almanac; American Muslim Council

QUESTIONNAIRE
LISTENING TO CHRISTIANS

RELIGIOUS PLURALISM
IN THE AFRICAN-AMERICAN COMMUNITY

Q-1. Which one of the following words best describes you?

  _32_ Pastor   _06_ Deacon   _22_ Church member

  _08_ Elder   _00_ Bishop   _08_ Church staff

  _04_ Other _____

Q-2. Which one of the following words best describes your church?

  _20_ Pentecostal   _00_ Evangelical   _28_ Mainline

  _06_ Liberal   _02_ Charismatic   _16_ Conservative

  _08_ Non-denominational   _04_ Other (which?) _____

Q-3. Please check your age group:

  _08_ 12-19   _12_ 20-29   _14_ 30-39

  _14_ 40-49   _12_ 50-59   _18_ 60-69 _02_ 70 +

Q-4. Are you: _32_ male   _48_ female

Q-5. According to the latest information, there are more than 1500 different religious groups in the United States. Which of the following non-Christian religious groups are most active in the African-American community where you live or worship? (Check three)

_8_	Bahai's	_72_	Jehovah Witnesses
_52_	Nation of Islam	_20_	Orthodox (Sunni) Muslims
___	Yahweh Ben Yahweh followers		
___	Ethiopian Jews	_06_	Buddhism
___	Other _____		

Please circle the ONE religious group listed above which threatens or seeks to undermine the Christian belief and practice MOST.   Jehovah Witnesses

Q-6.   How should Christians primarily relate to followers of other religions? (Check one only.)

   _14_   Join them in efforts to help feed the hungry and work for justice

   _30_   Seek to share the gospel with them whenever possible

   _07_   Seek to convince them that Christianity is the true religion

   _21_   Seek to understand their beliefs and practices

   _08_   I don't know.

   _00_   Other _____

Q-7.   Check only one choice. Should your church take part in interdenominational events with other Christians, in order to:

   _53_   Affirm that we are all part of the one Body of Christ.

   _19_   More effectively respond to human needs.

   _06_   Present a united front in evangelism.

   _00_   No, we should not participate.

   _02_   I don't know.

Q-8. Which are the two most biblically faithful ways for Christians today to live with religious diversity and pluralism, so that it enhances the Church rather than fragment it? (Choose two.)

  _32_   Respond to human needs

  _12_   Participate in religious dialogues with others

  _42_   Clearly proclaim the gospel in the community in relevant ways

  _00_   Dismiss all other religions as unimportant and of Satan

  _06_   Seek to find if the biblical God is present in other religions

  _16_   Emphasize that Christians worship One God only

  _32_   Demonstrate what it means to live in the Kingdom of God

Q-9. Which two Muslim groups or movements are you MOST familiar with? (Choose two.)

  ___   Hanafi   _2_   Moors   _78_   Nation of Islam

  _46_   Orthodox   _15_   American Muslim Society

  ___   Sunni

Please circle the above Muslim group which is most active in the community in which you live or worship. Nation of Islam

Q-10. In general, do you hold a positive or negative opinion of orthodox African-American Muslims?

  _38_   Positive   _24_   Neither positive or negative

  _12_   Negative   _06_   I don't know any Muslims.

Q-11. The following chart recently appeared in the *U.S. Today* newspaper. Read what it written here, and reflect on it. (Please refer to the pie chart in Appendix A.)

According to this information <u>42.0% of all orthodox Muslims in the U.S. are African Americans.</u> (Orthodox Islam is also known as the American Muslim Society and Sunni Islam.) As high as 90% of the new converts to Islam were African Americans.

Prior to receiving this questionnaire, does the high percentage of African Americans choosing to worship in orthodox Islam come as a surprise to you?

   _16_   Yes, definitely   _42_ No   _22_   Somewhat

Why or why not? (Please write your answer clearly here.)

Q-12. Do you think Christians should be concerned about the fact that Islam has drawn Christians away from a personal commitment to the biblical God as revealed in Jesus Christ?

   _64_   Yes, definitely   _02_   Not sure

   _04_   Yes, probably   _00_   No, probably not

   _10_   No, definitely not, because Muslims and Christians worship the same God.

Q-13. Malcolm X was first a member of the Nation of Islam, and later he converted to orthodox Islam. Were you aware of this?

   _64_   Yes   _16_   No

Do you think that the current popularity in Malcolm X among the youth reflects <u>any</u> interest in his religion journey also?

   _39_   No   _35_   Yes

Q-14. Do you know personally of someone who has converted to orthodox Islam?

   _46_   Yes   _33_   No

Was this person a _08_ female or _36_ male? (Check one.)

What was/is your relationship to this person?

   _16_   Family member/relative   _10_   Friend

   _02_   Co-worker or fellow student   _13_   Acquaintance

__03__ Other (identify) ____2 church members, 1 boss____

Q-15. Which reasoning or argument is most frequently used by Muslims when they share their faith with others? (Check two only.)

__30__ The Bible is not the true Word of God.

__24__ Deny the divinity of Jesus

__44__ Christianity is the religion of White people.

__02__ It's impossible to live as Jesus taught in today's world.

__14__ Denominations are evidence of Christianity's contradictions.

__18__ I don't know.

Q-16. When a Muslim says that the Christian church represents more of a barrier to African-American progress than Islam does, what do you think that Muslim (usually a former Christian) means? Please write your answer clearly here.

Q-17. Orthodox Islam, as indicated in the chart above (see Q-11.) is growing fast among African-American converts. What factors do you think BEST account for or contribute to this situation? (Choose four.)

__42__ Christianity is thought to be no longer relevant.

__16__ Islam is considered as a viable spiritual option.

__58__ The suffering of African Americans related to Christianity and racism

__04__ Muslms are getting help from Muslims overseas.

__30__ The Muslims have schools, centers, mosques, bookstores, worship in homes, etc. in the local community.

__40__ The average Christian is weak in his/her faith in public.

__26__ Muslims communicate their faith better than Christians.

__36__ Christianity is seen as the White people's religion and Islam is seen as the Black people's religion.

__30__ Muslims are more serious and aggressive in sharing their faith.

__18__ Christians are viewed as worshipping Jesus and not God.

__18__ Christians don't allow the Holy Spirit to direct them.

__26__ Muslims practice spiritual and physical discipline daily.

Which concerns listed directly above must Christians today address strategically for the well being of the future Christian generations of Los Angeles County? Please circle the three most crucial.

1st   The suffering related to racism and Christianity

2nd   Christianity no longer relevant

3rd   Average Christian weak in his/her faith

Q-18. In general, what is your opinion of the Church's ability (leadership/resources/knowledge) to meet the challenge of Islam?

__17__ Very good   __23__ Good   __25__ Not so good

__11__ Poor   __04__ Dont' know

What will it take to increase the church's ability to meet this challenge? Write your answer clearly here:

Q-19. In general, what is your opinion of the Church's willingness (desire/motive/hope) to meet the challenge of Islam?

__03__ Very good   __19__ Good   __22__ Not so good

__16__ Poor   __20__ Don't know

What will it take to increase the Church's willingness to meet this challenge? Write your answer clearly here:

Q-20. How should Christians primarily express their concern for people who are drawn to Islam and other religions, and away from a personal commitment to the biblical God as revealed in Jesus Christ? (Check three only.)

__36__ Continue to invite them to Christ-centered worship services.

_16_ Concentrate on developing a ministry to Muslims

_22_ Confront them boldly and unapologetically with the Bible.

_30_ For pastors to teach and preach essential Christianity.

_28_ Emphasize the African people in the Bible.

_62_ To intentionally live by biblical values and moral daily.

_36_ Emphasize God as a Spirit and not as a person.

_03_ Other (write here) _New models of ministry need to be developed, genuine spirit of evangelism, continued acceptance and love in case they want to return to the church_

APPENDIX C

THE INFORMATIONAL NEEDS REGARDING MUSLIMS

I.   The Perceived Nature And Role of Religion

1.1   Who is a Muslim?
1.2   Why are you a Muslim?
1.3   How long have you been a Muslim? (What is your faith journey?)
1.4   What attracted you to Islam?
1.5   What is good about being a Muslim?
1.6   What is difficult about being a Muslim?
1.7   Why is it important to come to the mosque?

2.1   What is it important to know about God as a Muslim?
2.2   What activities do you participate in as a result of your faith?
2.3   How is your faith expressed in your personal life?
2.4   What is the most important thing you do as a Muslim?
2.5   What are your current religious activities?
2.6   What is meant by the Arabic word "daw'ah?"
2.7   What is the most important part of your spirit life?
2.8   How do you share you faith with others?
2.9   How does your mosque share its faith in the community?
2.10 What does it mean to be obedient to God?

II.   Current Perception About Christians

3.1   Do you know any Christians? How do you know them?
3.2   Which Christian leaders do you respect?
3.3   Do Christians and Muslims worship the same God?
3.4   What are the differences is there are any?
3.5   What is your opinion of Christianity?
3.6   What do you think is positive about being a Christian?
3.7   What do you think is difficult about being a Christian?
3.8   What do you want Christians to understand about Islam?

III.   <u>Worldview Needs of African-American People</u>

4.1   What are the most important needs facing African Americans today?
4.2   What are the solutions?
4.3   What deep needs does Islam satisfy for you?
4.4   Are there deep felt needs that Islam satisfies for other people?
4.5   What benefits does Islam offer to the African American community?
4.6   How do people in this community learn about Muslims?
4.7   What do Muslims contribute to the community?
4.8   Why is being a Muslim important to you?
4.9   How does being a Muslim help you to see life differently?
4.10   What is the Muslim's attitude toward life?

APPENDIX D

TAXONOMIC ANALYSIS OF THE KINDS OF PRACTICES
IN WHICH MUSLIMS ENGAGE

Worship → → →	*Shahada* *Jihad* (spiritual striving) Daily cleansing rituals Daily prayer rituals Almsgiving/charity Annual: *Ramadan & Id al-Fitr* *Hajj* (if possible)
Nurture → → →	*Jama'a* Week-day classes Arabic lessons Islamic history education Retreats Fundraising activities Sunday Islamic school Sunday forums/lectures Radio programs Publications/publishers Activities for men/women/youth Children
Daw'ah → → →	Beginners/orientation class Special publications Bookstores Prison outreach University outreach branches Islamic education classes Community lectures

Community Involvement	→ → →	Operate elementary schools Ecumenical involvement Islamic education Cultural education Political education Community representation Economic ventures (products and property) Conventions

International Activities	→ → →	University scholarships abroad
		Missionaries sent to the USA
		Mosque being built with
		    assistance from abroad
		Literature from abroad
		    disseminated
		International lecturers
		International spiritual leaders
		Financial support of international
		    Islamic work
		International Muslims'
		political advocacy

GLOSSARY

Adhan	The Islamic call to prayer
Allah	The Arabic word for God
Hajj	Pilgrimage to Mecca
Id al-Fitr	Commemorates the breaking of fast when *Ramadan* has ended
Islam	Submission (as well as containing the idea of peace)
Jama'a	Congregational prayer held on Friday
Jihad	Striving in the cause of God
Mujjaddid	Reformer
Niyyah	The worship intention
Ramadan	Observance of the revelation of the Qur'an to Muhammad
Salat	The ritual or prescribed Muslim prayer
Sawm	The Islamic practice of fasting during the month of Ramadan
Shahadah	The declaration of Islamic faith
Shirk	To associate partners with God
Tasawwuf	The path of sufism, a branch of Islam
Wuduu	Act of purification
Zakat	Obligatory almsgiving or charity

BIBLIOGRAPHY

Adams, P. L. Review of *They Came Before Columbus*, by Ivan Van Sertima. *Atlantic Monthly* 239 (1977): 99.

Ajijola, Alhaj D. *The Myth of the Cross.* Lahore, Pakistan: Islamic Publication, Ltd., 1975.

Alexander, Paul. "Troops in Somalia Embrace Islam," *Pasadena Star*, 28 May 1993.

American Bible Society. *Good News Bible* (Today's English Version). New York: American Bible Society, 1976.

Ansari, Zafar Ishaq. "W. D. Muhammad: The Making of a 'Black Muslim' Leader, (1933-1961)," *American Journal of Islamic Social Sciences*, 1985.

Asante, Molefi K., and Mark T. Mattson. *The Historical and Cultural Atlas of African Americans.* New York: Macmillan, 1992.

Ba-Yuns, Ilyas. *Muslims in North America: Problems and Prospects.* Plainsfield, IN: The Muslim Students Association of the United States and Canada, 1977.

Bellah, Robert N., and others. *Habits of the Heart: Individualism and Commitment in American Life.* New York: Harper & Row, 1985.

Benjamin, Lois. *The Black Elite: Facing the Color Line in the Twilight of the Twentieth Century.* Chicago: Nelson-Hall, 1991.

Bennett, Clinton. "Victorian Images of Islam," *International Bulletin of Missionary Research* (July 1991).

Bennett, Lerone, Jr. *Before the Mayflower: A History of the Negro in America: 1619-1964.* Baltimore: Penguin Books, 1969.

Bevans, Stephen B. "Doing Theology in North America: A Counter-Cultural Model?" In *The Gospel and Our Culture* (Holland: Western Theological Seminary, 1993).

290

_____. *Models of Contextual Theology*. Maryknoll, NY: Orbis Books, 1992.

Birchett, Colleen, ed. *Biblical Strategies for a Community in Crisis: What African Americans Can Do*. Chicago: Urban Ministries, 1992.

Blassingame, John W. *Slave Testimony: Two Centuries of Letters, Speeches, Interviews, and Autobiographies*. Baton Rouge: Louisiana State University Press, 1977.

Bosch, David J. "Toward a New Paradigm of Mission." In *Mission in the Nineteen Nineties*. Grand Rapids: Wm. B. Eerdmans, 1991.

Buttrick, George Arthur, ed. "The Epistle to the Romans." *The Interpreter's Bible*. New York: Abingdon Press, 1954.

California Institute of Public Affairs. *Ethnic Groups in California: A Guide to Organization and Resources*. 2d ed. Claremont: By the Author, 1988.

Campbell, Bebe Moore. "Finding the Faith," *Essence*, December 1992.

Carey, Wilfred and Martin Kilson, eds. *The African Reader: Independent Africa*. New York: Vintage, 1970.

Cone, James H. *Martin and Malcolm and America: A Dream or a Nightmare*. Maryknoll: Orbis Books, 1993.

_____. *Speaking the Truth: Ecumenism, Liberation and Black Theology*. Grand Rapids: Wm. B. Eerdmans, 1986.

Copher, Charles B. "Three Thousand Years of Biblical Interpretation with Reference to Black Peoples." In *African American Religious Studies*, ed. Gayraud S. Wilmore, 105-128. Durham: Duke University Press, 1989.

Costen, James H. "Muffled Mandates." Lecture II, Austin Presbyterian Seminary, October 24, 1989.

_____. Missionary Influences." Lecture III, Austin Presbyterian Seminary, October 25, 1989.

Costen, Melva Wilson. *African American Christian Worship*. Nashville: Abingdon Press, 1993.

Cragg, Kenneth. *The Call of the Minaret*. 2d ed. Maryknoll, NY: Orbis Books, 1985.

_____. *The House of Islam*. Belmont, CA: Dickerson Publishing Company, 1969.

_____. "The Riddle of Man and the Silence of God: A Christian Perception of Muslim Response." *International Bulletin of Missionary Research*, October 1993.

Crockett, Joseph V. *Teaching Scripture from an African-American Perspective*. Nashville: Discipleship Resources, 1991.

Cruz, Virgil and Jean Cooley. *Breaking Down the Walls: Responding to the Racism That Divides Us*. Louisville: Presbyterian Church (USA) Peacemaking Program, 1992.

Dawood, N. J., tr. *The Koran*. New York: Penguin Books, 1990.

Denny, Frederick Mathewson. *An Introduction to Islam*. New York: Macmillan, 1985.

Dixon, Rita. *Evangelism in the African-American Experience*. Unpublished paper, October 1992.

Donovan, Vincent. *Christianity Rediscovered*. Maryknoll, NY: Orbis Books, 1982.

DuBois, W. E. B. Review of *Africa and the Discovery of America*, Vol. I, by Leo Wiener. *The Nation* 111 (September 25,1920): 350-352.

Ela, Jean-Marc. *My Faith As an African*. Maryknoll, NY: Orbis Books, 1990.

Ellis, Carl F., Jr. *Beyond Liberation: The Gospel in the Black American Experience*. Downers Grove, IL: InterVarsity Press, 1983.

Esposito, John. *Voices of Resurgent Islam*. New York: Oxford University Press, 1983.

Essien-Udom, E. U. *Black Nationalism: A Search for an Identity in America*. Chicago: University of Chicago Press, 1963.

Felder, Cain H. "The Bible, Re-Contextualization and the Black Religious Experience." In *African American Religious Studies: An Interdisciplinary Anthology*, ed. Gayraud S. Wilmore, 155-171. Durham: Duke University Press, 1989.

Fleming, Bruce C. E. *Contextualization of Theology: An Evangelical Assessment.* Pasadena, CA: William Carey Library, 1980.

Fortosis, Steve. "A Developmental Model for Stages of Growth in Christian Formation." *The Journal of the Religious Education Association and Association of Professors and Researchers in Religious Education* (Spring 1992).

Gehman, Henry Snyder, ed. *The New Westminster Dictionary of the Bible.* Philadelphia: Westminster Press, 1970.

Gelpi, Donald L. *Inculturating North American Theology: An Experiment in Foundational Method.* Atlanta: Scholars Press, 1988.

Gerloff, Roswith I. H. *A Plea for British Black Theologies: The Black Church Movement in Britain in Its Transatlantic, Cultural and Theological Interaction.* Frankfurt, Germany: Peter Lang, 1992.

Gilliland, Dean S. "Contextual Theology As Incarnational Mission." In *The Word Among Us: Contextualizing Theology for Mission Today.* Dallas: Word Publishing Co., 1989.

Gite, Lloyd. "The New Agenda of the Black Church: Economic Development for Black America." *Black Enterprise* (December 1993).

Grant, Jacquelyn. "Womanist Theology: Black Women's Experience As a Source for Doing Theology, with Special Reference to Christology." In *African American Religious Studies*, ed. Gayraud S. Wilmore, 208-227. Durham: Duke University Press, 1989.

Greenway, Roger S. *Discipling the City: A Comprehensive Approach to Urban Mission.* Grand Rapids: Baker Book House, 1992.

Gudel, Joseph. "Islam's Worldwide Revival." *Forward* (Fall 1985).

Haddad, Yvonne. "The Muslim Experience in the United States." *The Link* 22 (September/October 1979): 1-3.

Haddad, Yvonne Yazbeck. "Muslims in the United States." In *Islam: The Religious and Political Life of a World Community*, ed. Marjorie Kelly, 258-274. New York: Praeger, 1984.

Haddad, Yvonne, Byron Haines, and Ellison Findly. *The Islamic Impact*. Syracuse: Syracuse University Press, 1984.

Haddad, Yvonne, and Adair T. Lummis. *Islamic Values in the U.S.: A Comparative Study*. New York: Oxford Press, 1987.

Haines, Byron, and Frank Cooley. *Christians and Muslims Together: An Exploration by Presbyterians*. Philadelphia: The Geneva Press, 1987.

Haneef, Suzanne. *What Everyone Should Know About Islam and Muslims*. Chicago: Kazi Publications, 1979.

Hedaithy, Mesaid Ibrahim. *New Muslims in America: A Study of Religious Conversion from Christianity to Islam*. Ann Arbor, MI: University Microfilms International, 1985.

Hedland, Thomas, Kenneth Pike and Marvin Harris, eds. *Emic and Etics: The Insider-Outsider Debate*. Frontiers of Anthropology, vol. 7. Beverly Hills: SAGE Publishers, 1990.

Heim, Mark. *Is Christ the Only Way?: Christian Faith in a Pluralistic World*. Valley Forge, PA: Judson Press, 1985.

Hesselgrave, David J., and Edward Rommen. *Contextualization: Meanings, Methods and Model*. Grand Rapids: Baker Book House, 1989.

Hiebert, Paul. "World View and World View Change." Lecture notes. Pasadena: Fuller Theological Seminary, School of World Mission, Fall Semester 1988.

Hiskett, Mervyn. *The Development of Islam in West Africa*. London: Longman, 1984.

Hood, Robert. *Must God Remain Greek? Afro Cultures and God-Talk*. Minneapolis: Fortress Press, 1990.

Hunter, George C. III. *How to Reach Secular People*. Nashville: Abingdon Press, 1992.

Iqbal, Muhammad. *The Achievement of Love: The Spiritual Dimension of Islam*. Canada: Editions Islamiques. 1987.

"Islam in America: Time of Opportunity and Trial?" *The Los Angeles Times*, 25 January 1991.

Islamic Center of Southern California. "First Muslim 'Pow Wow' Held." *The Minaret* (July/August 1993).

Jones, Lawrence. "The Black Church in America." *Progressions: An Occasional Report*. Indianapolis: The Lilly Foundation, 1992.

Jones, William R. *Is God a White Racist?* Garden City, NY: Doubleday/Anchor, 1973.

Joyce, Raymond H. "Islam Is Here in North America." *The Link* (December 1977).

Kane, J. Herbert. *Understanding Christian Missions*. Grand Rapids: Baker Book House, 1978.

Karenga, Maulana. "Black Religion." In *African American Religious Studies: An Interdisciplinary Anthology*, ed. Gayraud S. Wilmore, 271-300. Durham: Duke University Press, 1989.

Kearney, Michael. *World View*. Novato, CA: Chadler and Sharp, 1984.

Kelly, Marjorie, ed. *Islam: The Religious and Political Life of a World Community*. New York: Praeger, 1984.

Kraft, Charles H. *Christianity in Culture: A Study in Dynamic Biblical Theologizing in Cross Cultural Perspective*. New York: Orbis Books, 1979.

Kritzeck, James, and William Lewis, eds. *Islam in Africa*. New York: Van Nostrand-Reinhold, 1969.

Ladd, George Eldon. *The Gospel of the Kingdom: Scriptural Studies in the Kingdom of God*. Grand Rapids: Wm. B. Eerdmans, 1987.

Latourette, Kenneth Scott. *A History of Christianity*. Vol. I: To A.D. 1500. New York: Harper and Row, 1975.

Laue, James H. "A Contemporary Revitalization Movement in American Race Relations: The Black Muslims." In *The Black Church in America*, ed. Hart M. Nelsen. New York: Basic Books, 1971.

Lee, Martha. *The Nation of Islam: An American Millernarian Movement*. Lampeter: The Edwin Mellin Press, 1988.

Lilly Foundation. "The Black Church in America." In *Progressions: An Occasional Report*. Indianapolis: By the Author, 1992.

Lincoln, C. Eric. *The Black Muslims in America.* Rev. ed. New York: Kayode Publications, 1991.

_____. "The Muslim Mission in the Context of American Social History." In *African American Religious Studies: An Interdisciplinary Anthology*, ed. Gayraud S. Wilmore, 340-356. Durham: Duke University Press, 1989.

Lincoln, C. Eric and Lawrence H. Mamiya. *The Black Church in the African American Experience*. Durham: Duke University Press, 1990.

Lovell, Emily Kalled. "Islam in the United States: Past and Present." In *The Muslim Community in North America*. Alberta: University of Alberta, 1983.

Luzbetak, Louis J. *The Church and Cultures: New Perspectives in Missiological Anthropology*. Maryknoll, NY: Orbis Books, 1991.

Mamiya, Lawrence. "The Black Church and the Poor." *The Auburn News* (Spring 1992).

Marsh, Clinton Ernest. "The World Community of Islam in the West: From Black Muslims to Muslims (1931-1977)," Ph.D. diss., Syracuse University, 1977.

Martin, Sandy. Review of *King and Interfaith Dialogue. The Journal of Religious Thought* 48 (Winter 1991/Spring 1992).

Mbiti, John S. *African Religions and Philosophy*. London: Heinemann, 1971.

McClung, L. Grant, Jr. "Theology and Strategy of Pentecostal Missions." *International Bulletin of Missionary Research* (January 1988).

McFadden-Preston, Claudette. "The Rhetoric of Minister Louis Farrakhan: A Pluralistic Approach," Ph.D. diss., Ohio State University, 1987.

Meier, August. *Negro Thought in America: 1880-1915*. Ann Arbor: University of Michigan, 1988.

Melton, J. Gordon, ed. *The Encyclopedia of American Religions*. Detroit: Gale Research Co., 1985.

Mitchell, Henry H. *Black Belief: Folk Beliefs of Blacks in America and West Africa*. New York: Harper and Row, 1975.

Morris, 'Abdul-Qadir. Personal Letter to Author. Inglewood, CA: 14 April 1992.

_____. Personal Letter to Author. Inglewood, CA: 1 June 1992.

Mott, Stephen Charles. *Biblical Ethics and Social Change*. New York: Oxford Press, 1982.

Muck, Terry C. "Religious Studies and Theological Education." *Insights* (Fall 1991): 5-16.

Muhammad, Elijah. *The Fall of America*. Newport: National Newport Publications, 1973.

Muhammad, W. Deen. *An African American Genesis*. Chicago: Zakat Publications, 1986.

_____. *Al-Islam: Unity and Leadership*. Chicago: The Sense Maker, 1991.

_____. *As the Light Shineth from the East*. Chicago: WDM Publications, 1980.

_____. "Education and Sister Clara Muhammad Schools." *The Muslim Journal*, 21 November 1993.

_____. "Farrakhan's Message Will Not Help Blacks." *Los Angeles Sentinel*, 1993.

_____. *Focus on Al-Islam*. Chicago: Zakat Publications, 1988.

_____. *Religion on the Line*. Chicago: WDM Publications, 1983.

Muldrow, William F. "Introduction." *Church and Society* (May/June 1990): 1-2.

Murphy, Kim. "Islam Rising: A World Report." *The Los Angeles Times*, 6 April 1993.

Musk, Bill. *The Unseen Face of Islam: Sharing the Gospel with Ordinary Muslims*. Great Britain: MARC, 1992.

"Muslims: Isolated in U. S. Culture." *The Los Angeles Times*, 24 January 1991.

Nazeer, Yussuf. *Islam and Black Muslim Roots in Azania*. Johannesburg: African-Islam Research Foundation, 1986.

Newbigin, Lesslie. *The Gospel in a Pluralistic Society*. Grand Rapids: Wm. B. Eerdmans, 1989.

Osman, Fathi. "Islam and Other Religions." *The Minaret* (July/August 1993).

Padilla, C. Rene. *Mission Between the Times: Essays on the Kingdom*. Grand Rapids: Wm. B. Eerdmans, 1985.

Pannell, William. *The Coming Race Wars: A Cry for Reconciliation*. Grand Rapids: Zondervan, 1993.

_____. *Evangelism from the Bottom Up*. Grand Rapids: Zondervan, 1992.

Pearstone, Zeena. *Ethnic Los Angeles*. Beverly Hills: Hillcrest Press, 1990.

Pelto, Pertti J., and Gretel H. Pelto. *Anthropological Research: The Structure of Inquiry*. Cambridge: University Press, 1993.

Pemberton, Prentiss, and Daniel Rush Finn. *Toward a Christian Economic Ethnic: Stewardship and Social Power*. Minneapolis: Winston Press, Inc., 1985.

Peterson, Michael, William Hasker, Bruce Reichenbach, and David Basinger. *Reason and Religious Belief: An Introduction to the Philosophy of Religion*. New York: Oxford Press, 1991.

Pierson, Paul E. "Class Syllabus" for Historical Development of the Christian Movement. Pasadena: Fuller Theological Seminary, School of World Mission, 1988.

Placher, William C. *Unapologetic Theology: A Christian Voice in a Pluralistic Conversation*. Louisville: Westminster/John Knox Press, 1989.

Posten, Larry. "Islamic Daw'ah in North America and the Dynamic of Conversion to Islam in Western Societies. " Ph.D. diss., Northwestern University, 1988.

Qutb, Syyid. *Milestones*. Delhi: Markazi Maktaba Islami, 1991.

Raboteau, Albert J. *Slave Religion: The Invisible Institution in the Antebellum South*. New York: Oxford University Press, 1978.

Reid, Stephen Breck. "You Can Keep Your Mouth Open, but Don't Swallow Any Flies: The Bible and Religious Pluralism." *Insights* 107 (Fall 1991): 31-35.

Sachs, Moshe Y., ed. *Encyclopedia of the States*. New Jersey: Worldmark, 1986.

Sanneh, Lamin O. "Christian Experience of Islamic Daw'ah, with Particular Reference to Africa." *International Review of Mission* 65 (October 1976): 410-426.

_____. "Muhammad, Prophet of Islam, and Jesus Christ, Image of God: A Personal Testimony." *International Bulletin of Missionary Research* (October 1984): 169-174.

Schlorff, Samuel. "Muslim Ideology and Christian Apologetics." *Missiology: An International Review* (April 1993).

Schreiter, Robert J. *Constructing Local Theologies*. Maryknoll, NY: Orbis Books, 1985.

Sernett, Milton C. *Afro-American Religious History: A Documentary Witness*. Durham: Duke University Press, 1985.

Shaw, Daniel R. *Transculturation: The Cultural Factor in Translation and Other Communication Tasks*. Pasadena: William Carey Library, 1988.

Shenk, Calvin. "The Demise of the Church in North America and Nubia and Its Survival in Egypt and Ethiopia; A Question of Contextualization?" *Missiology: An International Review* (April 1993).

Shu'aib, Tajuddin. *The Prescribed Prayer Made Simple*. Los Angeles: Daw'ah Enterprises, 1983.

Shulman, Albert. *The Religious Heritage of America*. San Diego: A. S. Barnes, 1981.

Siddiqi, Muhammad Iqbal. *Ninety-Nine Names of Allah*. Pakistan: Kazi Publications, 1991.

Sow, Fatou. "Muslim Families in Contemporary Black Africa." *Current Anthropology* (December 1985).

Sowell, Thomas. *Ethnic America: A History*. New York: HarperCollins, 1981.

Speight, R. Marston. *God Is One: The Way of Islam*. New York: Friendship Press, 1986.

Spradley, James. *The Ethnographic Interview*. Fort Worth: Harcourt Brace Jovanovich College Publishers, 1979.

Swann, Darius L. Personal Note to Author. Atlanta: February 1994.

Tapia, Andres. "The Myth of Racial Progress." *Christianity Today*, 4 October, 1993.

Thernstrom, Stephen, ed. *Harvard Encyclopedia of American Ethnic Groups*. Cambridge: Harvard University Press, 1980.

Tienou, Tite. "Themes in African Theology of Mission." In *The Good News of the Kingdom*. Maryknoll, NY: Orbis Books, 1993.

Tingle, Donald S. *Islam and Christianity*. Downers Grove, IL: InterVarsity Press, 1985.

Tonna, Benjamin. *A Gospel for the Cities*. Maryknoll, NY: Orbis Books, 1985.

Tracy, David. *Blessed Rage for Order*. New York: Seabury, 1979.

Trimingham, J. Spencer. *Islam in East Africa*. Oxford: Clarendon Press, 1964.

Turner, Harold. *Bibliography of New Religious Movements in Primal Societies*. Vol. 6. New York: Macmillan, 1992.

Tutu, Desmond. "The Role of the People of God in the Divine Enterprise." In *Mission in the Nineteen Nineties*. Grand Rapids: Wm. B. Eerdmans, 1991.

Ujvarosy, Helen, ed. *Signs of the Kingdom in the Secular City*. Chicago: Covenant Press, 1984.

Van Engen, Charles. *God's Missionary People: Rethinking the Purpose of the Local Church*. Grand Rapids: Baker Book House, 1991.

Van Sertima, Ivan. *They Came Before Columbus*. New York: Random House, 1977.

Walsh, Brian J., and J. Richard Middleton. *Transforming Vision; Shaping a Christian Worldview*. Chicago: InterVarsity Press, 1984.

Waters, Maxine. "Malcolm X". *Newsweek*, 16 November 1992.

Watzlawick, Paul, and John Weakland. *Change: Principles of Problem Formation and Problem Resolution*. New York: W. W. Norton and Company.

Waugh, Earle H., Baha Abu-Laban, and Regula B. Qureshi, eds. *The Muslim Community in North America*. Alberta: University of Alberta Press.

White, Joseph L., and Thomas A. Parham. *The Psychology of Blacks: An African American Perspective*. Englewood Cliffs, NJ: Prentice-Hall, 1990.

Whitefurst, James Emerson. "The Mainstreaming of the Black Muslims: Healing the Hate." *The Christian Century*, 27 February 1980.

Whitehead, James D., and Evelyn Eaton Whitehead. *Method in Ministry: Theological Reflection and Christian Ministry*. San Francisco: Harper, 1980.

Williams, John Alden. *Islam*. New York: George Braziller, 1962.

Williams, Walter L. *Black Americans and the Evangelization of Africa: 1877-1900*. Madison: The University of Wisconsin Press, 1982.

Willoughby, William. "Moslem Profile Low, But They're Growing." *National Courier*, 4 March 1977.

Wilmore, Gayraud S. *Last Things First*. Philadelphia: The Westminster Press, 1982.

Winter, Ralph. "Fifteen Changes for Tomorrow's Mission." In *Mission in the Nineteen Nineties*. Grand Rapids: Wm. B. Eerdmans, 1991.

Woodberry, J. Dudley, ed. *Muslims and Christians on the Emmaus Road*. Pasadena: MARC Publications, 1989.

Woodson, Carter G. *The Mis-Education of the Negro*. Trenton: African World Press, 1990.

Zwemer, Samuel. *The Nearer and Farther East*. New York: Macmillan, 1990.

INDEX

302